IMMACULATE PATHS

Profiles of 30 ordinary lives embraced
by Our Blessed Mother and Marmora

Sister Alice Johnson
RegN; BScNE; MScN; MPC(HCS); FCCHS

Copyright 1995

ISBN # 0-969-8934-2-6

This book is dedicated to the
Merciful Heart of Jesus
our Peace and Reconciliation

Books written by the same author:

In Pursuit of Love

Marmora Canada:
Is Our Blessed Mother Speaking Here to Her Beloved Children?

Cover Design by Wade Raley

Published by Amor Enterprises Inc.

1279 Royal Drive
Peterborough, Ontario, Canada
K9H 6R6, 705-748-2723
FAX 705-749-1614

TABLE OF CONTENTS

		Page
Map Illustrating A Cluster of Phenomena in Central Ontario		9
Chapter One:	Introduction	11
Chapter Two:	Steady Growth	15
Chapter Three:	A Full Happy Life Of Priesthood (Father Karl Clemens)	21
Chapter Four:	Touching Base with Some Early Visionaries (Dory, Marci, Branca)	31
Chapter Five:	A Rose Bud Which Continues To Unfold (Veronique Demers)	37
Chapter Six:	Chosen For Conversion (Stephen Ley)	45
Chapter Seven:	Family Response (Gerry Muldoon and Erin Ley)	67
Chapter Eight:	Elect From Childhood (Father Peter Coughlin)	73
Chapter Nine:	Evangelization and Healing (Allan Young)	89
Chapter Ten:	Rosary: Direct Line to God (Wade Raley)	103
Chapter Eleven:	Messages For the Holy Father (Sandra Ruscio)	113
Chapter Twelve:	Our Lady Shows That She Cares (Marian Rodrigues)	121
Chapter Thirteen:	Living in Union With Jesus (Eddie Virrey)	129
Chapter Fourteen:	Marian Leadership (Bishop Roman Danylak)	145
Chapter Fifteen:	Our Lady Changed Our Lives (Ron and Janet Brown)	165

		Page
Chapter Sixteen:	Attraction To Marmora (Jun and Diding Quiming)	173
Chapter Seventeen:	Nucleus Of Spiritual Growth (Emma De Guzman)	179
Chapter Eighteen:	A Healing Community (Mila Bueno)	197
Chapter Nineteen:	Jesus, My Way and My Life (Hilary)	215
Chapter Twenty:	A Call To Plan Pilgrimages (Mary Dollard)	225
Chapter Twenty-One:	Grace Flows Onward (Jeff and the Boys at the Group Home)	233
Chapter Twenty-Two:	Summary and Conclusion	241
Appendix One:		247
Appendix Two:		251
Bibliography:		253

Front Cover

Painting Of Our Lady As Seen by Josyp Terelya at Marmora.
With permission from Josyp Terelya.

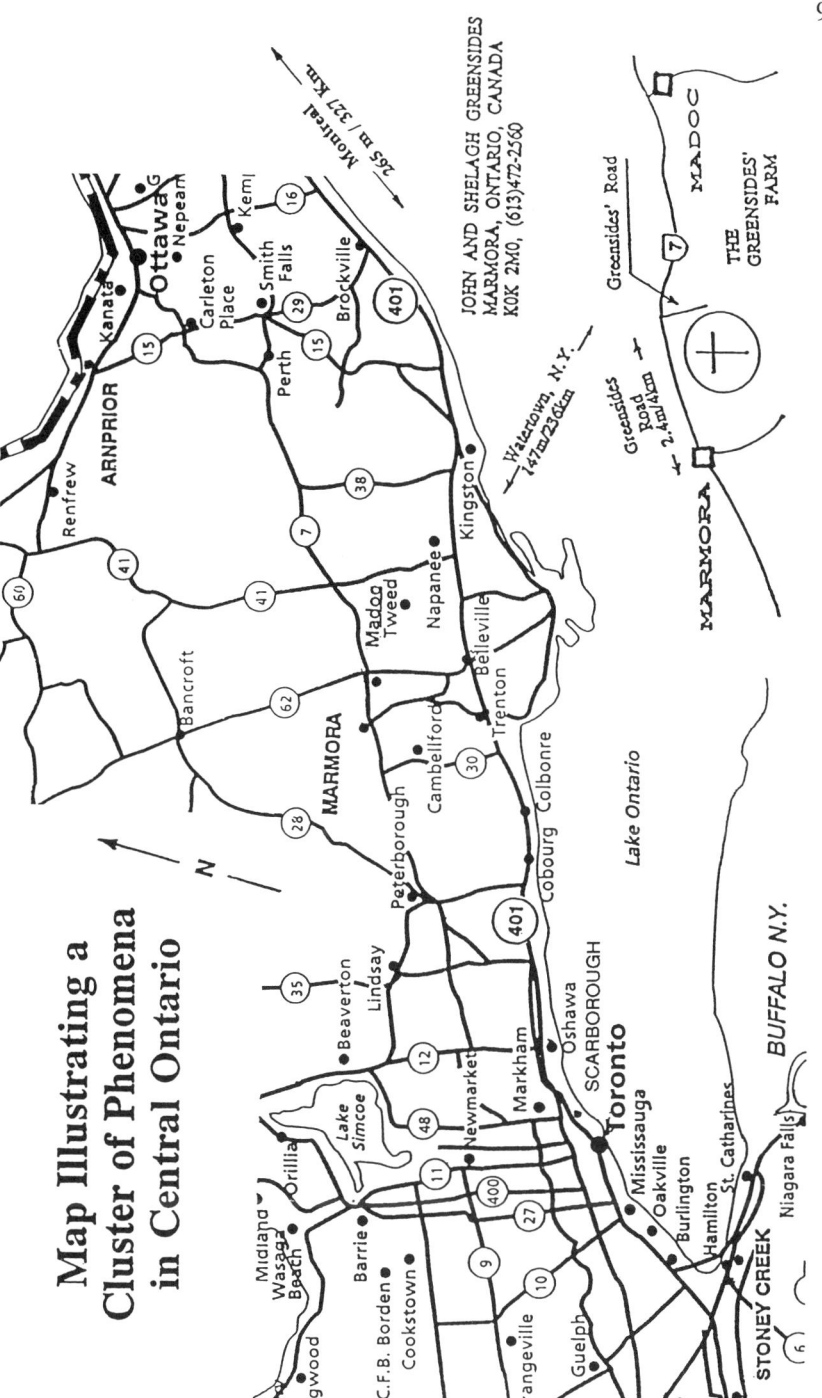

CHAPTER ONE

INTRODUCTION

Following the publication of my first two books, many people asked for a sequel to them. During a five week pilgrimage to the holy places of France, Belgium, and a return to Medjugorje, I was graced with the commitment to write again. This awareness impressed itself on me particularly at those sites which honour the Sacred Heart of Jesus, namely Montmartre in Paris and Paray-le-Monial, where Saint Margaret Mary had her apparitions of the Sacred Heart and His loving messages for the entire world. It seemed that Our Lord Jesus wanted this book dedicated to His Heart, which is God's chosen means to reveal divine love to all humankind.

The Heart of Jesus, formed by the Holy Spirit in the womb of the Virgin Mother, refers directly to the core of Christ's humanity. At the same time it is the real symbol of His interior life, His thoughts, will, and sentiments, as well as the living temple of God. (1) Through the Heart of Jesus we grasp His obedience to His Father and His brotherly love for all people. It is the sign of the fullness of His love, and the symbol of new life given to humankind through the Holy Spirit and the sacraments, especially Baptism and the Eucharist. (2)

The merciful Heart of Jesus was revealed in a remarkable manner to Sister Faustina Kowalska who was beatified in 1993. The Chaplet of Divine Mercy which is prayed particularly at 3:00 in the afternoon, is a means of tremendous grace to those who honour this devotion, and for those who approach their time of death. The Feast of Divine Mercy, celebrated on the second Sunday after Easter is honoured in a special manner all over the world.

It seems fitting that this book be dedicated to the Merciful Heart of Jesus because the participants in the interviews are involved in an affair of the heart. Each one experiences a personal conversion of the heart as well as of the mind. In some instances the conversion is so complete as to impact on the bodily senses as well. In every instance the participants are drawn more profoundly into the love of God which satisfies their deepest longing yet causes them to hunger for more of that infinite love. Their experience of God's mercy leaves them keenly aware of their sinfulness and invites them to repentance. In some cases it allows them to participate in the suffering of Jesus, and stimulates their compassion for others. This entire book is a manifestation of God's merciful love. May the merciful Heart of Jesus bless all those who read these testimonies with an increase of divine love.

The cover is a reproduction of a painting done by Josyp Terelya, and illustrates the apparition of Our Blessed Mother to Josyp at the Greensides farm. Our Lady's arms are extended in a welcoming embrace to all her children, as she draws everyone to her Immaculate Heart and to the Sacred Heart of Jesus. Our Blessed Mother holds the rosary in both hands, symbolic of the twofold path of prayer at the farm, namely, the Way of the Cross and the Rosary Path. As Our Immaculate Mother embraces each of her children, she invites us to incorporate into our daily lives the path of grace experienced at Marmora. Since people throughout the world recognize the CN Tower as a symbol of Canada, Josyp includes it in the background of the apparition.

As in the first book about Marmora, the messages in this edition describe the impact on peoples' lives during and following their visits to the Greensides Farm. Some supernatural phenomena continue to occur there. In certain instances, visitors received supernatural experiences in their home prior to and independent of their time at Marmora, which they recognize as a place of prayer and intercession for others. The real focus of this book is the ongoing conversion of individuals and families, their experiences of inner and physical healing, and their deeper commitment to personal prayer and spiritual growth.

This book makes no effort to seek out all visitors who come to Marmora, nor to select an official random sample of visitors who relate soul-touching experiences at the farm. Those activities are left to the discretion of the authorities who are charged with official investigations. Through word of mouth, individuals heard that my third book was being compiled. They agreed to describe their experiences, with the firm belief that this is the desire of Our Blessed Mother and Our Lord. Where individual visionaries prefer to retain privacy for the time being, their confidence is respected. Anonymity is also enhanced by the use of first names rather than the full names as with clergy or doctors who care for interviewees.

The author records in open faith the stories of conversion and healing as they are shared, for the single purpose of giving glory to God and enhancing the faith of all people. Twice during separate interviews in private homes, Jesus appeared to the visionaries and encouraged the furtherance of this work. Four times in different homes, Our Blessed Mother spoke to the visionaries, blessed the author and this documentation.

When referring to apparitions, the word alleged is not used in this book, though it may be implied by the reader. It is recognized that such apparitions and messages are private revelations for the edification and possibly deeper conversion of the faithful, and are not objects of faith. However, where these experiences result in manifestations of God's presence, such as peace, compassion, generosity, healing of minds and memories, they are credible and worthy of acceptance by everyone.

It is admitted that everyone who has a religious experience has the opportunity to grow in discernment with regard to the development of grace in that person's life. With the passing of time, new meaning may well be given to prior events and even alter the recipient's earlier understanding of the event. The personal statements recorded in this book reflect the recipient's thought at the time of the interview, with recognition that grace continued to unfold and would reveal new meaning of each occurrence. The author simply recorded the truth of the events expressed at the time of the interview, and returned the document to each contributor for verification before final editing. An effort was made to retain the original flavour of the interview including language and cultural expressions. If these statements allow the reader to be touched by God's grace, this book is well served.

In some instances local clergy and bishops conducted personal investigations into the phenomena reported to them, or into the fact that significantly large prayer groups occurred in private homes. Should official ecclesiastical investigation be conducted at those sites, the author submits to the conclusions of the Catholic Church.

This book would be incomplete without a word of thanks to those who contributed to its research, writing and publication. I praise and thank God for all those people who welcomed me and gave me hospitality in their homes during the many interviews. In particular I thank Bonnie Klettke and Anne Marie Pearl for their constant love and support throughout this endeavour. The Donald, Heckel, and Manion families and Stanley Smith provided vital equipment which enabled me to accomplish this task with ease. In a special way I thank God for my parents and family who from my infancy nurtured my faith and my devotion to the Sacred Heart of Jesus and the Immaculate Heart of Mary.

Most profoundly I praise and thank God for the privilege which was granted me to enter into the mystery of grace in the lives of these individuals and their families, which increased my personal love for God and the Church, and expanded my joy. May God bless, with profound peace and abundant love, all these loving people, and all those who read this book.

CHAPTER TWO

STEADY GROWTH

It is the third year since friends of the Greensides Family first witnessed the phenomenon of the sun at their gathering to commemorate the anniversary of Our Lady's appearances at Medjugorje. Visitors continue to come to the Greensides Farm by the thousand. Tour buses from various parts of Ontario, Canada and the United States arrive on feasts of Our Blessed Mother and on week-ends, particularly the first Saturday and first Sunday of the month. People of all ages and nationalities are attracted, possibly at first through curiosity about the rumours of supernatural phenomena. After a few moments at the farm, they experience the profound peace which characterizes the simplicity of this site.

Visionaries recorded in the previous book continue to receive apparitions and messages, which are made public according to the discretion of the visionaries and their spiritual directors. Hundreds of women and men experience unusual phenomena, including those persons who received apparitions or locutions prior to their visit to the farm. People of differing cultures, Sri Lanka, Hindu, Catholic, Protestant, or of no specified religious belief come with hesitant hope that their lives will be touched by the supernatural. Their faith is rewarded.

Collective Witnesses

On occasion, a group of people collectively witness an apparition. Such was the case in September, 1994 when approximately seventeen Filipino visitors saw the face of Our Blessed Mother at the same moment. Hundreds of people focus their cameras on the sun, and discover on their film silhouettes of the Blessed Virgin, the Cross, a door of light. On occasion, a large Host appears at the top of the photograph, in a picture almost identical to the miraculous appearance of the Eucharist in the sky above the sun, as recorded in Naju, Korea. (3)

Honeymooners come to the farm and seek a blessing on the lives they begin to share lovingly. They take with them a bottle of water from the spring which was blessed and which continues to flow. As Our Lady promised, this water is used for healing.

A group of at least six visitors from New York State of Chinese descent came for the first time in November 1994. They heard about Marmora from someone in Calgary and wanted to investigate for themselves. It was a little late on a cloudy day. They made the Stations of the Cross and walked the Rosary path. Two women in the group saw the miracle of the sun. They saw it spin, its gold rays spread outward, with gorgeous colours forming an aureola around it. One of the men rubbed his eyes because he couldn't look at the sun.

A young boy about thirteen years old couldn't face the sun and looked at his mother. He was amazed when he saw the reflection of the sun miracle in his mother's glasses. The family was excited about that. They remarked, "Some people go to Medjugorje to see these phenomena, but we see it right here."

Phenomenon in the Sun

Yolande Bekkers and her husband Harry from Greely, Ontario visited Marmora for the first time with her sister-in-law and her husband. Yolande commented, "My husband carried the camera. At one point I met a gentleman I knew from Medjugorje. He told me that he came here every first Saturday of the month. Then he said, 'It's time!' Yolande asked, 'Time for what?' He answered 'I know when to take my pictures.'"

To her husband Yolande said, "If he takes pictures, they must be good. Why don't you take some too? My husband took a lot of pictures. We brought them to be developed, and didn't see anything unusual. We brought them to my brother-in-law who exclaimed immediately, 'Look! That's the Virgin Mary!'"

"We were surprised that we had not seen the picture of Our Lady in the centre of light among dark clouds. With the same negative we requested ten reprints, and none of them showed the central picture of Our Lady.

We asked for a single reprint to make sure it was the right negative. The print showed Our Lady clearly in the centre. We ordered ten copies."

"To our amazement, the same thing happened again. The two first prints came out without Our Lady's picture and the others were clear." The enlargement of the photograph is included in the section of the book with photographs.

Accompanying Yolande was Lise Brisson from Cornwall who visited for the first time. She was drawn to Marmora because of Yolande's story. Lise commented, "There was no sunshine that day, so we were unable to see the phenomenon. I have the same feeling here as when I go to Notre Dame du Cap. I have been there several years in a row for the novena, and experienced the same feeling there as I have here today. I believe it is Our Lady's presence."

Message of Healing For Colleen

On Tuesday afternoon people from Hamilton came with a priest from the Philippines. Mila Bueno, a visionary from Hamilton, was experiencing oil oozing from her hair. John Greensides saw the oil on Mila's head, touched it and blessed himself with it.

The group made the Way of the Cross together and returned to the reception centre. John thought it would be wise for their daughter Colleen, who was undergoing treatment for cancer, to have Mila pray over her. Apparently by coincidence Colleen and Bob had the feeling that they ought to be at the farm. As soon as Colleen walked through the door of the reception room Mila walked over to her, embraced her and stood with her for about five minutes. Then they both went to the kneeler and prayed. Mila embraced Colleen again while they knelt together. Colleen rested in the Spirit and lay on the floor for a while. Mila had an apparition and was in tears.

Mila interpreted that the Blessed Mother said to tell Colleen that she wrapped her mantle around her, and that she would be cured. She gave Colleen a tiny rose which she drew out of her chest. People in the room smelled the scent of roses from the oil.

Feast of the Immaculate Conception

On December 8, 1994 between six and seven thousand people came to the farm in honour of Our Blessed Mother. Two parking lots were filled with cars, and forty five buses were chartered to transport pilgrims. Many people arrived in time for the 11:00 a.m. Mass in the Sacred Heart of Jesus church at Marmora. Others came in time for lunch which they enjoyed outdoors in the beautiful sunshine.

Shortly after 1:00 p.m. various groups began the Rosary or the Way of the Cross. Clusters of pilgrims gathered around visionaries and climbed the hill, meditating, singing, praising, praying in a variety of languages. One could hear French, English, Italian, Spanish, Croatian, mingled together in universal music. The Lourdes chorus 'Ave Maria' drew voices together, regardless of the refrains in differing languages.

Hundreds of people gathered at the Tenth Station where solar manifestations captivated everyone's attention. People gazed fixedly at the sun for long periods of time, observing its green disc, image of Host, tremendous rays encircling it, and an array of rainbow colours forming a gigantic aureole around it. One could feel one's own heart beat in harmony with the universal pulsating of the sun. There was deep peace and silence on that holy hill, broken only by the sounds of "OH! AH! Beautiful!"

Another phenomenon grasped the peoples' attention. It was the vision of huge golden energy fields in the sky, encircling the hill. Stephen Ley witnessed this event and saw clearly the figures within the energy fields. He described them as angels, some of whom were six feet in height, with wings, and beautiful features. Then Our Blessed Mother showed herself to him and to some children. People were overcome at the awareness of Our Lady's presence. Their joy and love flowed over in their tears.

Two women carried twelve inch statues of the Mystical Rose which they purchased at Josie's store. During the Way of the Cross many people witnessed that both statues wept.

Later, Dory Tan's apparition of Our Lady at a tree behind the Tenth Station indicated the spot chosen by Our Blessed Mother where she wishes a small chapel to be built. It will likely accommodate twenty people for prayer and worship, but will not house the Blessed

Sacrament. This tree is to be cut down to make way for the little oratory.

When the day ended and the tour organizers drew pilgrims back to their buses, it was with obvious reluctance mingled with joy that the visitors returned to their homes. Each one carried heartfelt renewed faith, and a strong sense that Our Blessed Mother was pleased at her children's manifestation of their personal love for her and for Jesus.

CHAPTER THREE

A FULL HAPPY LIFE OF PRIESTHOOD

Father Karl Clemens, pastor of Stanleyville and Dewitt Corners, grew up on the farm which is now owned by the Greensides. He left the farm after high school and became a school teacher in the Niagara Peninsula. Father describes his early years.

"We were ordinary people who worked for a living. Our parents made sure that we had an education. Because my father's health was poor there was a great onus on my mother to do extra work at home and in the neighborhood. She went out to work for low wages to ensure that my three brothers and I had an education."

"We had a regular Catholic upbringing, with Mass, Rosary and devotion to the Blessed Virgin Mary. When the movie "Miracle of Fatima" was shown in Marmora I was very struck by it. It was one of the most powerful influences on my childhood. As I stood on the hillside at the back of the farm I asked the Blessed Virgin why she couldn't appear in our own area and make her presence known more eminently here. I never dreamed that years later I would see people from close by, far and wide, experience something special there and take it back to the church communities in their own areas."

"Our Catholic faith teaches that wherever there is a community, Our Lord is present. And so wherever there is a Catholic church with a tabernacle home for Our Lord in the Blessed Sacrament of the Eucharist, His Presence is truly there. We don't necessarily have to look for special phenomena, such as Fatima, Lourdes, Medjugorje and Marmora, but Our Lord made it possible to renew and strengthen the faith and restore the Church by these means. All through the centuries these types of experiences were provided."

Call To The Priesthood

Father felt a call to the priesthood during his teen years but was uncertain in his discernment at that time. He wanted to teach school as well. He explains, "My pastor, Father Tim suggested that teaching would be a good experience if I were eventually to be a priest. There was such a shortage of teachers that out of Grade Twelve I took a six week summer course in Toronto and got a job in the Niagara Peninsula. The following summer I returned for the six week course and taught in the same school that fall. After a year in Peterborough Teachers' College I was invited to return to the same school for a six year period. After my first year they appointed me principal. It was a tremendous experience."

"Our family was also politically minded. The topic of politics prevailed whenever a group of us gathered. It is still so today. When I was 21 years old, in 1963, the first provincial elections of the New Democratic Party were fielding a slate of candidates to hopefully form a government one day. I was chosen in the riding of Niagara Falls to run for the N.D.P. This was a valuable experience, and an education which I could never have gained in any institution or books. I received opportunities to mature in my own life, faith, community living, people skills, and got a lot of things out of my system. During this time the call to the priesthood became stronger. The more I was involved in Catholic education and the Catholic Church community, the more I felt the priesthood to be my calling. It was hard to let go and say 'Yes' because I enjoyed my teaching career and community involvement."

"In Centennial Year, 1967, I decided that it was time to enter the seminary. I was attracted to the Conventual Franciscans, but decided to study at St. Augustine's Seminary for the Archdiocese of Kingston. At that time the system was quite set with three years of philosophy and four years of theology. St. Augustine's College was open for its last year and I took a make-up year in Philosophy during that transitional period."

"The following year St. Augustine's was closed. The Toronto School of Theology opened on campus, and I began my theological studies in the main seminary. This was a tremendously enriching experience because of the fact that there were seminarians from the Anglican, United, Presbyterian traditions as well as several religious orders of Catholics and our diocesan seminarians. I made it a point to take at least one course in every college to have the experience of other Christian traditions, and had the privilege of serving as President of the Student Council from the School of Theology for two years. Today I still have friends from other denominations with whom I have kept contact through the years. We have a tremendous spirit of ecumenism among the churches of this township."

Charismatic Renewal

Father's experience with the Charismatic Renewal dates from its inception in Toronto. He recalls, "While I was at the Toronto School of Theology the Charismatic Renewal emerged in the Catholic church. I was taken to it from the beginning. Through some of the Pentecostals, Kevin Renahan came from Notre Dame University to Toronto. We arranged to have Kevin speak at the seminary and had a time of prayer with him. From there we started the first Charismatic Prayer Group in Toronto. It began in a home on Glenholm Avenue and within four to five weeks our group of approximately 100 went to facilities provided by the Sisters of the Immaculate Conception. The movement continued to grow from then on."

"When I finished my third year of Theology, which signified my academic completion, Archbishop Wilhelm and I talked about the possibility that I would not take my fourth year because it was a pastoral orientation year at the seminary. He appointed me to Smiths Falls where the pastor was quite ill. The associate who was new also worked at the Rideau Regional Centre. Quickly I got thrown into looking after the parish. People were waiting to take instruction to become Catholic before marriage. Couples needed marriage preparation immediately. There was a large confirmation class coming up. I had a lot of good experiences."

"When the archbishop came for Confirmation he was pleased with everything. The pastor revealed that because of his own incapacity, I was the one responsible. The archbishop invited me to his office the following week and assigned me to the cathedral as a deacon. He ordained me on December 8, the Feast of the Immaculate Conception. After the new year he transferred me to the Chancery Office to work as his secretary and Vice-Chancellor. He also asked me to look after Catholic Charismatic Renewal to enrich it in its church appreciation and in the life of the church. He was very supportive and went to many prayer meetings. We conducted two conferences in the archdiocese of Kingston to host people who wanted to come from around the province, and provided many services for the Ontario Catholic Charismatic Conference. Bishop Windle became Spiritual Director."

"We continued to host conferences for the fifteen years that I was Diocesan Director. The beautiful part was that the emphasis was on parish renewal. As people became renewed in their own faith I encouraged them to take it back to their own parish and help the post-Vatican II renewal. Until that time the renewal was physical, such as turning the altar around and translating the Mass into English. At the Second Vatican Council Pope John XXIII asked people to pray for a new Pentecost in the Church, and we saw it emerge. Members realized that prayer groups were a means, and not an end. From there they went out to renew the face of the earth through the Church."

"The renewal was Eucharistically centered. We celebrated a regular Friday night Mass, with some liturgies focused on the healing gifts, and people were enriched in the Spirit. I was blessed with Charismatic ministry and experienced many events which happened in peoples' lives. They renewed or recovered their faith, experienced emotional healing, healing of memories from issues that caused them to suffer. Maybe the Lord was preparing me for Pro-Life because there were times when people had difficulties conceiving children. In a number of cases we prayed for couples to be able to have a child, and they did so even when medically speaking they were incapable of so doing."

"One day I was called to Kingston General Hospital. A couple was there, crying, holding their dead baby. I prayed with them, saying 'This is very tough and there's nothing I can say to make it easier, except that I know you love children and you want to have a child. God is going to give you a child.' The nurse spoke up, 'Father, they can't have any more children. That's why this one was born so deformed. They shouldn't have had a child in the first place.' I was happy to see that within the next three years they had two children who are healthy and good."

"A couple I married were having great difficulty and wanted a child very badly. It was a day when the Mass readings were about Abraham and Sarah. I prayed with the couple that day. She conceived and had a child, and a second child afterwards."

When I pastored previously in this parish Bob and Shirley wanted to have children. She had one miscarriage after another. They tried to adopt through the Children's Aid Society, but there were no children for adoption. One day Shirley told me that she quit her Medical Records job at the Health Centre because they were doing abortion referrals. She took a lower paying job in a factory. I advised her, 'I know that God will bless you with a child because of your faith conviction and your sacrifice through conscience."

"It wasn't too long before she became pregnant. Since this small community knew what Shirley and Bob had gone through, I asked the congregation to pray really hard for them. The child was not to be born until the end of January. On Christmas Eve they were at the family Mass and Shirley felt the child leaping in her womb during the whole service, especially as I did the Christmas story with the children. Before the night was over, Bob had to take her to the hospital and Julie was born on Christmas Day. These are the phenomena where it is wonderful to see the Lord at work."

Devotion to The Divine Mercy

Father Karl commented on the rich spiritual heritage of the Catholic tradition. He stated, "I felt strongly how the Lord has provided through the ages. Having been raised in the Sacred Heart parish we knew of St. Margaret Mary Alacoque and her visions of the Sacred Heart. In this century we received the phenomenon of Sister Faustina Kowalska and her whole journey with the Lord manifesting Himself as the Lord of Mercy. Father Kosicki spoke at the Kingston Charismatic Conference. I introduced devotion to the Divine Mercy in St. Paul the Apostle parish."

"In 1990, when I was transferred to St. Francis church in Smiths Falls, devotion to the Divine Mercy caught on like wildfire. I preached on it during Lent the following spring, and held the novena of Divine Mercy from Good Friday to Mercy Sunday. It was a beautiful celebration. People came from other parishes and took prayer booklets home. The following year an artist painted an icon of Divine Mercy which is in a niche over the tabernacle at the central altar. Devotion to the Divine Mercy continued with First Friday Mass at 7:30 a.m., Exposition of the Blessed Sacrament, and the Hour of Mercy at 3:00 p.m. In such a small place it is edifying to have up to 150 people attend the Hour of Mercy and pray throughout the day before the Blessed Sacrament."

Our Lady of Perpetual Help

Another great devotion which animated Father Karl's priesthood is his love for Our Lady. He actively cultivated devotion to Mary among his parishioners and helped them grasp Mary's role in the economy of salvation. He continues, "Thank God for people with Marian devotion. After Easter 1991, I obtained material on Perpetual Help and preached on its origin, with the tradition that St. Luke was given the vision and painted the original icon of Our Lady of Perpetual Help. The Redemptorists became the custodians of the Perpetual Help devotion."

"I knew that we would have the best response to this devotion within the context of the Mass, and introduced it on the first Monday of May at the 5:00 p.m. Mass. I discovered that the opening prayer of the novena is a perfect opening prayer for the Mass. The first three prayers of the novena are perfect as penitential prayers in the penitential rite. Each week we used the readings from the Votive Masses of Our Lady. The intercessions 'Help Us O Loving Mother' came in place of the Prayers of the Faithful. After the Consecration and Communion we had the Perpetual Blessing."

"Shortly before the 5:00 Mass, Sister Marlene, Pastoral Assistant, told me, 'I need to take out more booklets.' I answered, 'They're all out on the tables on both sides of the church.' She replied, 'No. Take a look. They're all gone.' We had to order more books. At that time there were more than one hundred people at the 5:00 p.m. Monday in a parish the size of Smiths Falls. We retained close to two hundred people for the nine weeks of the Perpetual Help Novena. I have been really blessed with the richness of our heritage of faith, and the way God allows me to be able to cultivate it with our people. I look forward on my return to Stanleyville to develop it, because there is strong Marian devotion in this parish, and it would be remiss not to cultivate and enrich it with more teaching."

School Ministry

Aside from his parish duties Father Karl maintained involvement with school ministry. He noted, "As a pastor I always spent a lot of time in schools and with the children. In St. Paul the Apostle parish there were fifteen hundred elementary school children in three schools. On the night they held my farewell celebration the principal gave me real affirmation when he said that in his seventeen years of principalship he never worked with a priest who took not only interest but a leadership role, and did so much to bring school and church together in sacramental preparation and the continued ministry of presence with the priest in the school. Children are our future. I was not blind to the fact that the majority of children did not come from religiously active families. The church had to go to them."

A year ago Father was transferred from Smiths Falls to Stanleyville. He explained, "I could not remain as chaplain at St. John's Catholic High School which was growing in leaps and bounds and be a pastor of a place the size of Smiths Falls. Now the high school is ten minutes down the road. It's a tremendous combination to have high school ministry which I love very much and is so important. The ministry of presence is the presence of the Church for most of those young people. St. John's Catholic High School is their experience of Church."

"In terms of ecumenical activity St. John's has probably the highest percentage of non-Catholics of any high school in the province of Ontario. We operate a full agenda and students of all faiths are part of it. They're here by choice, and their parents want them here. They know when they register that they will take Religious Education every year from Grade Nine to Twelve. They assist at all school Masses. They're part of all spiritual development; it's part of the package."

Father recognizes the need for spiritual maturity in ministering to students. He recalled, "When I was in church administration it seemed to me that young priests could have effective ministries in high schools or universities. Now I'm glad to be in the high school at middle age. I would not have had an effective ministry in my late twenties because I did not have the experience, the maturity, the cultivation of the different dimensions of priesthood and people skills necessary for this work."

Reflection on Prayer

Father underlined his personal spiritual development and his love for the prayer of the Church. He commented, "The one thing I always felt strongly about is the Breviary or the Prayer of the Church. When the Breviary was in Latin, many priests said they read it under obligation or were committed to it but didn't get much out of it. I was lucky to have come into the priesthood when the new Breviary was in the process of being developed. The Prayer of the Church in four volumes is so rich. It is an important part of my prayer life because the priest prays in union with the whole Church. He has a continuum of the unfolding of the Church's year, the reliving of salvation history."

"The Breviary, Rosary, devotion to the Divine Mercy bring so much to the Celebration of the Eucharist. Sundays never have to be a surprise. I don't find myself scrambling. I don't suggest that I'm the greatest evangelist, but I find that I'm not scrambling around on Friday or Saturday because I've had a continuum of prayer, scripture, spirituality throughout the week, which comes to the high point at Sunday Eucharist. I build up to it all week long and start afresh each new week in that salvific area."

Visits to Marmora

After many years away from the farm Father Karl returned in 1993 when Maria Esperanza was present. He remembered, "I was preparing to transfer from Smiths Falls and thought I would go to Marmora for the feast of St. Anne. I was overwhelmed when I drove off Highway #7 into the laneway to our farm and saw all our hay fields filled with buses, cars and thousands of people."

"I was asked to participate in the devotions and led the 3:00 chaplet of Divine Mercy that afternoon and sang a Marian hymn which I enjoyed doing, because as a child I sang in the choir. People showed great love and respect for the priesthood and what we offer by virtue of our vocation and ordination. It was quite an experience to have swarms of people come to have their religious articles blessed or have a blessing for themselves. The day was very uplifting for me."

"In 1994 the feast of the Assumption fell on Monday. I had spoken briefly to the parishioners about Marmora. At the last moment we filled a highway coach and drove to the farm. I was with my people and thousands of others. We made the Way of the Cross and I led the fifteen Mysteries of the Rosary for the community gathered there in the afternoon. I used water from the spring to bless people for quite a considerable period of time. Some beautiful things happened to enhance, enrich, renew or heal people's lives. We had a good spiritual pilgrimage and a wonderful day for the people of the parish."

"At the Eleventh Station of the Cross Veronique Demers received a message that Our Blessed Lady was pleased that we came on the Feast of her Assumption to honour her Divine Son and His journey of the cross, and that our parish would receive many blessings because of our journey that day. Our parish is coming back to what I had once known. The congregation is growing stronger. One necessity in my journey is to learn to be patient. We have to move ahead and do things but need to discern the appropriate timing. I can see some things that are in the forefront that will be very good for this community."

"When my mother first heard about the events at the farm from Father Grainger, the only thing she remembered were the hay fields, the gardens and the hard work. She was sceptical of the whole thing. She, my step-father, aunt and uncle were at the farm when we arrived. It was an emotional experience for us. The day was difficult for her, until after the fact when she was able to digest it. It was traumatic for her and for me too."

"There is obviously something special happening at Marmora. We need to be present to appreciate these pilgrimages. However, people ought not cling to the experience of the pilgrimage, but let it become part of their lives so they can share it. Wherever there's a congregation Our Lord is present and so is Our Lady. I believe very strongly that these manifestations are for a purpose that recurs in every age. Once we have an experience in our life, it's history. It is necessary for people to move forward to their own community, and share what Our Lady is doing, so that her mission is accomplished. This can happen only if we participate and cooperate with her intercessory power, her presence, and whatever she does in her mission on behalf of her Divine Son."

Vocations to The Priesthood

Father Karl did not only comment about Marmora and his valued experiences there. He testified to the happiness of the priestly vocation. He recalled his twelve years as Director of Vocations for the Kingston Archdiocese and his agenda in fostering vocations. He reminded the pastors of the archdiocese, "You're the vocation director in your own parish. You must discern young men whom you believe have a call to the priesthood."

"I had an awareness day in the spring with thirty-five to fifty young men from university or working people. During winter and Lent I held a couple of retreats with six or eight young men. Each fall, we sent two, three or five people to seminary. This diocese always seemed to have twelve to fifteen people studying for the priesthood. That was a real blessing. Recently a man told me of his son who is finishing his basic university program and wants to enter the seminary to study for the priesthood. It gave me a real boost and affirmation when he said to his dad, 'I want to be a priest like Father Karl.'"

CHAPTER FOUR

TOUCHING BASE WITH SOME EARLY VISIONARIES

Those individuals who received apparitions during the initial manifestations of Our Blessed Mother at Marmora continue to visit the farm on a regular or periodic basis, depending on the inner messages they receive and their own form of devotion.

Mrs. Dory Tan experiences apparitions and inner locutions at her own home, and is also a frequent visitor to the Greensides Farm. On the first Saturday of each month and feasts of Our Blessed Mother, Dory is present with her husband Henry. Together and usually with a reasonably large group of pilgrims, they pray the entire Rosary before beginning the Way of the Cross.

At the Tenth Station Dory continues to receive apparitions and occasional messages. On December 8, 1994, Our Blessed Mother fulfilled her promise to do something special on that day and revealed to Dory the site chosen for a small oratory.

Dory and Henry Tan have compiled their experiences and messages in book form, which will be made available to the public in due time.

Branca Cepo visits the Greensides Farm with members of her prayer group. Together they pray the Way of the Cross and pause reverently at the statues of the Sacred Heart and the Immaculate Heart of Mary which they have erected on the hill behind the Fourteenth Station, where Branca's first apparition took place.

Branca continues to receive apparitions in her home where she lives with her husband Ante and their two sons. Some of Our Lady's messages to Branca are personal, for herself and her family. The public messages are consistent with those of other visionaries. Branca emphasizes that Our Blessed Mother asks everyone to pray, especially from their heart.

Marci Guinto recently celebrated her fourteenth birthday, surrounded by approximately one hundred well wishers of all ages. Family friends formed a prayer group which developed at the home of Ernesto and Carmelita Guinto when statues and pictures began oozing oil in their home on June 28, 1993.

Marci has matured into an elegant, courteous, gentle yet effervescent young lady. When her group visits Marmora it is usually on a feast of Our Lady and on the occasional week-end, so that her school schedule will be uninterrupted.

She continues to receive apparitions from Our Blessed Mother every two weeks in their home, and occasionally has messages which are made known to the public. Our Blessed Mother begins and ends each message with the words, **Praise be to Jesus**. Some of these are as follows:

March 6, 1994:

I am very happy to see people praying from their hearts.

Saturday, March 26, at Marmora:

My child, pray from your heart from this day forward, because a lot of perscutions are going to happen in the future.

Sunday, April 10, 1994

This is only the beginning of your cross. You will be going through more trials. May my Son Jesus strengthen your heart for other people.

April 23, 1994, at the Healing Mass, St. Anne's Church:

My precious child, I know it is hard, but turn yourselves completely to my Son Jesus. Make many sacrifices to my Son Jesus, because I love you, and my Son Jesus loves you too.

April 25, 1994:

Jesus appeared and said, **This is the world.** And He showed people killing each other. **It will end, if you do not pray from your hearts.**

Friday, May 13, 1994:

Do not be sad. This is your trial. I am your Mother and will always be your Mother.

I come here this evening very sad because my children do not listen to my messages. Little children, I ask you to pray the Rosary.

Wednesday, July 6, 1994:

I beg you, pray, pray and pray, especially you, for Satan and all his followers are tempting you, not only you but your family and people who volunteer in your house.

My dove, make many, many sacrifices for my Son, Jesus. Fast, and especially go to Confession. Satan is trying to stop you from doing all these things I want you to do, so be prepared. I am very happy that you pray to my Immaculate Heart and continue the mission.

And remember, I love you and will always love you because I am your Mother.

Wednesday, July 20, 1994:

My dove, I know you are very tired. I will help you so you may not be tired.

My dove, I beg you, pray for the priests in the world, especially your community priest. I love my priests and I will always love them.

I love you.

Wednesday, August 17, 1994:

My child, hurry. Time is very short. Please pray the Cenacle daily, especially my young ones, for I will always guide and protect them from all evils.

Sunday, August 21, 1994, at the Eleventh Station, Marmora:

I thank all of you who sacrifice to come here. I hope that this will be the beginning of those who will come in growing numbers with true faith.

I love you so much. If only you knew how much I love you.

Wednesday, September 14, 1994:

My dear child, pray for the conversion of sinners, and also my child, try to go to Confession daily so that Satan my not tempt you in any way.

I love you.

Wednesday, September 28, 1994:

My dear child, be prepared, for many temptations from Satan will come upon you.

I am warning you now because I love you with all my heart and I will always protect you.

It is not only me who is protecting you, it is my Son too. You must have more faith in my Son, in order for me to protect you from evil spirits. My child, I beg you to listen to my messages. Each message that I give you is very important. I love you and will always love you, because I am your Mother.

Wednesday, November 9, 1994:

Tell all my other children to pray the Rosary daily, for the Rosary is the most powerful prayer to defeat the devil.

Remember I love you and will always love you because I am you Mother.

Wednesday, November 23, 1994:

Little children, I ask you to pray the Rosary. After saying the Rosary say, Jesus, I trust in you, three times.

The First 'Jesus I trust you' represents His love for us on the cross.

The Second saying represents the humility we should have towards one another.

And lastly, the Third saying represents the patience we should have towards others.

My dove, listen to my messages very carefully, for each message that I give you is very important to everyone in the world.

Remember, I love you and will always love you, because I am your Mother.

Wednesday, December 8, 1994, Vigil at home.

Praise be to Jesus.

Today is a special day. This day is a day of prayer for everyone. I am very happy to see everyone praying from their hearts.

May my Son Jesus be with them always.

Praise be to Jesus.

Note from Marci: Our Lady was all in white with yellow roses on her feet. When Our Lady said, **May my Son Jesus be with them always**, Our Lady laid her hands on us. When I saw her do that, I saw a bright light coming towards our heads. I'm sure Our Lady is very happy to see everyone praying.

Wednesday, January 4, 1995:

Praise be to Jesus.

My child, time is very short. Pray, pray, pray my child. Listen to my messages.

Have faith and never lose trust in my Son. That is what my Son wants you to have, trust.

Always be happy, for my Son loves you with all His heart, and remember, I love you and will always love you, because I am your Mother.

Praise be to Jesus!

January 18, 1995:

The Blessed Virgin gave me the third secret. (Marci had received the first secret in Los Angeles before Christmas in December, 1992, and the second secret in Rochester, N.Y., after Christmas). Our Lady said, **You can say only one word about the secret.** Marci said "It's about **Chastisement.**"

January 20, 1995:

Our Lady appeared, crying, with tears of blood.

My child, do not be sad. I am crying because the time is very, very close. Now is the time when you should turn yourselves completely to my Son, Jesus. Pray to Him every day.

Now is the time when you should also pray the Chaplet of Divine Mercy every day.

Remember that I love you and will always love you, because I am your Mother.

Praise be to Jesus!

CHAPTER FIVE

A ROSE BUD WHICH CONTINUES TO UNFOLD

Veronique Demers began receiving apparitions in 1992 and continues to receive visions, apparitions and messages from the Lord Jesus and Our Blessed Mother. Her original testimony is described in an earlier book about Marmora. (4) Apparitions continue during her visits to Marmora.

The Blessed Virgin Mary requested Veronique to be at Marmora on the Easter week end. She comments as follows: "At the Eleventh Station, Our Lady of Sorrows appeared and showed me Jesus on the Cross. There was no spoken message. It was difficult to see Jesus suffering so much on the Cross and Our Lady suffering in her heart and crying; to see how the people have mistreated Jesus so much; but there was so much love coming from Jesus. The love that Our Lord and Our Lady have for us is truly without end. It was really a great comfort through the suffering I saw. If it had not been for that love, I would not have been able to stand seeing Him suffer on the Cross as He was. Thank you Jesus and Mary for the great love You have for the world."

"Throughout 1994 my spiritual experiences increased in number with some differences. On Easter, April 3, at the Eleventh Station, Our Lady appeared very happy and smiling. It was the first time I saw her dressed in white. She was very beautiful. She had blonde hair, whereas until March 26 I saw her with black hair and a silver dress. She carried a beautiful Rosary in her hands. This was the first time I saw her with a rosary. The beads were white with gold lines and the crucifix and chain were golden. This was her Easter message":

The peace of the risen Christ, my Son, be with you all. I am very happy to see you here today and that you came this week end. This is a very special week end and it is beautiful that you came to pray in the company of my Son and Me here in Marmora. At the Fourteenth Station you will feel the glory of the risen Christ. I love you all and I bless you.

"At the Fourteenth Station, I had a vision of the risen Christ and He said,

Will you all please help me bring the people of the world back to my Father by your testimonies and the witness of your lives. Thank you dear ones for being open to my Mother's messages and to the call in each of your lives.

"In Marmora, on April 24, the Blessed Virgin Mary gave me an inner locution with the following message":

My children, may the peace of Christ be with you! I thank you for coming here today. Little ones, many of you have come seeking signs. The signs and wonders you should be seeking are the changes in your lives, in your hearts and those of your loved ones. These are the most important things my little ones, pray for these signs, these inner and everlasting healings.

In these days, my little ones, I ask you to pray for conversions, the healing of the soul and you, yourselves, my little ones, continue praying for and seeking a deeper conversion for yourselves.

Ask for Jesus' grace and He will help you too. Please, my little ones, continue praying. Always pray and also pray for Pope John Paul II and always support him. Thank you again my little ones for praying here today. I love you and bless you.

"On May 7, 1994, Our Lady gave me the following message through an inner locution at the Eleventh Station":

My dear children, I have come today to comfort you. Many of you suffer a lot because of the state of your families and of the world. Do not worry about that, hand these sufferings over to Jesus. He will take care of it all. Come, come, come to Jesus and me your Mother. Our hearts are opened to you. I want to keep you in my heart, but you also have to stay in prayer. Through prayer you will feel my protection and my support. Come to us my little ones and we will fill all your needs. Come to us and we will show you many things. I love you my children and I bless you and all of the things that you have brought here today to get blessed.

"Our Lady appeared on May 22, 1994, the feast of Pentecost, at the Eleventh Station. For the first time I received signs before the apparition, three flashes of light. The first flash was a cross, then I saw a door of light like the doors on the polaroid pictures taken at Marmora. The third flash was a triangle of light which turned into a dove symbolizing the Holy Spirit. Our Lady appeared. For the first time I saw her with a crown. She had blonde hair, blue eyes, and was dressed in white."

"Our Lady, Queen of Peace, gave the following message:

My dear children, I am happy to see you here today. It is good that you came here on this week end of Pentecost. I love you very much my little ones. Never doubt my love and Jesus' love too. Pray, pray, pray my children, always continue praying. It is prayer that will bring you to a closer life with Jesus.

My children, I thank you for the prayers that you prayed for the Holy Father. Continue praying for him. He needs your support. Know that he can feel the power of your prayers and he is happy to know that you support him.

Also pray for conversions, the conversion of the world because, dear children, time is running out and Jesus would like to see His flock gathered together.

My children, always pray. I love you my children and I will always keep you in my Motherly heart. I will protect all of my children. Jesus is sending His spirit over you. I love you and Jesus loves you. Go in peace!

"While giving her message Our Lady said that Jesus was sending His Holy Spirit over us, and she placed her hands over her heart. When she removed them the Holy Spirit in the form of a dove was in her hands. She raised her arms and the Holy Spirit flew from her hands and over the group that was with us. It was very beautiful. When I talked about this matter to my spiritual director he said that it's very significant, and a beautiful way of showing that in the Church all graces which Jesus gives us, including His Holy Spirit, He gives through the Immaculate Heart of Mary."

"On August 13, 1994, Our Lady appeared in the church of the Sacred Heart of Jesus at Marmora at the end of the hour of adoration of the Blessed Sacrament. It was the first time I saw her without her veil. It was so special and beautiful to see her beautiful long blonde, wavy, sparkling hair. She left a special message for a couple who were scheduled to have an abortion on August 15. Our Lady came to try to save the child and told me that the child, whose name would have been Matthew, would have been born on December 8."

"That night I called the parents and told them the message from Our Lady, and how she said that if they kept the child that Jesus would heal him from spina bifida with three holes in his spine. Doctors were discouraging them from keeping the child. The parents decided their course of action and proceeded with the abortion. It was a very difficult decision for them. Our Lord told us to forgive them, and that it was hard for them. They are suffering very much from this experience. We must try to understand their position. I thought it was beautiful for Our Lady to come and try to save one life. It shows us how important is each life."

On the following day, August 14, Our Lady appeared to Veronique at the Eleventh Station and gave her the following message.

My dear children, I have come today to thank you for all your prayers. Pray, pray, pray my children. Pray the full Rosary every day. Also pray for unborn children and those who have been aborted.

Jesus gave His blessing to those assembled and blessed all the religious articles they brought with them. Jesus and Mary thanked their beloved sons for coming today.

Veronique continues, "On November 20, 1994, the feast of Christ the King, I had a vision while resting in the Spirit; I saw Our Lady and Jesus as Christ the King wearing a magnificent crown and holding a sceptre in His hand. I brought two roses to present to Our Lady, one yellow and one red. As I presented them to Our Lady she kissed them. I presented them to Jesus and He also kissed them. Jesus told me to give the petals of the yellow rose to everyone in our group. Yellow represented glory and He wanted to show His glory to every one of us. I was to give the red rose to my father as a gift of love and strength."

"After this Jesus gave me a message for our family. My father saw the miracle of the sun and two sets of gold footprints coming down from heaven and forming a V, touching the ground between him and me. Then he saw the gold footprints go back to heaven and two gold silhouettes in the sky. When he got to the Fourteenth Station he saw the two gold silhouettes again. It was a special grace for my father. It was also his first experience of this kind. He doesn't know who the silhouettes represented."

Mission of Visionaries

Veronique said that visionaries of different nationalities seem to have a mission that is unique to their own people. She observes, "Dory is Filipino, Branca is Croatian, Ivetta is East Indian, and I am French Canadian. Dory is closer to the Filipino people, and Branca to the Croatian people. My mission is mainly to the French speaking people, but also with the English people because I am bilingual. Many French speaking people come to Marmora from Quebec, the Gatineau, Hull and Ottawa."

"From August 24 to September 2, I was on a speaking tour with one day in Ottawa, two days in Gatineau and the rest of the time in the Eastern Townships. At each speaking engagement there were about 80 to 400 people with an average of 200 people each night. On the first night in Ottawa there was a group from Haiti with 200 people in a room that would normally accommodate 50 to 100 people."

"I spoke for two nights in the Gatineau, once for adults and the other night for children and a good representation of young people. They asked questions such as Our Lady's age, appearance, messages, purgatory and heaven. Some Haitian children asked why Jesus and Our Lady appear to me as white rather than black. I answered that Our Lady appears to people in a way in which they can identify with her. For example, in Kibeho Our Lady appeared to the children with a dark complexion."

"Most assemblies were held in prayer houses, though some conferences were scheduled outside. The indoor conferences were more satisfactory because there was more control and security. When we were outside, people tended to get excited by the end of the talk and I needed to be protected from those who wanted to touch or take hold of me. It is particularly difficult after visions or apparitions when I need some time to write the message and interiorize the experience and people want to pull me from one side to the other."

"Similar conduct took place in Marmora. After the Stations of the Cross people recognized me and asked me questions. Groups of people gathered around and won't let go when it's time to leave. It's understandable because people look for what will make them feel peace, and Our Lord and Our Lady bring them that grace and peace. People want to know what Our Lord and Our Lady want of them."

"Their reaction is understandable. But some people think that just by touching the visionary they will be healed. That is an act of faith in one sense, but Our Lord and Our Lady touch people in other ways too. A visionary is a regular, normal person, only an instrument. It's Our Lord and Our Lady who provide miracles."

Veronique comments on her experience of public speaking. "Sometimes I am very nervous before talking in public, but as soon as I begin talking I feel great peace as though I am not the one speaking. The words simply come to me and flow out of me. I find this fact amazing because I am not one to be comfortable even with school presentations. This is a wonderful grace from Our Lord and Our Lady. Many times during my talks I smell the perfume of roses and I feel Our Lady close to me. I sense that she is there to support me through the talk and the questions. The Holy Spirit inspires me with answers which I can't make up. If I don't know the answers I admit it."

"What I find difficult about being a visionary is being recognized publicly and asked the same questions over and over. Sometimes I wish I could wear a mask and have some privacy. It's not annoying so much as repetitive. But most importantly after I speak to groups and answer their questions, I feel a great joy, knowing that I have served Our Lord and Our Lady and that they are happy that I have done this for them. It's a great feeling, knowing that I have done what is right. It's a blessing of obedience."

Louise Demers noted that during one talk given by Veronique, "there were a lot of tricky questions and I thought it might be difficult for her to answer them. But her answers came so easily that one of the priests who was present commented, 'This girl is only sixteen. How can she answer these questions in such a beautiful way? The wisdom that she has is not from her.' It's really beautiful to see Our Lady working through her."

"In the afternoon Father told everybody what he experienced during the Way of the Cross with Veronique and me. Emanating from her he smelled a beautiful perfume of roses. It was Our Lady's perfume. That was real confirmation for him, a sign that he needed in order to discern whether or not Veronique was authentic. He stated, 'I believe 100% in the authenticity of Veronique.'"

Personal Reflection

Veronique has matured significantly during the past year, while she retains her gentle simplicity and openness. She reflects, "In the past year my greatest growth was my ease and confidence in speaking publicly. I'm not as shy as I was during the previous year. I feel the need of more time to pray. My spiritual growth is very gradual, since Jesus and Our Lady do not push a person to grow quickly."

"My favourite flowers are roses and lilies. The lily symbolizes purity for me. I have always loved roses and their simplicity. They remind me of Our Lady's perfume and of the simplicity that Our Lord asks from each one of us."

As Veronique reflects on her favourite flowers, she equates herself with a little rose bud which continues to unfold and blossom under the gentle care of Our Blessed Mother, without haste, and with tender love.

CHAPTER SIX

CHOSEN FOR CONVERSION

To speak face to face with Stephen and Maureen Ley is to be made welcome in their active household of three daughters aged eighteen years to one month, and one thirteen month old son. Maureen and Stephen provided me with an interview during an afternoon when Stephen returned early from work. The older children were still at school, and the two youngest were sleeping. In a short time their household became filled with the children's voices and activities, as Father Peter arrived before supper for a visit. Last to join the family were Maureen's parents, Betty and Gerry Muldoon, who alternated with Maureen in caring for the younger children.

Period of Preparation

Stephen states that he was never a "religious" kind of guy; he never went to church when he was young; he attended Sunday Masses when he became a Roman Catholic for only a few months after he was married; then he became a self-confessed "pagan". At the time the apparitions began, Stephen could best be described as being completely "unchurched". He had no idea how to pray even the "Our Father" or the "Hail Mary". He was simply indifferent to religion. He was sceptical of what he was supposedly seeing and told Our Lady if she was real to prove it by appearing to him during the day. The next day around noon, as he was preparing lunch for himself in the kitchen, she appeared and spoke to him again.

Stephen relates his experience as follows. "I began to change a year before the first apparition. My family noticed it but they said nothing because it was a slow change. I became more mellow, more content with things. I approached people differently. At the same time, I had some weird dreams and never knew what they represented. They seemed to be dreams of mystical experiences but I didn't pay any attention to them or attach any importance to them."

"When the apparitions began everything started coming together. I recognized the inward connection and the gradual process to prepare me for my first apparition. After Our Lady appeared to me for six to eight months I asked her, 'Why?' She told me she had interceded for me since I was eight years old without my realizing it."

Apparitions

Stephen began receiving apparitions on March 25, 1992. These phenomena continued nightly until the first Friday after Easter of the same year. Stephen's initial experience was somewhat unusual. He was asleep on the couch in the living room of his apartment when he was awakened at 4:00 a.m. by a young woman who seemed to be hovering on a cloud, and who told him, "I am Mary, Queen of Peace, the mother of Jesus Christ Our Lord". Stephen thought this was some kind of dream and answered, "Right. And I'm the Pope".

One of the first questions he asked her was, "Why me?" She replied, "Why not"? He objected, saying he wasn't a believer. She said, "Then why are you talking to me?" He had to admit she had a good point. Then she told him she was here to help him take a good look at his life, to instruct him in the ways of the faith, and to use him to bring messages to others. She said he was part of an "army" that she was raising up.

Stephen continues his story. "In the beginning Our Lady appeared nightly between 4:00 and 4:30 a.m.. She taught me about her Son and prepared me to meet Him. The first night she taught me the Our Father, then the purpose of divine praise. Through inner locutions angels taught me to pray the Rosary. At night I prayed the Rosary and Our Lady appeared during the Fourth or Fifth Sorrowful Mysteries. At first she taught me only the Sorrowful Mysteries and I didn't realize that there were others. When I prayed the Rosary with other people and they said the Glorious Mysteries I wondered what they were doing."

"I prayed the Hail Mary and Our Lady prayed the Our Father and the Glory Be with me. When I continued the Rosary she disappeared, and reappeared when it came to the Our Father and Glory Be. At first she gave me her Rosary to pray with. That was quite neat. When she came at night I told my wife that it was happening, but Maureen couldn't see anything. She knew something was going on by the way my body responded. I was very scared and would shake. Maureen knew that the apparition was taking place. I was confused and concerned, yet happy and very peaceful. Eventually I always looked forward to seeing her."

"How did I know it was Our Lady? She told me who she was. There was a lot of love and peace about it. I wasn't scared. I thought I was cracking up, and had a lot of difficulties with it. So I didn't really say anything for the longest time. On Good Friday 1992 she appeared with swords piercing her heart. With my sense of humour, my response was "Gee that must hurt!" She was sad and crying at the time and I didn't know what it represented. Later that morning when my mother-in-law telephoned, I asked Maureen to ask her mother what it represented. "

"When Maureen's mother explained what it meant, my wife looked at me in a strange way, wanting to know why I had asked the question. I wouldn't tell her. They were very curious because I had never asked a religious question in all the years I knew my wife. My in-laws came for dinner that evening, and in response to my mother-in-law's probing, I revealed to them that I thought the Virgin Mary was appearing to me. Dead silence went around the table. My mother-in-law looked at me and didn't know if she should laugh or take me seriously. She paused and said, "Well, Steve, if anyone else told me that I'd think they were nuts. But knowing you and the way you are I believe you."

"I shared what happened. It meant nothing to me. To see Our Blessed Mother cry was sad, but not true sadness for me because I didn't understand why she was crying. I didn't have the knowledge to know the true hurt she was going through. It was sad to see her cry because she is such a beautiful young woman. It didn't touch home nor go into my heart. I felt no responsibility for her pain."

"Maureen and I stayed up together for the next two and a half weeks, waiting for her to come. She appeared around 4:30 a.m. for two to four minutes, sometimes longer. She encouraged and prayed with me. She gave me her rosary. I held the crucifix in the palm of my hand, and squeezed it tightly. When the apparition was over, I opened my hand to show my wife the imprint of the crucifix in the palm of my hand, and this would verify Our Lady's presence."

Spiritual Direction

"Between March and April 1992 Our Lady repeatedly asked me to seek out a priest and make my first Confession. I refused. I told her I didn't want to approach a priest. I had no use for them. She said, 'You have to seek out a priest or else I can't continue coming to you and working with you'. I answered, "Fine then. If you want me to see a priest, you arrange it". I left it up to her. A couple of days later she came back and said "It's arranged". She told me who the priest was. It was Father Francis. I laughed, and said "You arranged it"? She said "Yes". I called the parish and asked Father for an appointment. He asked what it was about and I wouldn't tell him. He said, "Well, I'm really sorry. I can't see you because I just had surgery done on my foot and I'm not seeing anybody." I said, "Well that's fine then." I hung up the phone and felt 'This is great. I'm off the hook. Our Lady asked me to do something and I did. She can't say I didn't do it."

"A couple minutes later Father called back and said, "I don't know why, but I'll see you to-night at 6:00 o'clock". I kept the appointment. Our Lady revealed some things for me to tell him so that he would be convinced that she sent me and that what I was going to share was from her. I sat in his office, looked at him and said 'Father tell me why I'm here. He looked at me very strangely and asked, 'Don't you know why you are here?' I answered, 'I do, but do you?' He said, 'No I don't.' I replied, 'Well I'm sorry, but I'm not going to tell you why I'm here until you reveal it to me.' He thought he had a crackpot on his hands. A couple minutes went by and nothing was said. He looked at me, then paused and exclaimed, 'No it can't be!' I asked, 'What do you mean?' He explained that the Lord revealed to him that morning, that He would send someone to him for general Confession, and that it was important for him to hear this Confession."

"Father wondered all day who it was. He thought he had to go out and find people. Then he said to me, 'You're here for a general Confession.' I agreed, 'Yes, I am.' I gave him the confirmation which Our Lady gave me for him. Dead silence went over the room. He got on the phone and cancelled all his appointments for the evening. We were together until after eleven thirty that night."

"When Father John returned from Rome Father Bob asked him to investigate me, discern everything and determine if the experiences were from Our Lord. During this process Father John prepared documents for the archbishop. They asked for a sign from Our Lady to confirm that she was appearing. One sign was conversion in the parish. The other sign was a request for her title. When it was time for me to reply to the clergy request, she revealed herself as Our Lady of Conversion. Conversion happened within the parish boundaries with increasing numbers. Eventually they accepted the fact that something supernatural was happening and took it more seriously. They investigated me; the changes in my life, and realized that the Lord was definitely working though me."

"Our Lady emphasized the importance of being with my family and praying together. We try to go to church together. I've had mystical experiences at Our Lady of Perpetual Help Church. I saw Our Lord walking down the aisle. During Mass I saw angels and saints. I had a message from St Theresa the Little Flower for one of the priests there. I had personal teachings. I prayed there in the evening with a couple of priests and had a mystical experience of souls from purgatory who revealed themselves to me and asked for prayer."

"Father John and I usually try to meet once a week. If I have any messages, locutions or teachings Father and I get together for a couple of hours afterwards so he can help me understand what happened. If that's not possible I speak to Father Peter. Father John guides my discernment and Father Peter helps me deal with sin in my life."

Gradual Conversion

Stephen explains, "I didn't come from a prayerful family. Maybe Our Lady knew I was on the road to destruction and she decided to save me. Her first comment to me was that she came to save me from hell, because I was already knocking on the door, more or less, and she wanted to turn me back to her Son before it was too late. Why did she do this? Out of love. Not much more. I think that is what's happening with Mary around the world. The whole purpose is love. I believe strongly that whenever Our Lord or Our Lady appears to someone it's not because they're in trouble nor because they're holy or special. The reason is that they feel they can use them as a tool of some sort. We can't see it but they can."

"With my life style I was a perfect candidate. I can relate with people who are into the bar scene or materialistic things, fast cars, travelling, partying, getting drunk, having a good time, living for today and not worrying about to-morrow. I can talk to them about it, and they don't feel I'm preaching to them. Then I say, 'Let me tell you something that happened to me'. They look at me with awe. At first they don't know how to handle it, but eventually they come around and ask questions. I don't normally push it. I just plant the seed."

"Before Our Lady's appearances I was always seeking something and had a hunger for happiness. I constantly needed a fix, a good time, a new car, or to get away, always searching. Through material things, travel, partying, alcohol, I sought happiness. I felt that I was happy, but as soon as the party was over I was lower inside than before. That was the only life style I knew and sometimes I still desire it. During the past three years I have grown, but I didn't change overnight. I still like to go out and occasionally travel. My desire for cars has pretty well disappeared and my hunger for the bar scene is gone. This was not due to my free will because I tried to hold on to it as much as I could. The desire slowly disappeared."

"It began in December 1992. Our Lady asked me to focus in another direction for true peace instead of emptiness. I said, 'You told me a long time ago that I had free will and my will is to go to the bars Friday and Saturday night'. She didn't say anything and I went out. At first I came home at three or four o'clock in the morning. Then I came home at one o'clock, or midnight, or eleven, then ten or ten thirty. Finally on Friday night my wife asked, 'Are you going out?' and I answered, 'No, I think I'll stay home tonight'. That's how it changed. It was very slow, very gentle."

Development of Prayer

"From the beginning, Our Lady's whole purpose was to introduce me to Our Lord. She prepared me for that. She taught me to pray and the importance and direction of prayer. She encouraged me and said, 'Pray from your heart. Pray for what's troubling you. Realize that my Son is listening no matter how you feel. The simplest prayer is what pleases Him.'" At first I had difficulties because I didn't like it. I thought praying was a drag. I talked to Our Lord, and said, 'You know how I feel. You know what my heart is saying. I can't put the words into prayer, so I'll talk to you'. I just talked to Him, and received a locution back from Him. I thought it really weird."

"One night I talked to Him and asked Him to give me hunger for prayer. Our Lady stressed the importance of that, but the desire to pray wasn't in my heart. It was there because Our Lady put it there, not because I put it there. The reason I had problems praying was because I had to learn why I was praying. I didn't truly understand the importance of prayer because at this point I had never met her Son and didn't know what He represented. I truly didn't know Him as a person in my life, so I couldn't relate to Him. That is why I didn't have the desire to pray because I didn't really know Him."

"This situation went on for months. My prayer time was simply talking to Him. Our Lord gave me hunger for prayer. Occasionally Our Lady appeared and asked me to pray with her. We prayed the Our Father or Glory Be or for the souls in purgatory. She always gave me direction as to what the prayer was for. I didn't take the initiative and do it for myself."

"I turned to a friend, Lil, and asked her to pray that I'd receive hunger for prayer. After that Our Lady taught me about her Son and said, "You have to learn to crawl before you can walk. You have to go back to the beginning and learn who my Son is. Learn what He represents. Once you learn about Him and truly understand Him then you cam begin to love Him. Once you begin to love Him you can relate to Him and start praying to Him. Then you can understand why you're praying."

"She gave me passages from the bible and suggested I ask Maureen or someone to read these scriptures and help me understand what they mean. (Stephen has dyslexia). She directed me to the bible to learn about her Son. I did this and asked Father John if he had tapes for me to hear. I listened to passages of the bible on tapes. Our Lady appeared at night and went through the different passages with me. She read them to me and taught me what the scriptures represented. This went on for a long time. I learned more about the importance of prayer and started to understand Jesus. I don't say I truly loved Him, but I started to admire Him. I prayed to Him, then received different mystical experiences during prayer."

"One night I prayed the Our Father, Hail Mary and Glory Be for the souls. I didn't know many prayers so I just repeated these. Then I said, 'Lord, teach me more. Give me hunger for prayer'. I heard as clear as day from the Lord, 'At least, try. Try. This is all I ask of you. Try'. So I tried. As I tried it became easier. As I surrendered, prayer became stronger and deeper. It took a while, almost a year. Now my prayer life is very strong. I really enjoy taking the time to pray and I don't neglect that time."

"As my prayer life developed Our Lady came to me and asked for prayers. She revealed to me individuals in purgatory who needed prayer, and I prayed for them. I had two types of prayer. At night when I first went to bed I gave thanks for my family and everything in my life, and asked for strength for myself and my family. My second prayer was for others. For the longest time I was wakened in the middle of the night by St. Raphael, who asked me to pray. Maureen has seen all this, maybe not with her physical eyes, but from my reaction and the change in me."

Intercessory Prayer

One message which Stephen received deals with the importance of intercessory prayer. He explains, "If I pray for my brother or sister or mum or dad and I feel that they need intercessory prayer, the Lord may say, 'Yes, it's important, but I need your prayers elsewhere.' He uses my prayers where they're needed, not necessarily for my father or mother. The reason is that Jesus knows their future. In His Heart He knows that He will convert them, so He uses my prayers where He feels they're needed."

"Suppose someone says, 'Let's pray for the souls in purgatory.' If I know someone who died and feel that maybe they went to purgatory, and realize afterward that they're not in purgatory but already in heaven, the prayers are not wasted."

Gifts of Ministry

"During the past year I received the gifts of seeing into people's souls, knowing if they're under stress or in sin, by the shape and colour of their aura. As the Lord so decides, I can tell when people had their most recent Confession. I see an aura with different rings, and the white ring is close to the body. If the person remains longer without Confession the aura goes into a grey then a total black ring."

"If persons are very prayerful I can see the aura expand each time they praise the Lord. What I sense about the different colours of the aura is the time of their last Confession. The Lord does not reveal to me the state of their soul. I think that the Lord is saying to me, 'This is a prayerful person but is building up sin in his or her body.' If it's a minor sin, the aura changes colour and becomes grey. If sin builds up, the aura gets darker grey. If a mortal sin is present, the aura becomes dark blue or black. The Lord reveals to me that it's time for them to go to Confession. If the person asks me to pray with them, I reveal to them the time of their last Confession, and suggest to them that they seek out a priest for Confession. I have done this on a number of occasions."

"I think that conversion happens in many ways, at any time, to anyone, no matter how hard one's soul is, nor how strong is the will to stay away from the Lord. I believe that everyone gets converted in one way or another, either through sickness, death or desires they need to fill their lives. My old life style is an example of this."

"Last summer Father Gerry joined us for supper. Father Gerry had just returned from a wedding, and was dressed in his black shirt and collar. I noticed through his clothes that he wore a miraculous medal under his shirt, tied to a brown scapular. I asked him 'Would you like to play a game?' He agreed. I said 'I'm going to reveal something to you. Let me know if I'm right.' Through two layers of his clothes I revealed that he wore a miraculous medal tied to the left side of his scapular. I touched him where the medal was. He opened his jacket and sure enough there was the medal with the scapular."

Mystical Experiences

"There's a presence that Our Lord and Our Lady give when they are with me. They manifest themselves to people around me, so they can physically feel the energy which comes from them. It manifests itself in different ways, through tingling up and down their back or through smells. From Our Lady comes a strong smell of roses. Different smells of flowers come from Our Lord. The smell that is most common is incense. Besides the smell of incense from Our Lord is the warmth and peace that He gives as He appears in the evening, when Maureen and I are in bed or if we're downstairs watching television. Peace comes over the room, and anyone in the room at the time can feel it and know there's something going on."

"Many times Our Lady filled up our bedroom with the smell of roses. Whoever went upstairs smelled the roses. During the summer it was there almost all the time. Sometimes Our Lady appeared at night and wakened me. I talked to her and continued to see her after the apparition. I yelled, 'Look at the roses! Look at all the roses!' Maureen sat up in bed, looked at me, and said, 'What roses?' I repeated, 'Look at all the roses!' She laughed at me and told me to go back to sleep. Jesus and Mary also manifest themselves through other ways such as silhouettes of energy forms which other people have seen. Maureen has seen silhouettes of Our Lady and angels."

"The difference between apparitions, visions, and locutions, is that they come in many ways. An apparition is a physical life form of Our Lord or Our Lady, and I'm brought into their dimension, with them in spirit. Inner visions come from the heart. A heavy feeling comes into my chest and I feel the Lord talking to me. I can't see Him but I feel Him. As I meditate, He becomes clear to the point where locutions come from my heart into my head and ears. At Mass the inner locutions come from outside. I have an inner sense by the peace in my soul and the air around me that the Lord is present, but I can't see nor feel Him."

"I always know when Jesus and Mary manifest themselves by the energy they give, or I feel them physically when they appear in front of me. I don't know when they are coming. Suddenly they're there. I receive inner locutions through my ear, and other locutions when they talk through my soul rather than through my ear. I think that the reason for this is to try to help me understand the different feelings, because these manifestations aren't going to last forever."

"At times during prayer Jesus and Mary reveal things to me through an apparition or vision, and communicate to me the answer to my questions. Now they answer only through locutions of the heart. Through my heart I feel that Our Lord talks to me and answers my questions, but I'm not positive it's from the Lord. So the next time He appears to me I raise the matter and ask, 'Did this come from You?' He answers, 'Yes. This is how we communicate with you.'"

Discernment of Spirits

Stephen explains, "I have many dealings with the evil one. He appears as Our Lady and there is absolutely no way of physically telling the difference between the two. The only way I discern is through the excitement and stress in my soul. I get uptight and agitated, and know that something is wrong. I discern by asking Our Lady to tell me that she loves Jesus, and how much she loves Jesus. The evil one refuses to do this and changes the subject. With him the feeling is different. He is angry and very demanding.

"Our Lady calls me by my name, or she calls me "My child, please do this for me, or can you do this for me, or are you prepared to do this?" She always asks. When Satan appears in her form he says, "I want you to do this. I expect this of you". I feel really uncomfortable until I realize that something is wrong."

"I looked for other signs. When Our Lady appears she always has her rosary. It goes across her chest and into a little pocket on her left side with the crucifix. The rosary hangs from her clothes. When the evil one appears, the image is the same. I see the beads of the rosary but not the crucifix. Sometimes he appears as though he holds the crucifix in his hand. He really holds the beads, but there is no crucifix at the end. When I ask Satan for the crucifix he refuses. Yet in the past Our Lady gave me the crucifix to hold. That's how I detect him."

Use of Blessed Articles

The Church has always honoured the use of blessed objects. Stephen also made use of these. He comments, "Every time I receive an apparition or vision I denounce it in the Lord's name and ask them to reveal themselves to me. If it's the Lord or Our Lady they don't mind and usually respond. Many times I use holy water and holy salt. During the first couple of weeks after I told Maureen that Our Lady appeared, her mother said that I should use holy oil or holy water as soon as the image appears. That night Maureen came home with a little bottle of liquid. I thought it was holy water, and when Our Lady appeared I splashed it all over her and she laughed. She didn't mind. Later I realized that the bottle was not filled with holy water, but holy oil which was sprayed across our bedroom."

"I have a large bottle of holy water and use it during my many demonic attacks, which can be psychological, physical, and mental. Physical attacks come in many ways. Satan appears in energy form as a person, but without a face. It's a very black soul in human form. He stinks with sulphur and has a very harsh voice. He does many things when I'm sleeping at night, screams as loud as he can in my ear, startles me and wakens me, or he growls horribly at me. He comes with other demons. One night four of them were in the room. They grabbed me, shook me, pushed me around, choked me. A number of times during the day as I sat with Maureen he attacked me physically, shoved his fingers down my throat, and choked me. I couldn't breathe."

"One night when Father John and I shared the messages, Satan appeared and started choking me. Father couldn't seen him, but could see my face turn blue and my breathing stop. He knew there was something wrong. The evil one did a number of things. Patricia and Maureen experienced him. He does stupid things around the house, slams cupboard doors, opens and bangs doors, goes into the basement and pounds the ceiling enough to lift the floor in the living room, runs up and down stairs. It scares the children and they wonder what is happening. In our bedroom he opens and closes cupboard doors, bangs on the windows or shakes the bed. Recently he touched Maureen physically on the shoulders, but did not attack her. He attacks only me."

"He does stupid things at night. I usually walk around the house without lights, and go upstairs in the dark. He stands at the head of the stairs. When I come around the corner he jumps out at me, screams, growls, and startles me. I back up a few steps and scream and swear at him. Then I realize that I am playing his game and call him names. There are so many attacks that I can't recall them all, but he's real. He manifests himself in many ways. He appears as Our Lord; Our Lady, or angels. He takes any form he chooses and it's hard to tell the difference. One thing that always gives him away is that he's very abrupt and demanding. He insists on what he wants. Our Lord and Our Lady are always very gentle and ask permission. Every time they give you something they ask "Can you? Can I share more with you? Can I teach you further?' They always ask, no matter what it is. What he does is insist. You can tell the difference right away."

Messages

Stephen received several messages during the past two years. Father John has copies of these. Last year the messages stopped. What happens now is in depth teaching about heaven, the Father, interceding for each other, how we all come to the Father through Jesus. Stephen continues, "During the last several months I bilocated to heaven regularly. I communicated with people in heaven, such as my in-laws' parents. They gave me messages in such a way that I had no doubt of their origin. For example, a woman gave me a message for my father-in-law, calling him Gervy. When I described her to my father-in-law, he went out of the room and returned with a picture of his deceased mother. I had described her to a 'T'. She was the only person who ever called him by that name. There were other parallel experiences which happened a lot during the last couple of months. They occurred any time, during the afternoon, at dinner, whenever the Lord wants. I didn't know how I got there. It was really strange." (See Appendix One)

"The first time I went to heaven was in 1992 on the feast of the Triumph of the Cross. Our Lady appeared to me and asked if I was ready to meet her Son. Then she asked, 'Would you like to?' I answered, 'Yes'. We landed in a huge open area. I saw people walking around praying, meditating. It was peaceful, with bright, soft colours.

Off in the distance Jesus stood with saints around Him. The whole crowd opened up and Jesus came toward me and His mother. He thanked me for surrendering and for coming. He said that I have a long way to go, and to be faithful to His mother and obedient to His priests. The next thing I knew it was over and POOF! I was back."

"After that experience I received more apparitions of Jesus. I haven't seen Our Lady since July 1994, other than two weeks ago when she appeared without words, to let me know she is still with me. When I go to church on week-ends I see Jesus and angels. Prior to this I saw Our Lady on the altar. Now I see Jesus on the altar. Many of my locutions, visions and apparitions come from Our Lord."

"My last teaching two weeks ago came through a vision during my night prayer, and dealt with how we are brought into heaven. I saw St. Michael the Archangel in heaven, with a young girl I was praying for at that time. He appeared on the left side of Jesus, beside the young girl. I couldn't understand why Jesus allowed me to see this girl in heaven with Him, but didn't give it much thought. On the second night the girl appeared again, on the right side of Jesus, with Mary and St. Michael. Jesus taught me that to come to the Father, it is necessary to come through His heart. His heart is on His left side. He receives on His left, brings us through His heart to the Father who is on His right. The reason why Mary is on His right side is because she is already assumed into heaven. When we die, we arrive on the Lord's left side and must go through His heart to the Father."

"Jesus exposes His heart a lot, and gives messages about His merciful heart. He talks about how His heart is scarred for every soul He has lost to hell. He said that it hurts Him very deeply. He talks about His love, and about the mercy of the Father. Most of these messages come through visions or apparitions. It's hard to explain without seeing it, but I understand completely by the time the apparition is over. Jesus appears with His heart exposed, in pure white silk garments, which are open to expose it. There are thousands of beams of light like laser beams from the heart, spreading everywhere. I saw the Sacred Heart of Jesus five or six times. It's very merciful. Our Lady exposes her heart too, but in a different manner. Rather than the beams of light as with Our Lord, a bright warm glow comes from her heart."

Impact On Family

The profound changes and supernatural phenomena which happened to Stephen were bound to have a significant impact on his family. Stephen emphasizes that the change in him and his family is as from night to day. He explains, "Erin was the only child Maureen and I had at the beginning of the apparitions. She was already scarred by my life style, because I was never home and not a father figure. I was more concerned about going to Jamaica, travelling abroad with my friends, or hanging out in bars and having a good time. I never spent week ends with my family. My wife and I were together for about fourteen years, but New Year's Eve of 1993 was the first one we spent together since Erin was born."

"The changes in me were gradual. I still went to bars after receiving apparitions. I saw Our Lady cross her arms, lower her head, and shake it back and forth very gently as a mother would, to let me know how disappointed she was in me for doing this."

"My behaviour had the greatest impact on Erin. When I wanted to go out on Friday or Saturday night Maureen got upset, and I deliberately provoked a fight so she would tell me to go out. I went out of my way to make her miserable. I went away for week-ends and Maureen prayed that I wouldn't return. It ruined our relationship. There was nothing to salvage. Erin was our only child, and we couldn't see ourselves being together and having more children. Who wanted to bring a child into a relationship like this?"

"Our Lady is the Lady of Conversion. She slowly changed my heart. The first thing that started to come back was the love that Maureen and I had for each other. We discovered one another all over in a new way through church and prayer. Taking time to pray together at night gave us a big bond. We sat down and talked, shared, were honest and open with one another. Erin was the first one to notice a change in me. It was difficult for her. On Friday nights she looked at the clock and asked, 'What time is it?' Maureen told her, 'It's 8:30'. Erin asked, "Why isn't Dad getting ready to go out?" Then Erin would laugh and say, "Ha! Ha! Dad's home, and it's Friday night! Mary doesn't want him going out!"

"Maureen and I spent more quality time together. Our Lady revealed to us that our family wasn't complete, and asked us if we would consider having another child. Maureen and I discussed it and we had another child at the request of Our Lady. He's a little boy named Kyle. Over a two year period Maureen gave birth to Andrea, who was born in October. In the past two years we had two children and now we have a household of six. We also purchased a home, thanks to Our Lord who provided the money. Our family life has stabilized."

Visits to Marmora

Stephen heard about Marmora but didn't believe in the events described there. He thought it hog wash. For the first Saturday of June 1994 Father John organized a pilgrimage, and asked Stephen if he would come with him and his parishioners. Stephen agreed. He commented on his experience as follows. "As soon as the bus pulled into the yard I felt the presence of something, but didn't know what it was. When I stepped off the bus I looked up into the woods and saw Our Lord crucified on the Cross. I told Father John what I saw. At this point Veronique and her mum came over to greet the bus and identified themselves. I asked her if she could see what I saw. She answered, 'No'. When I pointed out to her where I was seeing it, she indicated that it was the Tenth Station. Then I realized that there was something going on at Marmora and quickly became open to it."

"With Father John and the other pilgrims I prayed the Way of the Cross. I received visions of Our Lady carrying me through each Station with her. I perceived angels around me. Though I heard them, I didn't see them. I felt the presence of Our Lord very strongly, but couldn't see Him. I detected the smell of roses at each Station and as soon as I walked away from the Station the smell went away. This continued until the Ninth Station. When Our Lady did not appear, I felt that was strange."

"We continued toward the Tenth Station, which you can't see until you are right before it. As soon as I came around the corner of the tree before the Station, I saw Our Lord suffering on the Cross. It really hurt me and I started to cry. Father John looked at me and knew that something was going on. While the pilgrims read the prayer for that Station I watched the Lord."

"After the Eleventh Station Father John decided to take the pilgrims to the site of the blessed water. I had a strong desire to return to the Tenth Station, and said nothing to anyone. When I arrived, the Lord was still there. He talked to me and gave me messages of encouragement because I was crying. He said 'What you're seeing hurts you very much'. He shared the hurt that I felt in seeing Him suffer on the Cross. He let me know that on the Cross He suffered, but His suffering is even greater because He freed everyone from sin. More than His suffering on the Cross, it hurts Him to have His children turn their back on Him and continue to sin. I talked to him for roughly ten minutes. Then He said to me, 'You have to go back now to your group'. When I returned Father John said, 'You've been gone for almost twenty minutes'. Together we went on to the Twelfth Station and finished the Way of the Cross."

"I also received a locution from Our Lady. She said, "Father Peter's here and I would like you to find him". She didn't tell me where he was but I knew, without understanding how I knew. I left the hill and walked to Father as he stood in the midst of a large crowd. I told him, 'I'm supposed to be here with you but I don't know why'. Father replied that he said to Our Lady, 'It would be nice to have Steve make the Stations of the Cross with me and a group of seminarians.' When we reached the Tenth Station Our Lord appeared again on the Cross. I stood there and wept. It was hard to see Him that way. It was the first time I really cried for Him."

"At the Fourteenth Station Our Lady appeared. Father Peter and Father Roger were beside me with a couple of seminarians. Our Lady asked me to return on the first Saturday of July with my family and friends, for five consecutive months until December. I agreed to do this and many people have been blessed."

Stephen comments on organizing pilgrimages to Marmora. "The first time we advertised the trip to Marmora we ended up with four bus loads. We realized that this was too large an undertaking, since we wanted to focus on a pilgrimage for prayer and intercession. Now we don't advertise. By word of mouth people fill a bus within a week. We normally arrive in time for lunch, then start the Way of the Cross at 1:15 p.m. Somehow a group of about two hundred people connect with us and pray with us. They smell incense, flowers, see silhouettes, gold colours in the sky, a number of things. People who take photographs have different shapes come out in the picture. Many people have been deeply moved by it."

"During our November trip it was raining, so we prayed the Stations in the rain. No one got wet and none of the prayer sheets got wet. We lowered our umbrellas and still no one was wet. A lot of mystical things happened for our encouragement. The Lord revealed Himself to me through locutions and visions."

Experiences on Pilgrimage

It has been noted that visitors to the Greensides Farm actively search out visionaries almost to the point of embarrassment. Stephen comments on this situation, and provides his own suggestions. He claims, "I have a lot of problems with people who consider visionaries as saints and want to touch them. I think that people have to realize that the term visionary is exactly that. The individual is only a visionary, a tool, a messenger in the Lord's army. It does not mean sainthood or special person or anything like that. The Lord communicates with us in many ways. I guess He feels it's important that He chooses people to reveal Himself so He can use them as tools."

"My experience with people on pilgrimage to Marmora is that some of them do not focus on the purpose, the importance of being there. Every time I've been there, the first thing people do is look for a visionary. They ask the visionary to lead them in the Way of the Cross. I've been asked several times to do this, and I answer 'I'd be happy to go with you and pray with you, but I don't want to lead you. I want you to lead yourself and not concentrate on me but on why you're here. Let's do it together'. Some people put their arms around me, want to take my picture. I've had people ask me for my autograph, or ask me for my picture and sign it for them. It takes away from the purpose of these trips."

"I believe strongly that the Lord makes visionaries available to be with the people, but I don't think we're to be in the limelight. We're to encourage them and witness that the Lord is present at Marmora. He and Our Lady give messages to the visionaries for the people. We are people the Lord has chosen to communicate messages to His children. There is nothing special about me or any other visionary. I think it's important for people to realize this and not focus on signs and wonders or visionaries, but on the importance of prayer and why they're on pilgrimage. If a visionary is there that's great because it encourages people. Our Lady is now appearing to groups. She also is used as a tool and encourages people to realize that Jesus is really present at Marmora for all."

Resistance and Surrender

The path to ongoing conversion was not an easy road for Stephen to take. He continued to struggle for his independence from God and Our Blessed Mother. He describes his conflict and ultimate surrender. "During the summer of 1993 I had a lot of trouble with the apparitions and mystical experiences from saints and angels. I found it overwhelming. Each time Our Lady appeared I said, 'No, I don't want any messages.' My reason was that I was having difficulty with the responsibility she was giving me. Every time Our Lady, Our Lord or an angel appeared to me the first word that came out of my mouth was 'No. No. No. I don't want to hear it'. They listened to me and left as quickly as they came. They were very gentle with me and understood my wishes."

"One night during the summer of 1993 St. Therese, the Little Flower appeared. The first word out of my mouth was 'No. I don't want to hear it.' She said 'Please. All I want to do is show you something'. I said 'Fine'. A yellow rose appeared in her hands. It was three and a half to four feet high. She held it in the tips of her fingers, brought the rose forward and said, 'This is you'. Being a smart ass, I said nothing, but thought 'Yeah, I'm a rose.' She said, 'You are one with Jesus. As you learn to love and understand and surrender to Jesus you open up and grow.' As she said this the rose opened up and the head started to expand. She said, 'As you surrender, say yes and become one with Jesus, you open up and bloom further'. The head of the rose opened up to about twelve inches in diameter. She said, 'As you completely give yourself over and you're one with Jesus, you blossom'. The flower came to a full bloom. The head of the rose was about two and a half feet in diameter."

"St. Theresa continued, 'Just as you learn to bloom, you can also say No to Him. As you say No to Jesus', she pulled a petal off the rose, It began to close up. 'As you completely say No, and turn away from Jesus', she pulled another petal which dropped to the ground. The rose died. 'As you made that decision to turn your back on Jesus, you're no longer with Him. You are dead.' The head of the rose fell to the floor. That was it. That's when I finally surrendered. That teaching brought me where I am today."

"A few moments later, I had an apparition of St. Bernadette; she told me of her struggles and experiences, which encouraged me in relation to my rebellion. I felt the loss of my free will, and did everything in my power to hold on to it. The biggest part of my conversion was giving my free will to Jesus. Once I surrendered it from my heart, everything took off. The key is to realize that you have free will. It's also important to give it over and surrender it at all cost."

Investigation

An investigation was launched through the archdiocese of Ottawa Carleton during the summer of 1992, with a bishop, three theologians, a psychiatrist or psychologist who was on the board. Stephen notes, "They met with me, Maureen and Father Frank. The investigation is ongoing.

They have not yet prepared their final conclusion. Following the investigation the archbishop stated publicly in the Ottawa Citizen that I experience a private revelation. He did not deny nor promote this. He stated that as an individual I came forward to the diocese and described what was happening. The archbishop thought it worthy of investigation. I believe that as long as the apparitions continue, the investigation will be ongoing. The archbishop gave permission for Father John to continue to work with me. He also allows this event to grow on its own and because it is a private revelation, he does not want me to speak in the parishes or make public spectacles representing the archbishop or diocese."

"I have no problem with that, and think it ought to be done in this way. Apparitions and locutions are private and are not matters of faith as are the scriptures. Our Lady tells me to be obedient to her priests at all times, live according to the bible, and direct my life to Jesus. Guidance can come when based on the scriptures, not visions or apparitions."

"I do not represent the Church nor the archbishop's office in any way. This is a private matter between Our Lord, Our Lady and myself. It is something that I feel is important to be shared. I ask the reader to take everything with a grain of salt. If I can encourage you in any way, it is to let you know what is happening in my life. I plant the seed. Let it grow in your heart. Stay faithful to the Church. Don't let people mislead you from scripture."

Final Note

Stephen explained that he was not a prayerful person when Our Blessed Mother introduced herself to him. Gradually she taught him the meaning and purpose of prayer, and directed him to Jesus. Through his personal relationship with Jesus, Stephen grew in the knowledge and love of God. He was able to use his gifts in a parish service where he composed the following closing prayer for the end of the prayer vigil. The reader is invited to pray in union with him.

O Mighty God, Jesus Christ our Lord, we gather in prayer before you. We ask you to lead us and to give us strength to do your work. Grant peace to all our fellow brothers and sisters, especially those caught up in the fighting in Bosnia. Bring unity and forgiveness to the people who have caused the death and destruction of your children there. We pray too for those who have died. Help us not to judge or be judged, but give us the strength to do your will. We thank you for listening to our prayer, and for helping us to pray now and until your work is done. Amen.

CHAPTER SEVEN

FAMILY RESPONSE

Gerry and Betty Muldoon are parents of Stephen's wife Maureen. They are frequent visitors in the Ley home, particularly since the birth of one month old Andrea. They were present at Marmora during the scheduled bus trips from Ottawa, and they also experienced deeper peace and prayer in this setting which breathes the presence of Our Blessed Mother.

When commenting about his reaction to the change in Stephen's attitude and general behaviour during the past two years, Gerry states that he began noticing a difference in Stephen late in 1991, about six months before the first apparition. Stephen seemed to be more mellow, agreeable, cordial. He could sit and talk with a person, whereas prior to this time he always seemed to be under a great strain. Gerry asked his wife, "Betty, is it me, or is Steve changing?" Betty too, had noticed the difference in Stephen, and they were prepared when his behaviour truly underwent significant change.

Gerry remarks, "When I first heard that Steve was having visits from Our Blessed Mother, I thought, "Why Steve?" I thought she would visit someone who is a saint. If it were someone like Father Peter people would expect it. This way the whole thing is more believable. Steve is not reading books all the time. He's always on the go."

Gerry continues, "In my opinion, I was drinking too much. For a couple of years I had prayed to be able to cut down, not really stop, but be an occasional drinker. I prayed for this intention regularly and tried cutting down, but it didn't work. Some time around June 2, 1992 after Holy Communion I prayed, "Lord, I can't handle it. You have to".

"On June 14 I was having a drink after Mass. Steve said "I have a message for you but I'll tell Maureen and she can tell you". Maureen replied, 'That's your job". I urged him, 'Tell me. I might be able to guess what it is". Steve claimed "Apparently you've been praying for help with your drinking. Is that correct?" I agreed. Stephen continued, Our Lady told him that I was drinking too much for my health and I should quit. If I continue to drink I'll probably die before I'm 60 years old. I suggested, 'Find out how much I can drink and I'll live till I'm 70'".

"Steve answered, "I don't think it works that way, Dad". I accepted that and responded, "O.K. tell me the rest". Steve told me that it would be my decision. I had free will. If I chose to quit, then Our Lady and her Son would give me the grace to handle it. I quietly went to the sink, poured out my drink and never had another one. It's been unbelievably easy. If I ever feel that the desire to drink is breaking into my mind more than usual I say an Our Father and Hail Mary and the desire is gone."

Gerry claims that he feels differently about his family and spends more time thinking of them rather than centering on himself. He used to enjoy playing darts about three or four nights a week. In the fall of 1991 he suddenly lost interest in the game and hasn't played since then. That change also freed him from the bar scene. Gerry believes that now he is more understanding, patient, prayerful. He enjoys working on his own projects at home and at the trailer. After working for Atomic Energy of Canada for 35 years, he took an early retirement in December 1990.

In June 1993, Gerry had a sore knee, as though a nerve were exposed at the front of the knee. When he genuflected at church he couldn't touch the floor. Nor could he kneel completely at church. On June 9 he attended the full day of adoration at church. Gerry felt that it would be nice to kneel and pray, and so he went down on both knees and received a jolt of surprise. The pain was gone and hasn't returned.

Gerry describes the nice things that continue to happen since that time. After Mass, the family talks about these events, and quite often Steve tells them about the locutions he had received. Gerry continues, "One night in bed, Betty and I couldn't sleep, and so we thought we would say some prayers. Betty reached for her Rosary on the bed post and suddenly the room was filled with the smell of flowers. That happened to us on more than one occasion. Betty is a walking saint."

Betty and Gerry attend Mass daily whenever they are in Ottawa and not at their summer trailer. He notes, "Last year between Christmas and New Year's we went to a funeral Mass for a friend. When I went to Holy Communion and the priest placed the Host on my tongue, I tasted something different. When I tried to explain it to Betty, I told her that I had a different feeling, as though there were a saint in the casket. I mentioned the different taste of the Host in my mouth. It was as though Our Lord were saying 'Thank you' to me. A really nice feeling."

"Usually I pray the Rosary when I'm driving my vehicle. One day, while driving home, I saw a car coming toward me and stopped praying. My mind wandered a bit, as my hand rested on the seat beside me. Suddenly I felt a couple of tugs on the rosary as though someone reminded me to get back to the business of praying.

Gerry and Betty began visiting the Greensides Farm at Marmora in September 1992 purely out of curiosity. Steve had told them not to look for signs and wonders. Later they went with a priest from their parish, and a pastor from another parish in Ottawa. In 1993 they returned to the farm when Maria Esperanza from Betania was present.

More recently, when Our Lady asked Steve to arrange a pilgrimage to the farm on five first Saturdays of the month, Betty and Gerry returned in their truck, and joined the pilgrims who came by bus. Both Betty and Gerry claim that they did not experience anything great at Marmora until more recently, when they felt deep peace and contentment. Following their last visit, Gerry was awake for several hours that night, reliving their experience and enjoying the memory of their visit.

Betty recalls that their little group of six who made the Way of the Cross together smelled incense at the Fourteenth Station, and afterwards smelled roses. They were touched spiritually while saying the Rosary. They felt that they were being blessed by Our Lady and thanked for praying the Stations. It was her way of saying thanks. Several people on the bus claimed to have had the same experience. Betty explains, 'It wasn't someone wearing perfume. We can't even describe the joy we felt. It just catches in your throat. You couldn't ask for more.' They hated to leave the farm when they felt that peace and contentment.

On another occasion when Gerry and Betty were driving home from Marmora in their truck, they were praying as usual, when suddenly they received the smell of roses. It gave them such a feeling of joy. Again they felt that Our Lady was giving them her blessing.

The grandchildren are very affectionate with Betty and Gerry, and are comfortable about sharing the events of their day with them. Erin was present when both her father and grandfather were being interviewed and decided that she also wanted to contribute her comments about the changes which she had noticed in her dad.

I Watched My Dad Change

Nine year old Erin Ley was very specific about wanting to share her story about the change she has observed in her dad, since Our Blessed Mother began to guide his life in a new direction. She listened as her dad and then her grandfather shared their experiences, while occasionally hovering over Baby Andrea in her mother or grandmother's arms, and listened to their input into the family story. Then she wanted some time for her own version. It is as follows.

"My dad used to be so mad at times. When everything wasn't right my mum and I would leave the house and do things like go to church. When Mary started to come my dad really changed. He started to stay home and listen to people's ideas. He listens now to how we feel. But when he used to get mad at us he wouldn't care how we felt. That's why it's nice now."

"He still gets mad now and then, but God is trying to help him about that because his temper was the worst part. He usually gets mad about me crying, screaming around the house because he's really stretched out after work. I can't see why, but when he comes home from work he's sick or something like that, and I'm always getting worried about him."

"Now that we have only one person going to work we're losing money, so he's working hard trying to get us back together again, and get us moving like it used to be when my mum used to go to work. (Maureen was on Maternity Leave at the time) When my mum went to work everything was organized in the morning by my mum."

"I get too hyper and I think that's why he gets mad at me, because almost everything makes me hyper that has sugar in it, like caffeine and that. I really love him but some times he got mad and had to leave the house, or my mum and me left the house and went to church or to my grandparents. I understand that because some times we're always home and everything is confusing and he needs some time for himself."

"My dad is really nice. He is a good dad, but I'm scared because of what's happening. I'm always here and I know that something's happening and it makes me uncomfortable. Like if I knew that Mary was in the room, I would go to my friend or my cousin and I would get frightened at night. I would have to have a parent with me. I wouldn't go to sleep at night because I'm too nervous that she would come to me."

"When I was at church, kneeling after Communion, I saw Mary's shadow over her statue. I said to Mum, "What is that shadow on the wall over Mary's statue?" My mum said "There's nothing on the wall". My dad said, "Yes, there is something there." I asked him, "What is it?" He said "It's Mary's shadow". When we got to the car he asked me some questions. He asked what colour and shape it was. It was clear in the middle and had a ring around it, then it would be golden grey brownish colour, then it would turn white. It didn't scare me. Actually I didn't know what it was or what was going on."

"If I don't know what's going on I feel much better and more comfortable. It won't scare me then. This happened when I was at church. It was Mary's feast day and my dad was seeing things when it happened. Mary was standing somewhere but I didn't know where she was. I asked my dad but he didn't tell me because he was concentrating on Mary's message. Later my dad told me that Mary told him not to concentrate on her but on the Mass. When she said that, my dad concentrated on the Mass."

CHAPTER EIGHT

ELECT FROM CHILDHOOD

Father Peter Coughlin resides at Our Lady of Perpetual Help Church in Ottawa. For several years he exercised leadership in the Charismatic Renewal, Healing Ministry, and Spiritual Direction. Beyond parish duties he is currently active with the Companions of the Cross. He describes himself as normally quiet, shy and reserved, but he turns on in front of people and is empowered from his various ministries. Father experienced supernatural phenomena since childhood and understands how these opportunities enhance the work of grace in people's lives.

When he was about eight years old he came home from church one day and told his pregnant mother that she would have a baby boy, and the date of her hospital admission. She asked how he knew and young Peter replied, 'God told me.' Even at that age he experienced a Word from the Lord. As a teenager he was active in nocturnal adoration, going to the church in the middle of the night for prayer.

Father claims, "I have often had the experience of the Lord, certain sense perceptions where you get goose bumps all over and you feel warm and glowing inside. You know that the Lord is present."

Eucharistic Manifestations

"In my second parish appointment in Hamilton, so few people attended daily Mass that I prayed to the Lord to reveal Himself in the Eucharist and perform a miracle so that people would see and understand. One rainy day I made hospital rounds and distributed Holy Communion. I approached one person and held up the Host between my thumb and forefinger. The Host pulsated. I could hear It, feel It, see It. I looked at the person to whom I was giving Communion. That person's eyes were closed with head bowed. I knew that it didn't happen for him, but for me."

"I gave the person Holy Communion, then went down the hall testing my thumb and forefinger together saying, 'It's not possible to get my pulse in that way.' About two weeks later while distributing Holy

Communion to someone else, it happened again though not as intensely. Over the years I've had the experience where it happened as confirmation that it truly occurred to me."

"Other Eucharistic miracles also took place . A fourteen year old girl attended Mass at a school for the deaf. She received Holy Communion for the first time under both species. Her mother told me that they had to leave the church because her daughter felt the Lord in every part of her being and it was overwhelming. Once on a C.O.R. retreat weekend the Host pulsated visibly in the monstrance. Some people were strongly affected by that. Once when my mother received the Eucharist, she experienced the Host pulsate in her hand."

"More recently I have seen images in the Eucharist. At a healing retreat in September in Round Lake, a woman prayed for the Lord to reveal his Face. During Mass I consecrated the large Host for the monstrance in the prayer chapel. Later, people saw the Face of the Lord in the Host when It was stored in the reservation chapel. A few weeks later I celebrated Mass at Our Lady of Perpetual Help Church. At the words, 'Through Him, with Him, and in Him' I held up the Host and saw in It the Face of the Lord outlined in black and white silhouette. At that moment the seminarian who served Mass experienced a sudden rush of the presence of the Lord. Others didn't see it, but Father Dennis knew that something was going on. I debated whether the silhouette was actually in the Host for everyone to see, but believed it was for me alone to witness."

"Last Friday in Winnipeg the celebrant held up the Host at the Consecration. I saw in the Host the image of the Lord in the tomb. Then the image shifted to Mary holding the Body of the Lord, as in the Pieta. That image continued all the time that It was elevated. The priest held the Host for a long time. It's amazing that more than twenty years ago I asked the Lord for miracles in the Eucharist to show that He is truly present, so that people would believe more and gather for Mass. I was the one to receive these different experiences. I have great love for the Eucharist."

"The Eucharist is very alive for me especially since my baptism in the Spirit. I was prayerful before then, but Mass really became alive for me after that event. A friend who was home from Peru was greatly changed from his experience of that baptism. I went to prayer meetings with him and during holidays we prayed a lot, discussed scripture and the renewal taking place in Peru. I attended a couple of prayer meetings at St. Joseph's Mother House in Pembroke, and stayed an extra day to be prayed over for the baptism of the Spirit, which took place on August 4, 1971. There was a dramatic change in my life. I experienced tremendous joy, peace, the Mass coming alive, scripture leaping off the pages at me, a whole new enthusiasm about the Spirit and about life in the Spirit. About three months later I started to speak in tongues."

"Last May or June I celebrated a Mass on Wednesday afternoon for the devotions to Our Lady of Perpetual Help. People were slain in the Spirit all over the church. It came to light because the secretary apologized for falling asleep during my homily. Other people who fell asleep came to her to describe their experience. It was a typical slaying in the Spirit. The seminarian who served Mass counted the bodies falling over. I was preaching and wasn't aware that it happened. Afterwards he talked about the people who were hung right over."(See Appendix Two)

"Many times in prayer I experience a cloud of glory or incense around me. I sense the Lord's presence and feel a sense of expectation. I don't know why I have that sense. Spiritually there are expectations but I don't know to what it refers. With regard to others' experience I know that Stephen sees a lot of visions in this church. One day as he drove into the parking lot he saw the Lord standing at the front door of the church."

Remarkable Occurrences

Father Peter's considerable travels occasioned several pilgrimages to Israel. He explains some unusual events. "On my second trip to Israel I felt like a tourist and couldn't get into the spirit of pilgrimage. Inside I felt cold, empty, dry, without spiritual dimension. It was raining. Our group visited the church of the Primacy of Peter which I had not seen on my previous trip. I went into the church and was suddenly overwhelmed with the Lord's presence. I fell to my knees on the big rock and prayed there. I prayed for such a long time that they had to rouse me to return to the bus. People were photographing me because I was heavily caught up in prayer. It was an overwhelming experience of the Sovereign Lord. My spirit literally flew when I left the church."

"The group went to the church of the Beatitudes where I celebrated Mass. There were so many people with colds and sniffles that I offered prayer for healing. Another bus load of people entered the chapel and they also gathered in the prayer line. By the time I finished praying for people we were late and had to catch the boat to cross the lake. We went to Capernaum where you have to pass along a stone walk which runs between a building and a stone wall. A storm was blowing. We couldn't even see where the boat was docked. The water was rough and rose up the walk."

"One woman wanted to take a picture of St. Peter's house in Capernaum. I ran with her through the water to the boat. A few people followed; the rest took the bus around the lake. As we walked the board walk to the shore some of them were hit by a wave. Not I. I wore my shoes, walked very gingerly on the water, and emerged from that storm completely dry to the soles of my shoes. My spirit literally soared. WALKING ON WATER was a great experience, and that passage of scripture could not be more real to me."

"The following day we went to the head waters of the Jordan. I ran across the stones, explored the cave on the other side and returned. Because of the greasy and slippery mud I carefully picked my way across the rocks in head waters. Somehow I lost my footing and fell straight down, jamming the calf muscle of my left leg into the rock. My leg literally exploded in size. I spent the remainder of the day in bed. My leg was badly swollen but I felt no pain. We left the next day. I walked in Tel Aviv and was amazed that I was able to do so. When I returned to Canada my doctor examined me and denied that a calf muscle was damaged. I have had problems with my left leg ever since then and developed a drop foot and sciatic nerve problem, without pain but with poor motor control. My leg was wasting. I continue to bear that damage in my left leg and believe that the drop foot is connected with it."

"Three years ago I was scheduled for back surgery. I went to Medjugorje and when the doctor examined me on my return he explained that my condition stabilized and that surgery was not required. Maybe he was in a good mood because he won the $5,000. hospital lottery that day."

Spiritual Focus

Deepening one's spirituality is a given for a priest who chooses to grow in response to God's inner presence. Father Peter describes some moments of grace which stimulated his growth. "There have been many experiences of the presence and the power of God at work in my life, which are an ongoing source of grace and spiritual growth. I'm known as a man of faith. Some times I think it's precious little but at other times I know that I've been blessed with very simple faith. Some people struggle with their own faith but can be towers of strength for others. Other people are always asking questions, seeking understanding. Once I saw a bumper sticker which read 'God said it. I believe it. That settles it.' That is where my faith is."

"Through the years my focus on the spiritual increased. When I was ordained I focused on youth work, working with men in the parish, all kinds of programs. In my first assignment I tried to bring a dying parish to life. People cooperated with me in this endeavour. I asked the priest who replaced me to make an appearance and keep it going in order to affirm the people. He did not do that. He worked only one on one with people and not at all with groups, whereas I had done a lot of group work. Life in the parish collapsed. This is sad but often the case."

"In the next parish there was increased sacramental ministry with the emphasis also on teaching in schools, as in the first parish. I had two successive pastors who required a certain number of house calls per week which I accomplished. In my next assignment I experienced tremendous spiritual explosion with people. The parish began with Movement for a Better World Retreat. At one point probably three hundred people went elsewhere to prayer meetings because the pastor would not allow prayer meetings. C.O.R., Youth activities, Cursillo, everything blossomed and it was a spiritually graced time. I started a prayer group in a neighbouring parish, and half of the two hundred were teenagers from Oakville."

"My life has been one of service, calling forth people for spiritual growth. That's always been my focus. Once a woman who was having difficulty spoke with her friend, who advised, 'You should go and see Father Peter.' The woman complained, 'You can't get anywhere with him. All he ever does is take you to Jesus and leave you there.' I took this as a great compliment. That's how my life has been."

"At one point in Hamilton we had a priests' prayer meeting on Wednesday every month. We gathered with an opening song, and a time to praise God. Then we sat down; all but one of us were slain in the Spirit. One priest periodically offered vocal prayers. We sort of knew he was praying this way. The rest of us rested in the Spirit, overwhelmed in the Lord's presence. That happened every month for two years. Then someone wanted to move the group to his parish. It did so then fell apart again. I consider it as a spiritual phenomenon that a group of eight or nine priests all rest in the Spirit at the same time."

Supernatural Phenomena

"I have experienced many things in praying with people, such as healings right in front of me, signs and wonders of food being multiplied. I learned the difference between coincidence and God incident, and see the hand of God at work in many ways. I have been part of miracles of transformation taking place simply, as with the multiplication of food. In one parish we had fifty teenagers for an after school retreat from four until seven. The Catholic Women's League coordinated the dinner and supplied rolls and milk. The students were supposed to bring food supplies. Only six small casseroles showed up for fifty older teenagers. Just before dinner I was told that there was not enough food and answered, 'That's O.K. We'll multiply it.' When I said grace in the church I asked the Lord to multiply the food. The young people ate, had seconds, thirds and fourths. Then the eight ladies in the kitchen ate and there was food left over. Afterwards the ladies talked about this impossible thing that happened."

"We held a Christmas dance and full turkey dinner with the same group of students. They expected a hundred people, and two hundred and fifty showed up. We had no choice but to start the food lines. I asked the Lord to multiply the food to everyone's blessing. The line-up started and people arrived with different kinds of food. One student's father was a cook at the Knights of Columbus Hall. He raided their larder, cooked up sausage and whatever else was available. By the time the last person went through the line the menu changed completely, the food was gone, but everyone ate. No one was limited in portions nor warned that the food was in short supply. That was another marvellous answer which shows the amazing action of God in our lives."

Healing Ministry

Father Peter's gift of healing has been used largely with the Charismatic renewal. He shared: "About three years ago I fell and suffered a concussion producing blurred and double vision. It happened on a Wednesday morning, and I was scheduled to speak in Edmonton on Friday night. With the doctor's approval I flew west. At the conference I spoke for an hour though I couldn't read my notes. Then I sensed that the Lord was healing people. I told them that I had a real sense that healing was taking place and asked 'How many people experience healing?' Of the five hundred in attendance about two hundred and fifty hands were raised. I asked people to share their experiences. A young man who was a college or university student testified that he had a stiff neck for several days and it disappeared. I responded, 'That's good because the Lord doesn't want any stiff necked Christians around here.'"

"After their testimonies a few of us anointed people. Through the crowd I saw a man being held up by three people. His body was limp and sagging. I went through the crowd, anointed him with oil and blessed him. I prayed in tongues and heard the Lord say, 'He has faith to be healed.' I opened my eyes and looked at him. There was no change. I continued to pray in tongues and the Lord said, 'He will be healed as they move away.'"

"I turned immediately and walked away. As I continued anointing, I saw the man and his companions stand there for a moment then move away. I lost sight of them but the cries of 'Alleluia!' and 'Praise God!' echoed through the place. Then I saw the man. His cane went flying. He was leaping, dancing and jumping, talking a blue streak. I went over to him and discovered he had suffered for six years from head injuries sustained in a car accident. The three people who brought him were like the men who brought the paralytic to Jesus and lowered him through the roof of the house. I returned to my ministry and heard afterwards that the cries of rejoicing and alleluia could be heard a block away from the cathedral. About six weeks later the sister in charge of the event saw the man on the street. He did a dance for her and said he was still healed, in great shape. He came from Chile and was returning there."

"Many years ago when I first got involved in healing ministry I kept a record of everything and showed it to Bishop Ryan in Hamilton. He approved what I did, and I didn't bother to keep a record afterwards. This ministry enhances my faith and enlivens me as a priest."

Medjugorje Visionaries

Father Peter has enjoyed visits to several Marian shrines, including Guadalupe, Lourdes, Fatima, Knock, and five times to Medjugorje. He first heard about Medjugorje at the 1983 priests' conference in Steubenville which he attended, because he wanted a deeper sense of conversion in his life. As soon as he heard a speaker talk about Medjugorje he knew it was exactly what he needed, and believed it completely. He comments further.

"The following year I had an opportunity to attend an International Charismatic Leadership Conference. A doctor from Toronto asked me if I would go to Medjugorje before the conference with him and Father Bob, if he paid the way. I accepted. We spent twenty hours in Medjugorje on that trip, which was an exhausting journey. I did not sleep on the plane to Italy, then travelled the milk run through that country. We rented a car in Dubrovnik and drove to Medjugorje."

"In the church of St. James I prayed. It did not matter to me whether or not I saw anything supernatural. I firmly believed in the apparitions. Sister Agnes invited us into the apparition room that evening. Father Bob who had been there before, headed for the window. Dr. McKenna remained in the corner, and I ended up in the middle of the room, which was packed with about sixty people. I had no idea where the visionaries would be. When they entered I knelt with them in the centre of the floor. Later I watched the video in the parish rectory where I was staying."

"When Ivan, the visionary from Medjugorje, was in Hamilton, I was about four or five feet away from him during his apparition, and had the same experience with Vicka in Moncton in May. The apparition lasted for thirteen or more minutes, rather long compared to recent ones. I intuitively knew that I would be there and that it would be a longer apparition. I often have that strong sense of knowing about events. I don't necessarily speak about them but I am astounded at how I know. I perceive it as a spiritual phenomenon happening within or through me."

Experiences at Marmora

Visitors to Marmora will be interested in Father Peter's point of view with regard to the farm and pilgrims. He states, "I have visited Marmora about eight times, on occasion with a pilgrimage. When I drive back and forth to Hamilton I pass by Marmora, and if I have time I stop to see who is at the farm. I have been there with Steve Ley and also with the Companions of the Cross. Twice I was asked to celebrate Mass for the pilgrims at the church in Marmora."

"It's good to minister to the pilgrims, because they need to know what a pilgrimage is and why they are there. They need to be able to put their experience into words and into context. I think it's helpful to do that. From the comments of the pilgrims who attended Mass, it was the first time they had that kind of opportunity, and they found it to be beneficial to them. I was also a little charismatic, prayed in English, and had people lay hands on the person beside them."

"I have led the Stations of the Cross at the farm and also made them privately. I have talked to the Greensides and visited in their home two or three times. The farm is a place of prayer, of spontaneous pilgrimage on the part of people. It's a blessing for many and gives them an opportunity to focus, especially today when so many churches are locked and people are unable to go to church and pray."

"The Greensides and their helpers do a great job in trying to serve the pilgrims. It takes a tremendous amount of commitment, dedication and dying to self, to put people first all the time and to give over your property in the way they have done. They never really have any private space or time for themselves. Caution needs to be exercised about the nature of literature which is distributed by some individuals. It needs to be carefully screened."

"I am the spiritual director of one visionary and confessor to another, so I'm surrounded by all these events. I am not concerned that the messages be screened by clergy beforehand, because it seems that a lot of what happens is fairly private. One caution I would make is that the Greensides should not advertise the fact that there is going to be a visionary present. There are a number of people who have visions there, and some people always want to be with the visionaries. I have requested that caution of Veronique's parents. She needs space to grow, to develop, and when she has a message, to speak it. It's difficult to be a visionary and be always pulled and pushed."

Cooperating With God's Will

There are mixed reactions to spiritual phenomena. Some people consider it weird, crazy or pure imagination. Others recognize God's intervention in their lives, but fear or resist it because they feel threatened, and don't want to change their current life style. Still others place conditions on the grace with which they will cooperate.

Father shares some thoughts on this matter. "Basically God can do what He wants. Too often we try to put God in a neat package, give Him limitations as to how He can move or operate in the lives of people. Many people fear the action of God because it is not yet part of their experience. It's something new. It challenges them to have faith and believe. The reason some people do not accept healing in their lives is that they when they recognize the touch or action of God, it means that they have to change, and they may not be ready to do that. Others do not understand, and claim that it's the power of the evil one at work. Some resist praying in tongues, and though they ask God for all the gifts, they reject that particular one."

"They tell God what He can and can't do. They come forward and ask for prayer, then stand there, resisting the flow of grace to be overwhelmed in the Spirit. My observation is that they ask for grace from the Lord, but are willing to receive only on their terms, the way they can handle it, and the way they want to be. God is truly sovereign and does not operate in that way. What He needs more than anything else is our permission to go ahead and do what He wants. Surrender and giving God permission are basically the same. However giving God permission implies action on our part. Surrender can sometimes indicate passivity. Surrender implies action but is not perceived that way in our vocabulary."

"Probably my strongest indication of resistance was when I challenged a visionary that he needed to go to Confession. It was revealed to me that he had to deal with something. He refused. He attended Mass at the church, returned to me afterwards, and said he did need to go to Confession. I spent some time with him and took care of the matter. It's not normal for me to tell someone they have to go to Confession, but on that occasion I sensed strongly that I was to do so. The next morning during prayer in the church I had an inner locution from Mary. She said, 'Thank you for helping my son', and mentioned him by name. I was totally enveloped by the presence of the one who spoke. Her voice was inside and outside me. I believe it was Mary."

"I've had inner locutions from the Lord. This is the only pronounced time I can remember a locution from Mary, though I have been strongly aware of her presence prior to this occasion. I don't know how to describe it. I was on retreat, sitting in a room with a view across the water. I sensed very strongly that she was coming. Afterwards someone asked me about my experience because they observed that something was going on with me. It was a very real and strong sense."

"Another occasion was a couple of years ago during the Hamilton Charismatic Conference. Veronique was in attendance and had a vision of Mary, who entered and danced with the liturgical dancers. Veronique described it to me and I shared it with the assembly. After the procession Mary stood at the right side of the altar. That evening when I conducted healing ministry I stood at that same spot and was very much aware of Mary's presence. When sharing that experience with the assembly, I basically knew it to be true because I saw it, not as an actual vision in black and white or technicolour. Rather it was a whole sense perception and awareness which I simply knew. I can still see the vision in my mind's eye."

Concluding Thoughts

Father Peter's life was guided by the Lord since childhood. His life of prayer preceded his call to the ministerial priesthood, and continued to deepen as he matured in grace by the power of the Holy Spirit. Being personally gifted with visions, locutions, and other supernatural phenomena, he is able to serve others in a variety of ministries. He understands the concerns of those who do not receive such unique graces. He is also confident in the actual gift of personal faith, which invites each person to grow spiritually according to God's design for their lives during this challenging time.

Father concludes "Many, many people experience spiritual phenomena in their lives and this increases as they grow spiritually, hungering and thirsting for union with the Lord. There is always more that the Lord has in store for us; surprises of His Spirit that move and encourage us as we open our hearts to Jesus, focus on Him, and give Him permission to act in our lives. It's important to see the "God-incidence" in our lives, not just the coincidence. Look to see how the Lord is at work, but don't look for experiences. Look for the Lord, the God of our experience."

Photo taken by Harry Bekkers, with image of Our Lady in center.

85

Photo taken at Marmora, almost identical to the photo taken at Naju, Korea.

Unusual Solar Phenomena.

Pilgrims at Prayer at Marmora: Raoul and Mauricia Yumul.

Pilgrims Gather in All Kinds of Weather.

Climbing the Way of the Cross.

45 Buses Brought Pilgrims to Marmora for December 8, 1994.

87

December 8, 1994: People Gathered at the Tenth Station.

December 8, 1994: Site Chosen by Our Lady for a Little Chapel.

Father Karl Clemens

Marci Guinto

Veronique Demers

Stephen Ley

Father Peter Coughlin

CHAPTER NINE

EVANGELIZATION AND HEALING

After thirty-five years in the teaching profession Allan Young retired in 1991. He is divorced, with a twenty nine year old son. As a young boy Allan wanted to be a doctor because of his desire to help people. Instead he became a teacher, a profession which he loved. He states that he always had an active faith even through rough times, bad times, and off beat times. He knew that Our lady would be there to help him. More and more, in teaching, he prayed quietly to Our Lady without anyone knowing it.

As a teacher Allan was lively and animated, and enjoyed leadership roles with the Teachers' Association, Red Cross and other groups. He continues to be an outgoing person, ready to share his more recent gifts, wherever God indicates the need for this ministry.

Allan began to experience supernatural phenomena in 1991 during his first trip to Medjugorje, which he had longed to visit for several years, and to which he returned two more times. The tremendous gifts of Medjugorje transformed his life into one of active ministry of evangelization and healing. Hundreds of people have been significantly moved, converted, or healed through Allan's intercessory prayer and healing touch. He shares his story as follows.

"I was dying to get to Medjugorje for about six years and there were no pilgrimages during the summer, but only in the spring and the fall. I was beginning to cuss a little at these people who organized the trips and asked, 'Why can't they go in the summer?' Later on I found out from a friend who had gone in the summer, that the temperature was around 95 degrees and the place was worse than Disneyland. There were between fifty to sixty thousand people all the time and they couldn't get about nor do anything."

"Prior to my visits there I listened to Father Bob's tapes about Medjugorje. A retired teacher friend of mine helped him with the Lamplighter, which sent Medjugorje news everywhere. We obtained some tapes of the apparitions, and being fascinated, I watched Vicka and the other visionaries. The truth of it all began to hit me that Our Lady appeared to six people every day for extended periods of time. All the supernatural phenomena which accompanied the apparitions truly struck me. I realized that something was happening far more than at Fatima and at Lourdes, although these are very important as well. There was urgency in the frequent messages. We followed closely the testimony of their authenticity from leading theologians, other people and experts who had been there, even though there was a particular problem at Mostar with the bishop."

Attraction to Medjugorje

Allan's growing attraction to Medjugorje led him to make his first pilgrimage in October, 1991. He describes his experience. "For several days we prayed there. I purchased a rosary in the Franciscan gift shop and the next day we visited Vicka. She took our religious objects to have Our Lady bless them during her apparition. When we got them back the next day, all the links of my rosary had turned to a lovely light gold colour. As each day went by the gold grew darker, as someone told me it would. The links are still a lovely rich gold in colour."

"After that I began to see the spinning sun. I saw the sun quite clearly, like a grey-white Host, with a dancing gold light flickering all around it in different directions. I can still see the spinning sun to this day. We made the Stations of the Cross on Mount Krizevac. At the end of that visit, there was time in the afternoon of that thanksgiving day to climb Apparition Hill, which I did. On my way down I watched the sun again. Afterwards I noticed that the sun descended toward the cross on Mount Krizevac. A lovely soft pink cloud, like a pink mist, came down on the left of the sun, moved along the ground and expanded outward. As I watched in amazement, a yellow mist formed on the other side of the sun, and very narrowly came down on the right side to the ground and moved toward the cross. As it reached the cross it filled out more and more. That lasted for about three or four minutes. Then I had to rush down to the evening Mass."

"On my return to Canada, I toured England and then the United States. I noticed that my rosary was even darker than the original gold colour. Out of curiosity I dropped into two or three jewellers. Each one told me it was either a gold alloy or gold plated or gold. One jeweller said there were white specks in it. I began to feel that perhaps it was gold. I was elated because not only did my rosary change but I had read about people whose rosaries were pure gold. I said, 'Perhaps this is gold.' When I visited my sister in Montreal there was a mall across the street where a jeweller was checking gold. Without telling the story I had him look at it. He tested it and concluded that it was gold. Then I told him my story. I was thrilled and told my sister and her friends."

"My friend's wife had a rosary which changed to gold and I asked to see it. I wanted to continue holding it for a while and pray to Our Lady, but had to return it. That almost broke my heart. When this happened to my rosary I decided that it wasn't just for me. I let people hold it and invited them to pray with it. The look on their face was incredible after doing so. Some kissed it!"

"Whenever I gave people the rosary to pray, I could see the peace and gentleness which came upon their face. Somehow they felt a contact with Our Lady or with God in a strange way. I felt that way when I held friends' rosaries which turned gold, but more so now when I tell them about how the rosary turned gold from Our Lady."

"Personally I hadn't prayed too much although all through my life I often prayed to Our Lady and Our Lord, especially Our Lady. To say the Rosary was a struggle for me so I decided to lead myself in very gradually. I imitated the Medjugorje villagers and prayed seven Our Father's, Hail Mary's and Glory Be's. Even with those prayers I struggled, though I noticed a change in my life. When we think back about what we've done and who we are or where we're going, and read the messages of Our Lady very carefully, our priorities shift. Now I always say the Rosary, very gratefully."

Impact of the Rosary

As Allan shared his rosary and the story of Medjugorje, things happened to him. He expands on this. "For example, Lucille a teacher, had a niece Susie with rheumatoid arthritis. She was a dental assistant in her twenties, and could do very little. Because she lived in Rouyn-Noranda I suggested to Lucille 'When she comes to town, tell me. I'll come over and we'll pray with her.' That night I gave her my rosary and requested, 'Susie, pray to Our Lady'. As she prayed her head went down. I knew that something happened to her, but deliberately talked to Lucille and Susie's mother and a few others, so Susie wouldn't be distracted. After about four minutes I stopped, and asked Susie what happened. She said, 'I felt heat in my right hand. It went up my arm, through my body and down the left arm. I said, 'Pray to Our Lady some more.' About three weeks later when she went to the doctor for tests, the blood samples revealed that everything was fine. As a result the Rosary took on increasing significance for me."

Return to Medjugorje

In 1992 Allan returned to Medjugorje, and experienced a new dimension of grace even before the flight landed. He notes,"On the way, I talked with people who were in our group. My companion Margaret told others about my rosary. Bob was a sergeant in the Mounties. When I showed him my rosary he said, 'I hope my rosary changes. I need it badly.' He talked about one or two problems. On the plane Bob and I were independently praying the Rosary. He gave me a nudge, and sure enough two or three links had started to turn gold. He was elated. By the time we reached Frankfurt a good third of his rosary turned gold. He said, 'I've got my wife's rosary here too. Maybe it will happen to hers as well.' At the end of the week it was turning to gold!"

"In Canada I had attended some charismatic meetings with friends who suffered a tragedy, and we went there to pray for them. I watched people resting in the Spirit and the different manifestations. In the Medjugorje group were four charismatic people. One was Doctor Bob, a dentist from Montreal who had a gift of healing. The mountie also belonged to a prayer group. Philemon had the gift of healing, as well as other people in the group. In the dining room on our second day there they said, 'Let's pray over people here.' The owner joined us and he, his wife, their parents and others prayed with us. I held my rosary and prayed with all my heart. Suddenly one person went down, then another and another. About five or six people rested in the Spirit that night."

"One man in our group had a difficult time. His wife left him. His lower back was completely ruined. He had a year to work in order to receive his pension. He told us his story and added, 'I'm cursing God. Nothing's working, and prayer hasn't worked here either. I looked at Bob the dentist and Bob the mountie, my roommate, and said, 'We have to get him in the room tonight.' We prayed and suddenly my hands were on fire. The more intensely we prayed the more my hands burned. I told Bob and he answered, 'Allan, I think you have the gift of healing.' I thought it was due to the rosary and let him hold it. When I prayed to Our Lady over him, he praised Our Lord and Our Lady with tremendous enthusiasm. My roommate Bob watched us, and when I prayed over him, he talked and sang in tongues non-stop. They both agreed, 'You have the gift.'

"The next day was the Feast of the Holy Rosary. Because of the war there were only two or three hundred people in Medjugorje, Americans, Italians, Europeans, and our group. After Mass I talked with an American and Bob the Mountie chatted with another chap about someone in their group who prayed over people, and things happened. I intervened with, 'You should see what's happening in our group.' He asked me to pray over him. I prayed to Our Lady to help him, and he went crashing down on the steps. I yelled, 'Bob! Bob! A lady came over for prayer and Bob was there to catch her when she rested in the Spirit."

"Tears formed in my eyes. A woman brought a picture of her niece, and asked me to pray over the picture. As I did so tremendous heat came out of my hands. She asked if I would pray over her. I prayed to Our Lady and she went down in the Spirit. I said to Bob, 'I have to go away for a minute.' I went to the statue of Our Lady and I was bawling, literally crying my eyes out and enjoying it. I said, 'With these hands you gave me this lovely gift.' I thought of the day we arrived in Medjugorje and I asked Our Lady, 'You gave me this lovely gift of your rosary. Show me what you want me to do.' I had no idea that this would happen."

"We went to see Father Jozo. When he laid hands on me I went down instantly and lay there in an aura of light, a strange light I've never seen before. I opened my eyes and it was too bright. I closed them and enjoyed it. Dottie had a terrible knee problem. After Father Jozo prayed over her, she said, 'My knee feels fine.' She began to cry. I told her, 'Dottie things happen that way. Our Lady does beautiful things especially through Father Jozo.'"

"Dottie wanted to climb the Apparition Hill again. On the way up I said, 'Dottie look at the sun." She said, 'I can't... then, Yes I can.' She saw the grey-white sun and the spinning gold light around it. On the way up I said to some people, 'Look at the sun' and they all saw the sun. This continued all the way up the hill. Everyone who looked at the sun saw it."

"Coming down the hill Dottie said, 'Look at the sun. There's a lovely soft pink cloud going down on the left side. Now there's a yellow one. It's going down toward the cross. Now it's filling out.' Tears were running down her face. I saw the soft pink cloud, but not the yellow one, and wondered why I didn't see the yellow cloud again. I believe it was to confirm in me the reality of what I saw earlier."

"On my return to Canada I found it awkward to explain to people what happened to me during my pilgrimage. I received looks of cynicism and doubt. But I had to tell them that I had the gift of hands. One or two of my friends and their wives snickered until they found out about the gold rosary. When I mentioned the gift of hands they thought, 'He's gone far out.' I told Father Bob about it. He told me to take the Life in the Spirit Seminar to find out about the gifts and fruits of the Holy Spirit. I did so. While at Father Bob's I offered to pray over him. Oddly enough he held up his wrist, because he was having trouble with bursitis or tendonitis. I held his wrist and said, 'Father, usually I just lay hands on the shoulder and pray to Our Lady.' He said, 'Whatever you want, Al.' As I prayed, he waved his wrist back and forth rapidly. At the end, I asked, 'How's your wrist?' He said, 'I don't know. It seems to be moving. I'll tell you in a couple of weeks.' I saw him a few weeks later and asked about his wrist. He said, 'It's just fine.' I was delighted with this because though Father reported everything that went on in Medjugorje, his rosaries did not change colour nor did he witness the miracle of the sun."

Charismatic Ministry

Although some people are hesitant about the manifestation of the gifts of the Spirit, people who experience the Charismatic renewal freely appreciate the use of these gifts. When Allan went to Florida he visited charismatic groups around Fort Lauderdale, and shared his story with them. He continues, "Almost everyone who asked for prayer rested in the Spirit. I went regularly to their meetings, until someone told me about Our Lady Queen of Martyrs Parish where every month they recite the Rosary, have various liturgies for Our Lady, then Mass followed by prayer. When I prayed over people there I felt the Spirit moving. There were several cures each time, at different meetings in the parishes."

"One woman had extreme difficulty getting into her chair, and two or three of us had to help her. I had noticed her at other meetings and she was always in pain. I prayed over her but didn't feel her going down in the Spirit. At the end of prayer she said, 'Thank you.' She went to get up and I offered to help her. She declined, got up and said, 'I am fine. Look!' She twisted around all over. It was beautiful to see her this way. Someone with arthritis and one or two with skin problems were also healed."

"Queen of Martyrs parish sort of adopted me. At one time they had the Tilma of Our Lady of Guadalupe which travelled through the United States. One of the girls' mother had bone cancer in the arm, which was cured in Medjugorje. It was recurring and protruding through the skin. The group asked me to join them in the hospital that evening when they brought the Tilma. We placed the Tilma on the wall and prayed over her. She had a lovely rosary from Medjugorje which turned gold. I gave her my rosary. Someone asked me to pray over her again. One of the girls put her hand on my shoulder, and I could feel the heat from her hand going through my body and into this woman. About a week later we found out that her condition improved, and later more so before I returned home."

"In Montreal one of my godparents' nieces had lupus and also other forms of arthritis. She suffered from it so badly that she had infection under her finger nails. I prayed over her one night, then continued praying to Our Lady for her. Later her nails also cleared up and the lupus was in remission."

"One visitor invited me to pray with their prayer group while I was visiting Gospa House in Merrickville. Until this time I prayed to Our Lady straight from the heart, without formal prayer. Suddenly it dawned on me, 'Why not use Our Lady's prayer, the prayer to the Holy Spirit?' "Come Holy Spirit, come by means of the powerful intercession of the Immaculate Heart of Mary, your well beloved spouse." As I began to use that prayer things happened instantly with amazing results at Gospa House and their prayer meetings later on."

"I visited groups, attended the Life in the Spirit Seminar with the Assumption group, then returned to join St. Mary's prayer group where all this began. I told my story, prayed over people, and they rested in the Spirit. Many cures happened which I listed at random as they came along."

"Des, a friend and a retired colleague, was visiting with his wife Joan at mutual friends. I prayed over Joan then over him. Des said, 'I have a terrible headache that goes all around the front of my head. Joan said 'I have the same headache.' They had prayed for their daughter who suffered from post-partum depression. Something told me to pray over them again. I did, and both headaches were gone. I found out a week ago that their daughter will be home from hospital soon."

New Grace At Medjugorje

The irresistible pull of Medjugorje drew Allan back again, in 1993. He wanted an extended period of time there, and flew a week earlier than the regular group, agreeing to meet them when they arrived. A change occurred in his prayer life. He explains. "Until then I had been praying to Our Lady constantly. Then I noticed the miraculous medals with the hearts entwined, and said to myself, 'I should be praying to Our Lord too. It's through His mercy and grace and His love that these things happen.' I recalled the beatification of Sister Faustina and the devotion to the Divine Mercy. I prayed to the Sacred Heart, saying 'I place my trust in You.' I was anxious about one or two personal things and asked Our Lord to look after them."

"In Medjugorje I prayed over people, with positive results. One time I prayed, sitting in the outdoor pews, when a voice said to me, 'Go to the Cross'. Behind the church is a log Cross in a pit with stone work around it, where people burn their candles. I went there and looked toward Mount Krizevac. As I looked up, I noticed that the Cross had no arms. Then there were arms again. Once again, there were no arms, and arms again. I said to myself, 'I'm diabetic. Am I seeing things?' It happened once more. Suddenly something about twice the size of a star flashed a lovely soft pink and red on the left of the Cross. I asked, 'Are you showing me something?' I prayed to Our Lady and Our Lord and it flashed again. On the other side another flashed a soft blue-white-grey."

"I didn't quite realize what was happening. I thanked Our Lord saying, 'I think You're answering my message,' and continued to pray. At the end I said, 'Thank you very much, Lord,' and it flashed that lovely soft pink red colour again. Six months later I realized that these are the Divine Mercy colours. I knew that somehow Our Lord, and not only Our Lady answered me at that particular time."

"I used to be a First Aid Instructor with the Red Cross. The next day after evening Mass I saw a priest holding a young woman about 25 or 30 in his arms, and thought, 'This calls for either first aid or healing.' I offered him my help. He said, one word to me, 'Stigmata.' This young Italian woman had multiple sclerosis or muscular dystrophy, perhaps both. She was in terrible condition lying in his arms. I looked at her hands and there was a tremendous round brown welt all over both palms. Apparently during Mass he went outside to give Communion and her guardian was with her. When he saw her in her condition he gave her a blessing. The guardian insisted she receive Communion, and she was able to receive It."

"Her guardian explained that the phenomenon began three months earlier and continued on the 25th of each month, the day of apparition. Occasionally her hands and feet bled. She was in terrible agony. Spontaneously I placed the rosary into her hands. I said to myself, 'I'm seeing someone with the stigmata here.' After about five minutes she came out of it and was full of joy. She hugged the Scottish priest. I reclaimed the rosary and she hugged me and the person who was with me. Witnessing the stigmata stopped me cold, because it followed so closely my recent awakening to the Divine Mercy and Sacred Heart."

"Later I prayed over Father Eddie from Scotland, lending him the rosary. His head went down in quiet prayer for about eight minutes, and he emerged peaceful and content. Every time I saw him afterwards he had a wave for me and sometimes a hug!."

Teamwork in Prayer

The movement of the Spirit builds Christian community. No one is a loner even when ministering personal gifts. Allan shared his experience. "St. Mary's prayer group decided that I continue to pray over people. They wondered why I placed the rosary in peoples' hands when I pray. I answered, 'It somehow brings people closer to Our Lady.' I told them the story of how I wanted to hold my friend's rosary for a longer time and couldn't then. They suggested that when I pray over people I have someone there with me for my own protection, someone who would pray, as well as one who could hold those who rested in the Spirit. I looked around at the group and couldn't spot anyone."

"I remembered a young lady, Risa, whom I had prayed over. Something told me she was the one. I invited her and she was elated to pray with me. Without my knowing it, the prayer group leaders had already picked her because of her healing gift. She prays to Our Lord, so we had a winning team. The regional meeting of all prayer groups in Ottawa drew about one hundred and fifty people. Heather, the group leader, asked Risa and me if we would pray. As we prayed over people, the Spirit really moved and people often fell in the Spirit. One man came forward and told his story. I thought, 'I'll pray to Our Lord this time.' We laid our hands on him, touched his shoulder and he went down instantly. I looked at Risa and said, 'I prayed to Our Lord.' She stated, 'I prayed to Our Lady.'"

"Some cures happened, arthritis, acne, eczema, and so on at other meetings also. We don't follow up too much. Sometimes people tell us, but we know it's happening, and there are a lot of conversions. Some people have an expression of peace reflected on their face after we pray over them. An inner peace seems to come upon them. They hug you afterwards and you know that something happened."

"I have been quite active lately with the Holy Cross group in Kemptville, the Assumption group and was invited to pray with the Ave Maria group in Resurrection parish. About two thirds of the people went down in the Spirit. One woman said, 'After that, when I went to Mass for the next few days, it was incredible. My personal approach to Mass changed. Even the way I pray is different.'"

Experiences At Marmora

Allan heard about the events at the Greensides farm at Marmora but had not the opportunity to visit until his last return from Medjugorje. When that flight landed in Toronto he stopped in Marmora on his way home, with only his light jacket for protection. He describes the event. "It was pouring rain and my umbrella was in Medjugorje. I went into the reception area and talked with Colleen. She complained about not being able to make that pilgrimage because the time was always awkward. I described a way she could travel independently, and told her where she could stay in Medjugorje. I explained briefly what happened to me, showed her my rosary, and gave her some medals. She was delighted, and I left for home."

"The Assumption group, Father Brian, Audrey, their leader, and others decided to drive to Marmora in September. We said the Rosary and ate lunch. Anne Marie was outside, and I asked for Colleen but she wasn't there. We made the Stations of the Cross and when we came back they wanted to go to the book store. Anne Marie was still outside so I chatted with her, told her why I wanted to see Colleen again, showed her the rosary and told her about my gift of healing."

"As soon as she heard that she explained, 'Colleen is not well. She has cancer and it's not a very good sign. Her husband Bob is in the house. I'll get him.' Bob came out and told me that they live in Marmora and he would get Colleen. I suddenly realized that I should pray over him. I asked, 'Do you mind if I pray over you?' He agreed. I prayed over him and felt something happen, but not too much. When it was over he remarked, 'I have to tell you that until this particular time I was a mess. My mind was just racing all over the place. My stomach was in knots. I was uptight, tense, and troubled by all that's happened. Since you prayed over me I felt nothing but peace all through me.'"

"He went into town and got Colleen as the group returned from the book store. I told them what happened. When Colleen arrived we went into the house and Father Brian, who has the gift of healing, myself, and the others prayed over her. She rested in the Spirit. We prayed over Mrs. Greensides who was wearing a neck collar at the time, and a woman from Toronto. On a subsequent visit to Marmora, Anne Marie told me that Colleen's cancer is shrinking. It's probably due to all the people praying for her."

A Voice From The Past

Allan recalls with fondness, Wade, a student he taught in Grade Six. Wade's mother told Allan that Wade and the family fell away from the church, and asked for prayer during Allan's pilgrimage to Medjugorje.

Wade had previously called Allan to obtain a letter of reference for a job he was seeking. Allan continues, "I agreed to do this and he asked what I was doing. I told him I was retired, and of my involvement with Medjugorje and healing. He was extremely interested."

"Several months after my return from Medjugorje, I received a call from Wade. After I described my pilgrimage, he told me he was praying the Rosary every day. In later telephone calls and visits, he told me about his conversion and, hesitatingly, about some unusual incidents and changes in his life. I gave him some Medjugorje literature, explained the graces and messages of Our Lady, answered his questions, and prayed over him and his family. Now he attends Mass daily and once in a while, spontaneously experiences the tears of love and joy. An incredible change happened to him and his family."

"Wade's anniversary was last week. He wanted me to go to Marmora with him and I couldn't that Monday, but we went on Thursday. I picked him up at Arnprior and we drove to Marmora, arriving at the farm around one o'clock. We offered a few intentions for people, went towards the grotto, then to the reception area. John Greensides was there. Shelagh was talking to a group of Italians. As I walked in she recognized me but couldn't quite place me."

"I talked with John and an Irish woman who was with him. I reminded John of what happened and the woman asked, 'You have the gift of healing?' I said, 'Well, I have the gift of hands. Sometimes healing happens.' She brought her husband who had kidney problems. We prayed over him and the strangest thing happened. I felt him going down and thought, 'He's going down in the Spirit.' He straightened up and seemed to gain about a foot in height. We continued praying. I could feel him starting to back up a bit, and thought, 'He's going.' Then he jerked up quickly again. When I finished praying, his eyes were closed and he went back to his lower position."

"One of the Italian women came over and asked if I would pray over her. She had a bad knee. We prayed over her. She went down in the Spirit and stayed there for a while. Another woman with the gift of knowledge looked at me, but I knew that she looked through me at the same time. She said, 'You have seen many beautiful things in your life. But you've also seen one or two terrible things.' I said, 'Yes.' She said, 'The cross is very important to you.' I agreed, thinking back to Medjugorje and the things that happened at the cross. Whenever I have doubts or things bother me, I think of the cross on Mount Krizevac and my own rosary, and the problems go away."

"We prayed the Stations of the Cross. One man had a polaroid camera. The group with him were crying out in exclamations. All of the pictures showed the sun with the open door and rays of light shining through. Without saying a word he took the picture out, took another photo of the sun and it happened again. After the Stations of the Cross we saw the woman I had prayed over and the Irish fellow dancing a jig at the Twelfth Station. I looked at Wade and said, 'Something's happened.' He said, 'Those are the ones you prayed over.' Returning towards the cabin, we noticed two young teenagers running out frantically with more pictures of the open door and the sun."

Through Mary To Jesus

Allan's prayer life underwent a change of focus, from Mary to Jesus. It took life during his second trip to Florida. He comments, "I was concerned about my own life and what was to happen to me. I prayed to the Sacred Heart, and was increasingly aware of Our Lord's mercy, kindness, forgiveness and the love, care, understanding and compassion He has for all of us. This was a few months before the beatification of Sister Faustina."

The Holy Sacrifice of the Mass took on new meaning for Allan, though it was always very important to him. He notes, "I'm more aware of the whole dynamic of the Mass, and appreciate the invocation of the Spirit before the actual Consecration. During the Consecration I realize that Calvary is still with us today. I wondered about this tremendous gift from Our Lord, and pray to Him directly, although sometimes I still feel unworthy. I suppose it's the effect of the devotion to the Divine Mercy which encourages everyone to draw closer to Him."

"The visionaries of Medjugorje confirmed that Our Lady draws people to herself for a time, then leaves them to Our Lord. That has happened to me, yet I find that I go back to Our Lady again because of this gift of healing. I prayed to Jesus and Mary in my ministry, and healing happens to people, though I recognize that the gift came to me through Our Lady. I believe that my role is to continue spreading the news about

Our Lady and sharing her gifts with people. Their responsibility begins from that point on."

Allan concludes with a reflection on gifts. "The gift is the Spirit through Our Lady in Jesus. Some charismatics get a little uptight when I pray to Our Lady. Our Lord has given her all the graces possible. He has made her Mediatrix of grace. I say the prayer she gave us through the Spirit. I still give people the rosary to bring them close to Our Lady and let her touch their hearts. From there things happen, through God's grace."

Personal Reflection

Allan became more reflective as he pondered the reasons why he should receive such gifts of prayer and ministry. He comments, "This is where the humbling part comes because I can't really say why. It was a pleasant shock for me that Our Lady would give me this gift of the lovely golden rosary and the gift of healing. I'm beginning to see why now because of my outgoing nature. Our Lady knew that I could not keep these gifts quietly to myself. I had to share it in such a way as to be objective with people regardless of their religious denomination. These are some results and signs of that sharing. I knew that I wouldn't stay still with it."

"I've gone through a tremendous change in my life; am more prayerful; aware of my past life and things that have gone on, and what I must do to sort of make amends. I really don't know why Our Lady picked me. It's hard to understand. I know that as I become more and more involved with prayer groups, tell them my story and pray over them, it has a tremendous effect. I'm glad because Our Lady has done some beautiful things for me. It's my way of saying 'Thank you', and doing it for her."

CHAPTER TEN

ROSARY: DIRECT LINE TO GOD

Wade and Penny Raley live in Arnprior with their three children and a fourth on the way. In 1993 Wade experienced employment difficulties and his job search led him to contact his former Grade Six teacher. From then on Wade has never been the same. He explains the sequence of events in the following pages.

" My parents are good Catholics and they raised my three brothers, my sister and me in the same way. They were active in St. Elizabeth's Parish and we became friends with the parish priest. It was that type of upbringing. As a teenager my rebellion didn't come with drugs or alcohol; it came on the spiritual level. I found church boring. My brothers and sister followed suit. After I got married in a Catholic church, I stopped going, and lost a lot of faith."

"A few years ago I began searching for answers to life's mysteries. While working as a magazine editor I came across a lot of things, for example, U.F.O.'s. During the summer of 1993 I was going through a rough spell. I was unemployed and going from job to job. I wasn't losing work because of any fault of mine, but because of the recession. I secured a lot of contract work but most of it was short term."

"I'm 33 now. By the time I reached my 30th birthday I was feeling a void in my life, and looking for something to fill it. Compared with other people, my life was okay, but I felt troubled. This feeling became more intense when I began having employment difficulties."

Connection With Allen

"In July 1993 I was looking through the classified section of the newspaper, and saw an ad for a communications job with the Carleton Roman Catholic Separate School Board. I told my mom about this job. She suggested that I should give Allan Young a call because she thought that he had worked for the board for some time. I hadn't seen him for twenty years or more, since Grade Six. I called him and asked for assistance. He said he had worked for the Ottawa Board, not the Carleton Board, and didn't have too many contacts there."

"During the course of the conversation he asked me if I was going to church and praying. I said 'No, why?' He said he had been to Medjugorje in May, 1993. I didn't have a clue what was over there and asked, 'Isn't there a war going on?' He said, 'Yes, but Our Lady has been appearing there since 1981.' I intuitively knew there was substance to what he was saying. It had an immediate impact on me. When he told me about his rosary turning gold I believed it. After the phone call I dug up my rosary and began praying with it, more cautiously at first. I simply asked for help."

The Knack Sack

Wade began experiencing immediate answers to prayer. He recounts, "In September a friend of mine received a U.S. patent on a toy bag he invented for children. He said, 'Why don't we get together and try to make this happen?' I agreed to help him market the product. At the time it seemed miraculous in a sense. Penny and I had just had our third child, bought a house and I wasn't working. Even though it was chaotic, I felt at peace and attributed a lot of this feeling to prayer."

"A lot of exciting things happened during this period. My friend Allen Abraham had the product in his hands for three years and couldn't come up with a name for it. One night I finished praying the Rosary, sat at my computer in the basement of my home trying to figure out what to call this thing. Right away the name came to me, 'Knack Sack'. It was a period when I needed and received a lot of strength and creativity. And Our Lady started making her presence known. We went to the welfare office because we wanted to get people who were also suffering to work on this project. We expected to get a flurry of calls for work and only one person called us three weeks after the fact, when we thought we might have to go the usual route of putting a classified ad in the newspaper."

"My partner went to see her. When he was in her home he saw a big statue of Mary. I had told him about starting to pray to Our Lady. While things were progressing they weren't happening fast enough. My bank account was running very low. I was getting distressed, so I began praying a lot more. My faith continued to grow. We placed a quarter page ad in The Ottawa Citizen for our product to try to test the local market. The ad appeared on page two of the Saturday edition of the Citizen. This was unbelievable. Usually that space is reserved for long-time advertisers, who pay a huge premium. I phoned the advertising department and they couldn't tell me how our ad got there, though obviously someone put it there."

Logos Land Resort

Events continued to lead Wade in a positive and forward direction. He notes, "After our ad appeared unexplainably on page two of the Citizen, I prayed at home, giving thanks to Mary. In August 1993 I tried to drum up some contract work at a four season resort near Cobden called Logos Land Resort. I visited the vacation destination, which is based on Christian values. I met one of the founders named Barbara Richardson. We talked for about an hour. She showed me the resort. I asked her if they had any work. She said, 'No. We do everything in house, and that was the end of it."

"One particular day when I was giving thanks to Mary, a few months later in November, I received an inner locution. At the time I didn't know what it was. It felt like a thought that came from without, not from within. 'Logos Land Resort' kept coming into my mind. I continued praying, but Logos Land Resort kept coming back into my head. This was replaced by the thought "Barb Richardson". This name continued to repeat itself in my mind until I said out loud, 'What?' The thought came back, 'She will help you.' It was really strange. The next thought was even more bizarre, 'Bring her to me.' I knew I was praying to Mary because when I pray to Mary it's different than when I pray to Jesus. I stopped praying and went into the next room where Penny was. She wondered who I was talking to. I was white as a ghost and sat down to have lunch. The fork was shaking in my hand. She asked me, 'What's wrong?' I answered, 'You're not going to believe this,' and told her what happened. I said, 'What am I going to do?' Initially I wasn't going to do anything about it because I thought maybe the pressure of everything was getting to me and I was starting to lose my mind."

"The message was so strong that it gave me a headache, but not the type of headache that really nags at you. I said, 'I've got to act on this or it won't leave me.' I summoned up the courage and phoned Barb. She didn't immediately remember who I was. I told her I had been there in August. She asked what I wanted. I said, 'I don't want to tell you over the phone. Don't worry, it's not another sollicitation, but I do need to talk to you.'"

"I knew Logos Land Resort had Christian roots but didn't know anything about Barb. Going back there with a "message" took a lot of courage. I thought, 'What happens in these situations!' As an ice breaker I brought a prototype of the Knack Sack."

"I got to the parking lot and said to myself, 'I'm not going to do this. I did decide to at least show her the Knack Sack. When I finished my demonstration, we looked at one another. I could tell by the way she looked at me, she thought 'What does this guy want?' I was nervous, and said, 'Look, I've got to tell you something.' She sat down. I told her about the inner locution. To my surprise she didn't bat an eye, and said, 'Don't worry. This happens quite a bit; people often cross spiritual paths here.' She said, 'Do you know what it means to have someone of your age come in here with this type of story?' She hugged me, saying 'Don't worry about this. It means something.' I answered, 'I wasn't sure about the Mary part because I was pretty sure you weren't Catholic.' She said 'I am Pentecostal, but taught at a Catholic high school in the early '70's.' She assured me, 'Don't worry I'll pray over this. I'm supposed to help you. I'm not sure how. Only God knows if I'll help you in a week, month, year or ten years from now. Don't belabour it too much.'"

"I took her advice, went home, and put the event out of my mind. She phoned me during the Christmas holidays and asked how I was doing. 'Why don't you come in and meet my partners? We'll see what we can do to help you with your Knack Sack project.' My partner Allen Abraham and I met with the resort's three founders. They agreed to help us find investment money by introducing us to many of the people who had invested in Logos Land."

"The next time I went to see Barb, after Christmas, I got in my car, put the key in the ignition, when BANG! I got hit by what people call a bolt of lightning. It was like a huge energy field inside my car, uplifting me. I felt peaceful. I drove all the way home singing praise."

Bad News, Good News

Wade's road was not altogether smooth and free of struggle. He continues his story. "By March 1994 things were not going well. We couldn't get investment money. My partner and I were broke and didn't have money to put into this project. I was bleeding to death financially, and beginning to fight a lot with my wife. Since the inner locution I was praying every day. It was giving me strength to get through this period of time."

"In March Penny suggested, 'Why don't you phone Barb and see if you can get a job to tide you over until the Knack Sack project gets going?' I called Barb, and explained 'I need some work. If it's flipping hamburgers in your restaurant or whatever, I don't mind. I just need something to keep food on the table and keep my house.' Barb answered, 'Give me a couple of days.' She called me back in a couple of hours and said, 'Can you be here tomorrow for an interview?" I agreed. They offered me a sales job. It was funny because Barb said at the time, 'We have been praying that someone like you would come.' Today I look after the resort's marketing effort."

Allan's Influence

Wade's recollection of that fateful telephone call with his Grade Six teacher continued to influence him. He notes, "One day in April 1994 I woke up thinking, 'I must meet with Allan.' Something was urging me to 'Get together with Allan.' I hadn't spoken with him for eight months. I called him and explained everything that happened since our initial conversation. I invited him to visit me at Logos Land. I carry my rosary with me every day. The day Allan was coming to see me, I looked for my rosary in my bedroom on my hutch. I couldn't find it, and thought, 'Darn! I wanted Allan to pray over it.'"

"After I dropped my wife off at her car pool destination, and the children at their baby sitter's, I drove back home, searched the house again, but couldn't find my rosary. I went to work. Allan met me later that day, and we had a nice visit. He prayed over me and I felt somewhat strange, but left it at that. He also prayed over Barb. That evening Allan agreed to follow me home after work to meet my family over dinner."

"While we prepared dinner I said, 'I have to look one more time for my rosary.' I went to the bedroom and there it was on the hutch. It had to have always been there, but for some reason I couldn't see it in the morning. As I walked down the hall looking at it, I was shocked to find that the four main links on my rosary (the one that joins the crucifix and three surrounding the medal) had turned gold in colour. I use it every day and I knew they were silver before that. Allan prayed over it with his own rosary, and we praised Mary and God for the miraculous sign. Later that night Allan prayed over Penny and me and we both went down in the Spirit. She was crying and I wasn't sure what was wrong with her. I went down, not expecting to. The thought crossed my mind that I must have looked like one of those turkeys on Sunday morning television. I was embarrassed by it, but it still happened."

Supernatural Phenomena

Wade describes some of the occurrences which happened to him. "During May and June of 1994 a lot of supernatural things occurred. One day I was working in the barn on my property, giving praise for a great day. Suddenly I felt something with me. I looked at the wall and sensed that there was a human shape there but couldn't visually see it. To me it was Mary, and I thought, 'OH! YOU'RE HERE!' I felt like I was going down in the Spirit. I ran out and didn't go in there for a few days. I had Allan check it out. Every time I'm in the barn now I say a few prayers. I don't go in there intentionally; it's not drawing me, but if I'm in there I say a few prayers and always feel light-headed in that particular location. Allan blessed the barn with holy oil and holy water."

"We live in the country. One night when the sun was setting, I glanced over and saw a cross in a rock garden at the side of our house. I looked away and did a double take. It was gone. I went into the house and said, 'Penny, I have to construct a cross.' As soon as I made the cross, I knew my work was done. I had to build up the courage to actually put it up, and did so three weeks later. It's five by three feet, in a nice setting. I pray at it every so often."

"After seeing Allan, and after my rosary changed colour, I began going to Mass every day, simply because I wanted to."

"In June we went to 7:00 o'clock Mass one hot Saturday evening. I wore shorts that double as swimming trunks because we were going swimming after church. I always keep my rosary in my left pocket. I went swimming with the kids at the beach at Arnprior. Later we went to a restaurant. On my way home I put my hand in my pocket and my beads weren't there. I exclaimed, 'My God! I lost my beads at the beach!' We drove back but it was dark. I was heartbroken and thought, 'They're gone! They're gone!' I liken the Rosary as a telephone to God."

"I didn't sleep well that night. The next morning I woke up and said, 'Come on girls. I've got to go find my rosary!' The girls got in the car with me. I took a rake, my mask and snorkel, and something to sift the sand with. I was disappointed and distraught when I got to the beach because it was cold and windy that day. There were white caps on the Ottawa River. I put on my mask and stood in two feet of water. The sand whipped up on the bottom and I couldn't see a thing. I thought, 'This is crazy!' I took all that stuff off me, and prayed, 'If it's meant for someone else to find my rosary and get graces from it, so be it, but I'd really like to have it back.'"

"I was praying silently when something pulled me ten feet out into the river. I stopped, turned to the right, and walked ten steps, then felt something under my feet. I reached down in four feet of water and there was my rosary! I started crying, 'I FOUND THEM! I FOUND THEM!' The girls screamed, 'Yeah! Yeah!' It was wild. That had the most profound impact on me. Under those circumstances, how could I find them? When I told my mother she said, 'It wasn't that you found them that surprised me. It was that you even had faith to go and look for them.'"

"Twelve years ago, when my wife and I were engaged, she bought me a chain with a cross on it for Christmas. About the time I had found my lost rosary, I asked, 'Do I still have that chain with the cross on it?' I hadn't worn it in about ten years. She said, 'I think it's in my jewellery box. She found the chain and cross which is a small gold cross, but beside it she found a larger cross which was gold. She said, 'I don't remember us having this.' What she had found was a sterling silver cross, but it turned gold. We moved to our current residence about six months before that. I remembered packing that particular cross in the jewellery box and it was silver. My parents were visiting us at that time. I said, 'Get out the silver polish. There's something wrong here.' We polished it madly, but it got shinier. It showed no oxidation. I have worn it ever since."

"With all this happening, my mom thought it was wonderful. She has always had a strong devotion to Our Lady. When I moved out of my parent's home I was in my early twenties. The phone rang very early one morning. I wasn't awake yet to get ready for work. It was my mom. She sounded frantic on the other end. As soon as I answered and said, 'Hello.' she said 'Oh Good! Your're O.K? Everything's fine?' I said, 'Yes.' She said, 'Great! I'll talk to you later.' That was the end of the conversation. Recently she said, 'Remember when I phoned you that morning ten years ago and sounded so frantic?' I had to think back and said, 'Yes, I remember. What was that?' She said that in a dream Our Lady came to her and said, 'I want Wade.' She thought, 'Oh my God! He's dead! She took him!' She bolted up and phoned me. When she told me that I didn't know what to think."

Staying Grounded

These supernatural phenomena were exciting and challenging to Wade. He was conscious of his growth in faith. He was also feeling stretched to his capacity and needed some breathing space. He explains. "Since last Spring, things have been quiet from a supernatural standpoint. I grew from all those experiences, but they had to stop. I've asked for them to stop to some extent because they were getting overwhelming. We have three children with a fourth one on the way and a new job. I've got to stay grounded. That's my belief. My capacity must increase before I can take more in."

"Also, while supernatural things were happening, negative supernatural things started happening. One night I was working at the computer and felt someone behind me. I looked over my shoulder and saw this decrepit little man. I can't explain it. I couldn't see it with my eyes but with my mind. I can still see what he looked like. He was gross. I cursed at it. I was saying the Rosary at the time. When I swore at it, it disappeared. I went back to praying the Rosary and it was only after I finished that I became very frightened. I thought, 'What was that?'"

"Whatever that being was, it represented everything that was holding me back, the reason that even though I'm a good worker and intelligent

I couldn't seem to get ahead. That event for me was important because it hasn't come back. Sometimes I'd be praying the Rosary and a lot of lewd thoughts would enter my mind, which weren't of my own design. I thought 'This is really bizarre.' Allan gave me the prayer of protection which I say every day now. It has helped."

"I say the Rosary every morning on my way to work. Some times I'll be saying it, feel really emotional and start crying. Other times I sing songs I don't even know."

Marmora

Wade visited the Greensides farm on a few occasions and each time experienced peace and other benefits. He describes this. "I first learned of Marmora from a Man Alive telecast. I went there for the first time in July 1994 with my parents and family. We were visiting Picton and decided to swing by Marmora on the way back."

"The first visit was pleasant, but I had my son on my shoulders and it was tough climbing the steep hills there. I couldn't really concentrate, but it was peaceful. In September 1994 while driving to work one morning, I felt compelled to go to Marmora. So I went, just like that. On my way down, I thought 'It's too bad Allan's not with me.' I got there about ten thirty and spent a quiet day by myself. It was wonderful, me, God and nature, nothing miraculous, just great. I felt that I needed the boost."

"Allan phoned me a week later and I said, 'Have you been to Marmora yet?' He answered, 'I was there last Thursday.' I exclaimed, 'I was there last Thursday!' I left at 12:30 to go back to work and Allan had just arrived. We didn't meet. It was the Feast of Our Lady of Sorrows."

"In August I struggled with doubts. Somebody told me that I was in the desert. I feel I'm almost ready to go further with my spiritual growth, but I have to resolve a few more things. I don't know what I mean by that. The majority of the people I work with are Pentecostal, who have no allegiance to Our Lady, though they have great allegiance to God and Jesus, which most Christians would be envious to have. I believe Mary wants me, but she wants Barb too. She is a remarkable person. I hope to be at Logos Land Resort for a long time. I feel that it's not my plan. Mary has asked me to be here. It's her plan."

"I meet people and something tells me to tell them my story. Other times I feel 'Don't say one word!' One time I was helping this guy put together a commercial for Logos Land. It was after midnight and I told him the story. I showed him the rosary and he held it. He said, 'This feels really good. It's warm in my hand.' He looked at me and said, 'You have a barn?' I said, 'Yes.' He said, 'There's something in it.' I said, 'I don't even keep my car in it.' Much to my amazement he described the positive presence of Mary in my barn."

Final Thoughts

Wade experienced total conversion within a relatively short but stormy period of time. He continues his life of prayer and reception of the sacraments according to the ongoing grace he receives from God. His mother's prayers have born rich fruit in abundance. More than ever are Wade and his mother grateful for Allan, his Grade Six teacher.

CHAPTER ELEVEN

MESSAGES FOR THE HOLY FATHER

Sandra and Domenic Ruscio moved to Mississauga six years ago, in order to live closer to their two sons and their families. They claim that their house is firmly founded on the rock of faith. When they built it they placed in each corner of the foundation rocks collected from their pilgrimages to Fatima, Lourdes and Medjugorje.

Sandra always maintained an active faith since childhood. A few years ago a cat scan revealed that she had an ovarian cyst about the size of an egg, and surgery was scheduled for its removal. As her friends prayed over her, Sandra promised Our Lady that if she were healed she would arrange a chapel in their home. The final cat scan results indicated that the cyst had disappeared, and so the operation was cancelled. Their lovely chapel is a central place of prayer in their home.

Illness and Healing

Sandra lived through a dozen surgical procedures. Because of inherited arthritis and disintegrating bones she required a total hip replacement about fifteen years ago. Seven years later she fell down the steps from the deck of a ship, while on a cruise between Miami and the Bahamas. A second hip replacement corrected her problem for a time. When she returned from Italy in 1993 with great pain, surgery was required once again. She offered the pain of these operations in honour of Jesus' five wounds and Our Blessed Mother's tears.

During Sandra's first pilgrimage to Medjugorje in 1988, she saw Our Lady in the church window during the evening apparition to the visionaries, and also witnessed the miracle of the sun. Prior to her second visit in September 1990 she suffered considerably from Hepatitis B for seven years. As she prayed before the statue of the Madonna in St. James Church she said to Our Lady, "Please ask your Son to heal me. Whatever you ask, Jesus will never say 'No'". She heard a woman's voice answering, "Sandrina, don't worry. You are already cured from Hepatitis." These words gave her great joy and peace. She continued her prayer to Jesus, "If you grant me healing power I will use it for your name and Your glory." Subsequently wonderful events occurred, especially when Sandra called upon the aid of the Holy Spirit.

Five months later she went to her doctor for her annual blood test for Hepatitis. After three days he called her for a return visit. He was puzzled and asked her to explain her healing. A little worried about her explanation, Sandra tearfully shared what happened in Medjugorje. At that time her doctor did not believe in the Blessed Virgin. After his examination, he told her that she was cured from Hepatitis B, and added, "Now I believe you and I believe in the Blessed Virgin's intercession." His May 27, 1991 signed document to this effect indicates Sandra's healing and immunity from Hepatitis B. It was sent to and acknowledged by visionary Vicka Ivankovic. The following month Sandra returned to Medjugorje to thank God, Jesus and Mother Mary for her healing.

Because of several years of pain in her hip prior to and following the surgery, and the prescribed medications ordered for her Sandra had become addicted to these pills. Her addiction and consequent depression had lasted for ten years. During prayer, Sandra told Jesus that she didn't want to take any more pills. When she spoke to her doctor about this matter he encouraged her not to take medication. When she felt a recurrence of depression, her doctor gently but firmly asked her, "Where's your faith?" Then he took his bible and they prayed together. Sandra relaxed in peace and contentment. She has been free of her addiction for three years.

In October 1993 Sandra made a pilgrimage to the Holy Land. After visiting the Holy Sepulchre, the group waited for Father Giuseppe to celebrate Mass. She explained, "Being somewhat apart from the group, I heard a voice calling me, "Sandra!" "Yes" she replied. The voice continued, "Sandra, are you willing to suffer for me"? This was repeated three times, and I recognized that Jesus spoke to me. Each time I answered "Yes, Jesus." He continued, 'From now on you are going to suffer.' At that moment I started to have pain."

Sandra notes, "Before I left for the trip I promised Jesus that I was willing to suffer for Him for all the problems that I was having in my family; in my husband's business; for all those who asked me for prayers; for all the sinners in the world and their conversion; for peace in this world and especially in Russia; but mostly because I wanted to help Jesus in His sufferings for all the sins in the world."

"When I returned home I had two operations on my feet for bunions and hammer toes, and the following year my third hip replacement. After each of these operations the doctor prescribed pain killers, but I took only four of them and discontinued them, remembering my promise to suffer for Jesus. Then Jesus, to my great surprise, removed all the pain."

Following the third operation on her hip Sandra was admitted to St. Bernard Convalescent Home. One night she felt very weak and sick, because of her loss of blood during surgery. On Easter 1994 she was wakened around 3:00 a.m. and felt someone touching her with tenderness. She continued, "When I opened my eyes, I saw the room totally bright and three visitors dressed in white, almost shining. They came close to me, smiled and we shook hands. Then they disappeared. Immediately I called the nurse, Frances. She switched on the light and told me that it was 3:01 a.m. I believe that these were three angels sent from Jesus on the day of His Resurrection. A few months later, my strength was restored.

During the summer of 1994 Sandra developed shingles and was confined to bed for one and a half months with intense pain. When her doctor suggested that the pain could last a year, Sandra replied, "No it won't. I will pray." Within two months the pain was gone, much to the doctor's astonishment.

Healing Ministry

In April 1993 Sandra heard a voice telling her to get in touch with Mrs Anna Maria Difebo so they could pray the Rosary together. Though it took some time to reach Anna Maria, the voice continued to insist that Sandra keep trying. Finally Anna Maria arrived at approximately 8:30 in the evening. Meanwhile Anna Maria's daughter Tina called her mother to tell her that her eight year old daughter Enia had not returned from her dance lesson which was usually over at 8:00 p.m. and her husband Richard had gone to pick her up.

It was raining heavily that evening. Around 8:45 Tina decided to leave home and go out in search of her family. She drove to Enia's dance school and no one was there. She called home to see if they had arrived. They hadn't. Tina drove for about a half a kilometre and saw her car at the gasoline station totally wrecked. She began to cry. The police officer stated that Richard and Enia had been taken to the hospital, but they were all right.

Tina was frightened and phoned her father to come and help her. He arrived with Anna Maria, Sandra, Domenic and together they went to the hospital. The police officer told them it was a miracle that they were alive. A tractor trailer had collided with them. Enia was wearing her seat belt which she never would attach. The doctor took them to visit Enia and Richard. Enia needed only twenty four stitches inside her mouth. Richard, lying on a stretcher had only some bruises on his body. The families truly believe that these lives were saved due to the intercessory prayer which was taking place for them at that moment. This was the first major grace which happened in Sandra's home chapel before the statue of Mary, Mystical Rose, through the Rosary.

From her home Sandra exercises a ministry of intercessory prayer for healing. She is also an active member of team ministry at the local parish, and prays over people at the healing Masses. In May 1993 Caterina Saccucci visited Canada, and was scheduled to have a coronary by-pass on her return to Italy. Together Sandra and Caterina went to the healing Mass at St. Wilfrid's Church, where Sandra joined the healing team led by Chris and Sharon. When Chris identified Caterina's symptoms she came forward and the team laid hands on her. After she returned to her pew Chris pointed to her husband Pompilio and stated, "In your heart you are crying. Please don't cry because your wife is already healed." When Caterina returned to her cardiologist in Italy he said, "I don't know what happened, but you don't need the operation any more."

Sandra visited Marmora five or six times and exercised her healing ministry there. While there she received messages from Jesus and Our Blessed Mother, which were subsequently taken to Bishop Lacey, Bishop Danylak and Archbishop Spence. She was also advised to take these messages to the Holy Father, and was able to do this personally.

Messages For The Holy Father

Sandra and Domenic's cousin Antonio lives in Rome. His friend Augusto arranged for an interview with the Holy Father so that Sandra could personally deliver the messages to the Holy Father, and tell him about Marmora and the apparitions which occur there.

Face to face with the Holy Father, Sandra presented him with a painting of his picture and miraculous oil from the home of Ernest and Carmelita Guinto and their visionary daughter, Marci. Sandra gave the Pope an envelope containing messages of the visionaries. The Holy Father blessed her twice during this visit. Subsequently Sandra wrote him twice about witnesses to the oil in the Guinto home, and received replies to both letters.

Messages: August 8, 1993

Sandrina, I am your Mother. My Son Jesus and I choose you to be our messenger to the Pope. Get together with Dory, Joan, Father Grainger, Shelagh and her husband John. All of you go to the Bishop. Dory has to write down the message I gave her at Marmora, and you Sandrina will bring the message in person to the Pope. Thank you.

May 6, 1994

Because you have just had an operation it is not possible for you to take the trip to Italy to the Holy Father. Your cousin Eugene will take all the messages and the two pictures of the Pope to his brother Antonio who will take them to the Pope. Go with Eugene and his wife Maria to Marci's house and get all the information pertaining to the miraculous oil. If they agree, send this information.

July 8, 1994

Sandrina pray a lot for the Holy Father because he is going to suffer very much and I, your Jesus, am ready. The earth is infected with a lot of sin. This is why I said I am ready to come. Pray, Sandrina, pray. I love you and I bless you.

October 26, 1994.

Sandrina, together with Carmel (who had received the identical message) go to the Greensides and say, I the Blessed Mother desire a small chapel to be built at marmora, where the Mass will be

celebrated as soon as possible. After that, write to the Pope and send the message I gave you. Go to Father Wasik and Bishop Lacey. They will help you. Remember, this is my desire. Sandrina, pray a lot. Receive my blessing and my motherly love. Your dear **Mamma Maria.**

November 10, 1994

My daughter, I am your Mamma Maria. I am so happy for your obedience every time I call you. Today I will wait for you at Marmora, together with my dear daughter Dominica, Frank, Benito, and his wife Philomena. Come my daughter, come. Jesus and I your dear Mother Mary bless and love you. Pray, Sandrina, pray.

After a pause,

To Domenic your spouse I give blessing and my motherly love.

November 29, 1994

Sandrina, on December 8, I will wait for you at Marmora. On the Twelfth Station I will give you a sign. You will see me on the tree. Sandrina you will go to Rome to the Holy Father to finish your mission. Remember to come that day. Pray Sandrina, for poor sinners, for the Holy Father, for young people and young children. I bless you with my motherly love. Your dear Mamma Maria.

December 7, 1994

Sandrina, tell all the people and the visionaries to be alert, because the enemy causes lots of confusion, especially to my beloved children. Help each other like one happy family. The enemy is trying to destroy my plan but he will not win.

My children, listen to my call. My Son Jesus is very sad because of the many sins of the world, and the cup is getting full, ready to spill over. I your Mother have to endure lots of suffering and pain in my heart for the salvation of many souls. Pray, Sandrina, pray. I your dear Mamma Maria love and bless you.

December 11, 1994

Sandrina, you and my dear son Luca will go to Rome to the Holy Father, and bring with you the message where I said I desire one small chapel at Marmora. Go to Mr. and Mrs. Greensides and say,

"Now is the time to give the message I gave you at Marmora." After that, Sandrina, bring the message to the Holy Father and you will have finished your mission. Pray, Sandrina, pray. I love you and bless you. Mamma Maria.

Ongoing Healing and Conversion

From childhood, Sandra suffered acutely from parental conflict and family discord. Through God's grace and the intervention of Jesus and Mary, she has been able to forgive her parents and family for the suffering she endured. The depression which this conflict generated in her has now been lifted.

Sandra knows what it is to suffer spiritually, emotionally and physically. Because of her own conversion and inner healing, she is able to exercise compassion on those people who suffer in a similar way, and give them understanding and encouragement.

She reminds people to keep the main focus of their prayer on God, on Jesus, and only secondarily on Our Blessed Mother who loves us very much. She wants everyone to know what Jesus is doing for us, and that Jesus is real.

Sandra is at peace with her past. She is joyful and loving in her present life. Toward the future she is filled with expectant hope. All this is through God's grace and Mary's intercession. Praise God.

CHAPTER TWELVE

OUR LADY SHOWS THAT SHE CARES

Marian Rodrigues originates from England and lives in Mississauga. Her recent manifestations at Marmora seem to indicate a turning point in her life, in which she experiences peace and trust at knowing that God was present with her throughout all her joys and difficulties. She shares her story in the following pages.

First Visit To Marmora

"It was Good Friday, 1994. I decided that my curiosity had peaked enough to visit Marmora. I had heard of Our Lady appearing there through a friend's mother, Mrs Mary Antao, and until this point had not been comfortable about seeing Our Lady. In all honesty, I was a little frightened. In my mind, appearances of Our Lady were always associated with holy people such as saints, mystics, and special people selected by Our Lady. I chose Good Friday for my visit to Marmora because there were no services in the church that day."

"I knew there were Stations of the Cross at the farm and thought 'What a perfect way to spend Good Friday', and asked my elderly parents, who were 81 years of age, to join me. When we arrived at Marmora I was relieved, as this was the first time that I had driven further than Weston Road on the 401. I was also elated to be at the farm which I considered a holy place."

"My parents are devout people. My mother converted to the catholic faith when she married my father. From my early years she taught me devotion to Our Blessed Mother. My father always impressed upon me the companionship which Our Lord provides for us if we allow Him."

"Upon arrival at the farm much of the land was covered with snow. I wondered how I would be able to make the Stations of the Cross, because the land was of undulating terrain. I proceeded with my parents to the building adjacent to the farm house, not knowing what to find there. I was pleasantly surprised to see chairs and an area set aside for private prayer. There was also a long table with reading material and other bulletins provided by the Greensides."

"I settled my parents and prepared myself to face the cold, having resigned myself that this would be a true and personal Calvary. I turned to my mother and said, 'Come with me Mum, and let's go as far as we can walk.' My mother is blind in one eye, and due to dislocated foot joints has a poor sense of balance. At that time my father was using a walking frame due to an arthritic leg. After much hesitation and fear on my mother's part, I finally persuaded her to accompany me, leaving my father in the warmth of the reception area."

"My mother clung to my arm, and we slowly walked to the First Station. The melting snow caused some of the ground to soften, and it squelched as our feet sunk into it. We prayed, proceeded to the Second Station, and went as close as we could to the Third Station. My mother became more anxious as she felt insecure with her footing. After praying, I decided to take my mother back to the reception area, since we could not climb the hill leading to the Fourth Station."

Miracle of the Sun

"As we turned around, I felt the piercing heat of the sun penetrate through my winter coat. I had heard of the miraculous sun at Marmora, and felt compelled to look at it. With all the faith I could muster, I asked Our Lord to permit me to look into the sun. It was brilliant white, a perfect sphere that resembled the Holy Eucharist. Suddenly a deep sapphire blue disc came over the sun and it began to pulsate. I knew I was witnessing a miracle. My mother, whose vision is weak, also witnessed this miracle. When we walked back to meet my father, we saw patches of gold intermingled with the colour of daylight. We suffered no blurredness."

"We told my father of our experience. Then I took my father outside to witness the sun, knowing that he too had poor vision. He struggled to look into the sun and exclaimed, 'I see the Host. It's dazzling white.' I returned my father to the reception area and asked my mother if she would consider walking uphill to the grotto. She reluctantly agreed, and I suggested that she offer this difficult walk to Christ as her Calvary."

"With each step toward the grotto my mother's excitement grew. I believe Our Lady rewarded my mother's effort, by allowing us another view of the sun from the top of the hill. As we gazed into the sun, which seemed closer to us, the pulsating blue disc appeared. 'Oh, darling Blessed Mother!' cried out my mother, with one hand raised to her eyes, clutching her rosary. My heart leapt for joy for my mother."

"When we descended the hill, everything around us beamed with patches of gold. My mother's fears had dissipated and were replaced by sheer ecstasy. The temperature had become much colder. With only a half an hour left before three o'clock, I felt it necessary that my parents take some warm refreshment, even though they were fasting, since my father has diabetes."

"We walked to the car, and as my father opened the door, I urged him to look again into the sun, and he witnessed the pulsating blue sun. In the car I began the Sorrowful Mysteries of the Rosary, as I stared into the pulsating blue sun, telling Our Lord that I would rather be blinded by this action rather than not witness it. During the last five Hail Mary's of the Fifth Mystery, a corner of the sun turned a vivid blood red. It was as though God were saying, 'I am here, Marian, and I know you are here at the farm.' I gasped, 'Oh!', and said to myself, 'Lord, that is Your Blood. It is the hour of your death.' When I finished the last 'Glory Be' the clouds covered the red sun. The hour of Our Lord's death transpired, and the sky became overcast. The sun did not shine for the rest of the time we remained at the farm."

"On returning to Mississauga, I stopped at my brother's home and told them of the day's exciting events. That evening as I watched television, I realized that I was not wearing my glasses. For ten years I had to wear glasses for light sensitivity, yet my eyes were not even hurting. From that day until this I have not required glasses to defer natural nor neon lighting. In gratitude for this miraculous gift, I promised Our Lady that I would tell all who cross my path about Marmora. Since then, many relatives and friends have visited the Greensides farm."

Grace Unfolds

Marian continued to experience God's grace unfolding in her life in a more profound way than she previously knew. She states, "What was so significant to me about Marmora is that I believe God wanted me there that day. A few days before going to the farm, I resigned from my employment because of victimization, which would soon result in dismissal regardless of my intervention. Though I had no prospect of a job I did not doubt that God would provide for me. I surrendered my entire life to God and lived one day at a time, with total abandonment to God's will. As a consequence I am freed of fear which previously handicapped me from living in God's light."

"The next exciting thing that occurred was with my brother. He and his wife have two young adult daughters. Two days after my visit to Marmora he went there also with his younger daughter. My brother is a highly organized and meticulous person who returns things to their proper place. The day following his visit to Marmora, as he prepared to take his wife to work, he could not find the shirt nor the jumper he wore the previous day. He searched fruitlessly and with increasing annoyance for these two garments, turning the house upside down in the process. To his absolute bewilderment he eventually found the two missing garments neatly folded, as though they had never been worn, in a spare room under a chair covering."

"During his visit to Marmora, he had asked Our Lady to give him a sign that would show him that she knew he had visited her. With great joy he received the answer in his folded garments. The two garments remain folded, and my brother intends to leave them that way until he dies. This experience brought him great inner peace and reinforced faith. Incidentally the spare room in which he found the garments was the former bedroom of his elder daughter, who had expressed fears of the supernatural. Our Lady seemingly also intervened to alleviate her fears and doubts."

"The younger daughter also received great graces at Marmora. At the time she was a Grade Thirteen student, and anxious about her university placement and the possibility of leaving her family and home. That fall, she registered at Trent University in Peterborough, less than an hour from Marmora. She became friends with a student who is a practising Catholic, and expresses genuine delight in their friendship. In her words, 'I'm so glad that I have a boy friend who is of the same faith. I could not be comfortable with one who was not Catholic.' Surely this relationship is under the guiding hand of Our Lady, possibly in reward for that earlier visit to Marmora."

Continued Blessings

Marian claims that many wonderful things happened in her life. She comments, "I always saw the hand of God and His Blessed Mother with me through many of my darkest moments, and subsequently found that my faith was strengthened through these times. I believe that Our Lady directed me toward encounters with certain people who became inspirational. One such person is Donna. She became my friend and helped satisfy my quest for spiritual knowledge, which grew during repeated trips to Marmora."

"During my visit on August 14, 1994, I saw a lady talking to a group of people about the messages received that day by one of the visionaries. I moved in closer to listen, and began a conversation with Donna. She told me about Michael Brown's publications and about the St. Bridget prayers, the Pieta. I asked Donna if she had ever seen a golden rosary. She answered, 'Yes. My own rosary is gold', and showed it to me. I was overwhelmed. Donna suggested, 'Why don't you ask Our Lady in faith, to turn your rosary to gold?' I responded, 'How could I? Who am I to ask for such a gift?' Donna replied, 'If you don't ask, you won't receive. Ask for it, if it is Our Lady's will.' I agreed to do so."

"On the following two days, while reciting the Rosary, I asked Our Lady to turn my two rosaries gold, if it was her will. My second rosary is at my bedside. On August 17, I noticed that the links between each decade had changed to gold! That evening I realized that my bedside rosary had also changed. No words could express what I felt. I am a sinner and yet my prayer was heard. I prayed, 'Lord, I am not worthy to receive you.' From that point on I became more prayerful, and committed myself through Our Lady, to try to meditate on Jesus Christ every waking moment of my life."

"I share this experience because I was heartbroken that I could not be at Marmora on August 15, the feast of the Assumption. Nor could I be there on August 16, my birthday. As it happened I met Donna on

August 14, and she opened my eyes to more meaningful prayer. She inspired me to believe that all things are possible with God."

Statue of Our Lady of Fatima

Our Blessed Mother continued to show her gentle caring love to Marian and her friends. She shared as follows. "Mrs Antao reminded me of the tradition of housing the statue of Our Lady in one's home for prayer and meditation, and through her I obtained such a statue. From the moment I received the statue of Our Lady of Fatima, my friends who are both Catholic and non-Catholic exclaimed, 'What a beautiful statue!' I was delighted at their response."

"One night while I prayed before the statue, I saw the lips moving. Our Lady was praying with me. I knew she was reciting the prayers with me because of the hollow between her lips. I rubbed my eyes several times, but never changed my position. This was not an optical illusion. Our Lady was letting me know that she was really present. Some days later I shared my experience with the person who gave me the statue. He answered, 'Marian, it doesn't surprise me. Many people witnessed the same experience when praying in front of this statue. I asked myself, 'Why is Our Lady giving me these graces? I'm no one special. Why me?' There is no answer. I promised Our Lady that whenever such happenings occur, I will share them with those who express interest in or belief in the faith."

Growth In Prayer and Service

Marian realizes that her prayer life continues to deepen. The closer she desires to be in communication with Jesus and His Blessed Mother, the more difficult it is to fulfil her call to pray. She notes, "I understand the meaning of 'pick up your cross daily, and follow me.' In day to day living the pressures of life can be overwhelming, and easily distract me from prayer. I call upon Our Lord and His Blessed Mother to strengthen me to overcome worldly distractions and focus on quality time in meaningful prayer."

"When I recite a prayer I am forced to think about the actual words, and not race through it. Prayer must be said with a contrite heart, whether it be traditional prayers or prayer from the depth of one's heart. Praying taught me that Our Lord and His Blessed Mother are my best friends. The time I give to them must be of the same intensity as I would give to one with whom I am in love, but with more far reaching rewards. A loved one can break your heart, your dreams, your aspirations. We can overcome disappointment and heartache by placing all our relationships in God's hands and Our Blessed Mother's trust."

"Prayer has enriched the meaning of my life. Through daily prayer I am made aware of the needs of others. For them I commit my services to the Lord Our God. Our Blessed Mother called me to be closer to her Son, and to listen carefully to His will. Through the intercession of Our Lady, my heavenly Mother, I dedicate this testimonial to the Glory of her beloved Son."

CHAPTER THIRTEEN

LIVING IN UNION WITH JESUS

Eddie and Ida Virrey with their two young children moved to a quiet location in Scarborough in 1991. Ida emigrated from the Philippines to Canada when she was twenty. Eddie went from the Philippines to the United States at age sixteen, and subsequently moved to Toronto.

Ida graduated from nursing in the Philippines in 1980, and since 1981 worked full time with the Extendicare Company. In the Philippines there are no nursing homes, because families take care of their own elders. Ida has the opportunity to pray with seniors, particularly those who are dying, and this action seems to give her patients considerable peace, regardless of their religious tradition.

Eddie's Difficult Childhood

Eddie's father died when he was one year old and his mother could not care for their seven children. Her brother and his wife, who had no children, adopted Eddie and his sister. Because Eddie was such a difficult child, they returned him to his mother. From then on Eddie lived with relatives throughout the Philippines. By the time he was eleven years old his mother gave up on him completely. He worked as a caddie for golfers, sleeping on the streets while waiting for golfers to arrive, and was the first boy to be hired. In this way he earned money to support himself.

When Eddie was fifteen years old, his grandmother wanted the family to emigrate to the United States. Eddie resisted, but his mother convinced him to move with the family. From January 1977 until 1984 Eddie and his family lived in New Jersey. He worked at a variety of jobs, such as Burger King, Kentucky Fried Chicken, and a factory. For a time his mother gave up on him again.

At twenty years of age, Eddie moved to Toronto to live with his aunt and help care for her children. Eventually he and Ida met and were married some time later. He worked in a Japanese restaurant; then he did silk screening; finally he worked in electronics. His employer's business failure in November 1994 resulted in Eddie's temporary unemployment.

Prior to the supernatural phenomena in their home, Ida and Eddie had a small altar in their home with four statues, according to their Filipino custom. However, they did not pray. Eddie states, "Every week-end my wife wanted me to go to church but I declined, making excuses like I had a headache or I said I'd go later, but I never did. One day my wife wanted me to go with her to a prayer group and I refused, saying 'No. Call your brother's wife. She always goes.'"

"They went to the prayer meeting and the next day, May 29, 1993, my wife was sick with a tooth infection, fever, and couldn't get out of bed. She asked me if I and my children would pray for her. That was the night of the Maple Leafs and Vancouver Play Offs and I intended to watch the game. I answered, 'I'll pray later, after the hockey game'. I didn't care about my wife or anyone else that night. I only cared about the hockey game."

Phenomenon of the Oil

Eddie was willing to pray for Ida when the hockey game was over. He states, "I came to the altar and saw that the face of Jesus on the crucifix was very wet. I asked my wife 'Did you do anything to the face of Jesus?' She answered, 'No.' I looked at the statue again, then went back to my wife and told her to get up, even though she was sick."

"Ida got up, touched the face of Jesus on the cross and realized that it was covered with oil. I was so shocked that I began praying for her. Ida didn't understand what happened, and thought it wise to call people from a prayer group." Ida continues, "I phoned my sister-in-law and she called some of her friends. Her sister was celebrating her birthday and drove from Whitby after their party. They agreed that oil was oozing from the figure of the crucified Jesus. I asked, 'What will we do about it?' They answered, 'We have to pray.' From then on we prayed every day."

"The next morning oil oozed from some of the statues in the living room. Three of our friends came to pray every day, and eventually formed a prayer group which grew to a large number of people.

Individuals brought their own statues, and approximately four hundred statues continued to ooze oil. Some statues remained dry, and eventually people took them back to their homes."

During Holy Week 1993, in imitation of the Church's purple coverings over crucifixes and statues, Eddie covered with purple the statue of the Infant Jesus on their altar. After Easter when Eddie removed the covering, the statue had disappeared. He asked the children if someone had taken away the statue. The children were too small to reach the shelf at the top of the altar, and they said that no one had been in the house to remove it. For two months they did not know where the statue was. A friend suggested that someone else needed the statue more than they, and that it would be replaced with something else. They never discovered where the statue went, and it was never returned. For a time they thought that it was a punishment for them because they were not praying. From then on they prayed the Rosary.

Eddie did not know his prayers. Ida taught him the Our Father, Hail Mary and other prayers, and gave him a booklet to learn the Rosary. They opened their home to people who heard by word of mouth what was happening, and who wanted to pray and witness these phenomena. Buses came from Windsor, Chicago, New York, California, and various parts of Toronto. Regardless of Ida and Eddie working all day, they welcomed visitors every day of the week, and prayed late into the night with people who came and went continuously to their home.

They share the oil with anyone who comes to visit, especially those who are ill. To some people Eddie gives cotton balls soaked in oil. He suggests that they pray the Rosary before they use the oil, and then to wipe oil wherever they have pain. It works. Some times he uses blessed water from Marmora with a drop of oil to bless people.

In the fall of 1994 the statue of the Blessed Mother with the Baby Jesus shed tears of blood for a few weeks. The owner of the statue collected the blood.

Trance

Eddie sometimes goes into what he calls a trance. On one occasion Our Lady asked him if he wanted to go with her, and he agreed. Our Lady showed him purgatory, hell and heaven. She was escorted by angels. Those who were with him said that the trance lasted forty-five minutes. Eddie describes what happened. "I was lifted up with a floating feeling as though I were carried up an escalator. I never stepped on the floor. I saw something like a very white church, with long stairs to climb. When I got tired, Mama Mary said, 'Don't give up. You still have a way to go.' When we reached the gate St. Peter, who held a rooster, opened the door. He looked at my name and said, 'Yes, it's here. This is your room if you want to stay.'"

"I saw St. Therese who wore a black dress and held a flower and cross, as well as other saints, but don't know all their names. I saw St. Michael and my guardian angel. He is a cherubim clothed in white with blonde hair. I always see him when I am in a trance. His name is Raphael and he protects me. Mama Mary said, 'Do you want to stay here now?' I said, 'No. Not yet. I have my family down there and I want to stay longer with them.' She said, O.K. Tell me whenever you want to stay here. Just ask and I will help you.' Then she brought me back again."

Eddie explains, "Some times I go into a trance when people pray here, and I receive a message for them. At other times people ask me for a blessing, and I respond with a blessing for them. When I touch people, they rest in the Spirit. Some people get healed. Other people who do not pray from the heart do not get healed. The Lord said 'Pray from the heart, not from your head. Love one another. Forgive one another and forget. If somebody bothers you, ask My Mother for help. Don't give up.' Some times you have to sacrifice before your prayer is answered. If you don't believe in prayer, you may not get well. Some people want to get well right away. Jesus says that it doesn't happen that way. Sacrifice is needed. When it is time for them to get well, they will."

In June, 1993, Eddie received a message that the three days of darkness are coming soon. In his trance, he heard Jesus say to him, "Pray hard. Remind people who forget to pray. Bring back to Me all those who forget to pray and I will forgive them and their sins. Tell the people to go to Confession and the Lord will forgive them. When you pray go straight to God, and go to Our Blessed Mother. If you listen to people who tell you that these things are not true, you go in the wrong direction."

Ministry of Prayer and Healing

Eddie and Ida describe some incidents of healing prayer. "In July 1994, Angelo was healed after using a cane for twenty one years. The doctor told him he could not walk without the help of a cane. By chance he was in Marmora with Eddie and a group of nine people at the Tenth Station and rested in the Spirit. Eddie touched Angelo's leg and the Lord told him to remove the cane because Angelo could walk without it. Angelo shook for a time then exclaimed, 'I can walk! I can walk!' He decided to join our prayer group, and comes every Wednesday and Friday."

"In August 1994, when we were in Marmora, a man with cancer and his friends came to our house, where Ida's father welcomed them. As they prayed, they saw a light over the doorway into the living room, facing the altar. They closed the window curtains and the light remained, with an image of the Blessed Mother. They prayed and realized that Our Lady was with them. They returned home and telephoned later, inviting Eddie and Ida to their home for prayer, and when Eddie touched him, he rested in the Spirit. The next day he visited his doctor, who examined him and told him that his tumour had shrunk. However, the man either gave up or it wasn't his time to be totally healed, and he died shortly after."

"A nurse from Windsor was disabled from lifting patients and was unable to work. In August we visited and prayed over her, and though she still has a problem with her back, she no longer needs her cane for walking."

"On November 19 Our Blessed Mother said that people came to our house out of curiosity, and were not really praying. She said that more people would visit our house but cautioned us to be careful because some were seeking signs and wonders. She wants people who come here to close their eyes, pray, concentrate on what they're doing, and not look around in distraction."

Eddie's First Visit To Marmora

Ida visited Marmora several times since 1992, but Eddie did not accompany her. He continues, "One day in the summer of 1993 no driver was available so I drove the group to the farm. They invited me to join them on the Way of the Cross but I declined. After a short while, I went into a trance and found myself following them up the hill. By that time I had learned the Our Father and Hail Mary but no other prayers. When I returned home, I rested in the Spirit on my bed, and my body took the shape of a cross. In that moment I confessed myself before the Lord as a sinner. In my trance, Jesus spoke to me and asked me to go to Confession. Then Jesus said, 'Trust me. I am always with you, watching you.' I answered, 'I trust You. I give myself to You and entrust to You my family.' Jesus asked, 'Can I use you to help all those who need help?' I surrendered to Him saying, 'Yes.'"

When Eddie awoke from his trance Ida asked him 'What happened to you?' Eddie answered, 'I was talking to Jesus.' Ida asked, 'How do you know it was Jesus?' He replied, 'I asked Him and He said, I am Jesus Christ.' Then Jesus asked, 'Are you willing to sacrifice yourself for me?' Eddie replied, 'Yes. I accept whatever you give me.' Jesus asked him to go to Confession because he had not been to Confession since he was a child in school. Eddie comments 'It was so good when I went to Confession. I told all my sins, my lies. I felt so good.' I still go to Confession weekly in my parish church and feel relieved each time."

One First Saturday Eddie and Ida were praying a mission at someone's house and were unable to be at church, so they went to Confession the following day, Sunday. That night when Eddie was at home praying he went into a trance. He explains, "Mama Mary and an angel who looked like St. Michael came and thanked me for praying. They said, 'Open your mouth and I will give you the Host.' I made the Sign of the Cross, opened my mouth and received Holy Communion. In 1993 Jesus gave me Holy Communion on the day I returned from Marmora after Angelo's healing. Jesus told me to close my eyes so I could see Him. I always ask the identity of the visions before accepting them. Jesus taught me this precaution."

Eddie remarks, "Wherever I go, I see angels with my eyes open and sometimes with my eyes closed. I know that I am never alone. My guardian angel Raphael guides me constantly and tells me that I am taking the right way. St. Michael, St. Gabriel and St. Raphael are always together."

On June 28, 1993, when Ida and Eddie returned from Marmora, they saw five beads of oil hanging on a string from the beard of Jesus crucified. They captured this phenomenon on video before the beads of oil vanished.

Stigmata

During Holy Week 1994 Eddie began receiving the stigmata, without external bleeding. He describes his experience, "Oil was oozing from my eyes, my ears, my hands, my feet, my side, and I was in great pain. My shirt and pants were soaked with oil. I was restless, and had to continue walking as though I were carrying the Cross. During that Holy Week we prayed the Rosary constantly. I knew that I could not ask anyone for assistance because that was my sacrifice to accept. I agreed to accept it without complaint during the two days that this pain lasted, until the Resurrection on Easter Sunday."

On November 1, 1994, Eddie was again in great pain. He recalls, "I was sitting alone, remembering that it was All Saints' Day. The next day was my birthday. I believe that the Lord gave me this special grace as a birthday gift. I asked the Lord for health, but that if the Lord needed help, I was willing. My hands were bleeding. I was in pain. I was lying in the form of Jesus crucified. My wife tried to lift me, but I was too heavy. She phoned Sal for help. After a while I felt better again. They tried to wipe the blood from my hands but it wouldn't come out. They used water from Marmora and were able to remove the blood."

"That day I was nailed to the floor. A lot of blood came out of my hands, and my shirt was filled with blood. I felt pain, but also great love. I love Jesus very much. He changed my whole personality. I am born again. I feel better, stronger. I can do things that are difficult and He helps me. He gives me words of prophecy when I need to speak them. Love is everything; love for the family; love for one another. Remember that God is always with you. If you have any problems simply ask Him and He'll tell you what to do. Twice I received the stigmata, but only once did the blood pour out of my hands, feet and side. Those in the room said that my body was three times its normal weight and could not be lifted."

Eddie and Ida respond to requests for their prayer group to visit and pray in people's homes. These visits are called missions. Eddie remarks, "This past summer we went to New Jersey in response to a request from people who requested our ministry. On the way home as I drove the car I felt pain, but said nothing to anyone. I saw that my hands were bleeding and knew that I couldn't drive. They saw the blood and immediately we changed drivers. I began to pray the Rosary right away and my hands stopped bleeding. During Holy Week we went to my brother's house in New York for our mission there. When I feel something I show it to people and they know that more prayer is needed. This is when they see signs on my hands and feet."

Effect on Eddie's Life

Eddie understands his contribution as follows. "I know that I suffer for people all over the world who forget to pray, and help bring them back to Jesus. That's all He asks of me, to help convert people who don't believe before it's too late, before the three days of darkness come. I don't know if I'm saved either. I still have lots of sins for which I must atone and make sacrifices. Even though I know that God is with me, it is still not enough to have God forgive your sins. You have to sacrifice for the rest of your life. Even if you go to church, nobody knows if they are truly saved. That's why we trust in the Lord to save us. He sustains us in life."

"How do I see myself differently? I am happy now, but before I was JUNK! Now I have no problems. I trust in the Lord. I believe that I will have a new job within the next month. The Lord never leaves me and He will find something for me in His own time. My work now is to pray and sacrifice. In my prayer I go first to Mary and then to Jesus."

"People who read this book might be touched by the Lord. Some may consider me a liar and doubt what I say. Others will know that I am honest. Everyone is not touched to believe in their heart. It is good if people believe. I believe that Our Blessed Mother is truly appearing at Marmora, but some people doubt these apparitions of Mary and Jesus. It was Our Lady at Marmora who led me to Jesus. That is why Jesus is using me. He trusts me and I trust Him too."

Phenomenon of the Rose Petals

Visitors to the Virrey home bring bouquets of roses for the altar. On some rose petals an image of Our Lady, the Divine Infant, Jesus Crucified, or the Holy Family emerges. Photographs of some of these rose petals are included in this book.

Additional comments about the rose petals are made in this chapter by Father Fernand Proulx, who describes holding a petal and watching the image take shape before his eyes. He claims that there are no two identical images on any petals.

Messages

Eddie shares with the reader some of his recent messages from Jesus:

December 3, 1994

Help me to carry my cross. I will show you how heavy the cross is to carry. Help me to bring back all the people who stopped praying.

Forgive and forget. Love one another.

Pray with your heart, not with your head.

Evil is all around the world. Help me to destroy it.

December 5, 1994

I am Jesus crucified. I am so tired already.

Pray to my Mother. (This message was repeated twice) I want you to pray to my Mother.

Bring people back to my Mother. I am calling you to pray with her. I am watching you and guiding you.

God the Father is already angry at the way things happen around the world, killings and murder. Bad spirits are all around the world.

The Three Days of Darkness are coming soon. Don't be scared. I will protect you all.

Spiritual Direction

Aside from regular Confession, Eddie receives spiritual direction from a priest who visits his home frequently. This priest also brings groups of people from his own parish, and confirmed to the author his conviction that Eddie's experiences are valid and faith-building.

In October 1994 the bishop of Toronto's Eastern Pastoral Region initiated an inquiry into the prayer groups being held in the Virrey home and asked Eddie to meet with him. This was done, to the mutual satisfaction of both parties.

Appendix Two contains a copy of a flyer which Eddie gives to people who are not familiar with the phenomenon of resting in the Spirit. It is included for general information and is not considered an official document from any authorized group.

HELPER IN EDDIE'S MINISTRY

Salvatore and Antonietta Papania live a few streets away from the Virrey home. Sal took an early retirement in 1994. He was present during my second interview with Eddie and assisted him as he came out of his trance.

Sal comments on his life and experience. "We have three boys, one of whom was married this year. I was not a religious person. Sunday Mass was about the extent of my religious observance. One day I was mowing the lawn at the front of my house and a man drove by asking for direction to the house where a crucifix was oozing oil. I told him I didn't know where it was. He said the house was near mine. I said, 'If you find it, let me know and I'll come to pray with you."

"I didn't hear anything more. One day when I was at Mass with Antonietta she approached a woman and the same subject surfaced. I asked where the house was because I wanted to pray. The woman brought us to Eddie's house in July 1993. I continued to return daily since then. My wife, mother, the three boys and my son's wife come here almost every night."

"We assist Eddie when he goes into a trance. I saw a lot of people who were helped by Eddie and who rested in the Spirit. Many people were cured in some way, not from Eddie, but from Jesus and their own prayers and faith. It has changed most of our lives. We are not the same as we were before."

Prayer Group and Personal Prayer

Sal explains, "I am dedicated to Eddie's prayer group. We go to different missions wherever people invite us, in the city, outside the country, anywhere. Our purpose is to encourage people to come together in prayer. We hold Cenacles as instructed by Father Gobbi. Prayer bonds our family together. Our children are no longer on the town at night with no time for prayer. Everything is set aside with the Rosary in this house as first priority. It is the same with our missions, which is our most important activity."

"We keep a calendar in the house for all requests from people to come to their home for prayer. Everything else is secondary. When we are on missions and pray the Cenacle, Eddie has a message for the people of the house and those who are gathered together."

"I don't know why the Lord has chosen me to help Eddie. It is His will, and He brought it about. I guess it is to make sacrifice for our sins. He was chosen to carry a heavy cross and we have to sacrifice our lives by helping him and pray at the same time."

"The initial group was about thirty to thirty-five people, and other people come two or three times a week from outside areas. The kitchen, halls, living room, the whole house is packed with visitors. The group is getting very large now. We are one big voice in prayer."

"Personally I am more armed with prayer. I consecrated myself to Our Lady. She thanked me for doing so and I'm more constant with my prayers. Whatever spare time I have I don't waste, but use it for prayer. We have an altar at home, not as large as Eddie's, but it is ours and we use it more often than we did previously. It has changed me and my family quite a bit."

"My wife was closer to Mary than I, but I go to Mary in prayer. Sometimes I ask Jesus a lot of questions and one way or another I get my answers. At times the answer is not an answer to the pain but thanksgiving as an answer for prayer."

"I read the Bible a little bit. Confession is to me something that we should do more often because it is a sacrament. I go as often as I can because I hate living with a sin in me. It bothers me until I get rid of it in Confession."

Witness to Eddie's Trance

Sal describes Eddie's trance during their trip to New Jersey. "I took over as driver when Eddie began to bleed. He started to pray the Rosary and suddenly he collapsed into a trance. He became the Baby Jesus, or Santo Nino as we say in Spanish. When Eddie is in a trance, you can tell by his body position if he is Our Lady, Jesus, or the Divine Infant. His voice also takes on a different tone with these different persons who speak through him. As Santo Nino his voice has a high quality, almost like a squeaky sound, though he can be understood. As Our Lady his voice is soft and feminine. When Jesus speaks through him it is a firm command. As Santo Nino he asked for milk when he was in a trance. We offered him Coke but he refused it. We prayed the Rosary on the trip there and he was in trance almost the entire time. On our way back from New Jersey he was drawn in once again.

Many times Sal went to Marmora with Eddie. Sal notes, "When Eddie goes into a trance in Marmora it is more difficult than at home, because of the trees, mud and different weather. If there is mud we try to protect him as much as we can but when he goes into a trance there is no warning. He has to be observed constantly. You can tell the moment before he falls. We help to lay him on the ground and bless him with oil. Although Eddie went into a trance at almost every Station, it was at the Tenth Station that he felt Our Lady coming."

Sal concludes, "My feeling is one of great satisfaction, not because it's a job. I love doing it because I know Who I'm doing it for and its outcome. More people are coming together in prayer."

Statement From Father Fernand Proulx

Father Fernand Proulx and the author met for the first time in Medjugorje, 1991. The following telephone interview reflects Father's estimation of Marmora, of the phenomenon of the oil and the rose petals and of Eddie's experiences.

Visits to Marmora

"I have been to Marmora many times and took with me small groups of people, two or three car loads at a time. We didn't have any phenomena there except that some of the people saw the sun dancing. I believe in Marmora, and there I met the visionary Veronique Demers and her parents. In October 1994, I met Shelagh Greensides in her house. She placed a statue of the Blessed Mother on the table. The statue had been in Scarborough for a few weeks and now it was home over a month. The head and the shoulders of the statue were covered with oil and the rest of the body was completely dry! People who went to Marmora with me experienced an increase of faith."

"In Marmora I made the acquaintance of a special person named Carmelle. We talked and we became friends. Later, one day, she phoned me and invited me to meet her prayer group. I accepted right away even though it was a three hour drive from my place. There we prayed and she told me about the two places, Scarborough and Mississauga, where the phenomenon of the oozing oil occurs. Later she introduced me to Eddie's place. It was on Easter Monday. 'Show Father your hands', she asked. He did so in a very simple manner. They were healing. He lifted his pants a little and I saw the marks on his feet. He lifted his sweatshirt and I saw the mark on his side, about two or three inches long."

Assessment of Eddie's Experiences

"On November 14, 1994, I went to Eddie's place. During the recitation of the Rosary, in the middle of the second decade, Eddie, who was kneeling, fell on his back and took the position of Jesus on the Cross: his left foot over his right in a very uncomfortable position with his arms extended. Both feet and arms were nailed to the floor. No one could move them. During the fifth decade his feet and arms slowly returned to a normal position. Some friends then pulled him to a sitting position against the wall, in order to rest his back. There was no bleeding that night, contrary to what happened fourteen days earlier."

"On November 1, there was the same scenario, but Eddie's wounds were bleeding profusely. After his hands were joined together and he was pulled to the wall, someone took pictures of his hands. (See pictures) In my mind there is absolutely no doubt about the veracity of his stigmata."

Phenomena of Oil and Roses

Father Proulx continues. "The Lord decided to give us evidence of His presence since May 1993 by covering statues and religious articles with oil. Nearly every statue of Jesus, of the Blessed Mother or any other saint, any crucifix, medal, rosary or even holy pictures will testify to the miraculous phenomenon. It seems though, that these articles must first be blessed. Last August 1994, I brought a couple of statues there, but they gave off no oil. 'Father, said Sal, were these statues blessed?' I answered, 'I don't think so.' He advised, 'You had better bless them. Otherwise they won't give out any oil.' I blessed them, left them there, and on my next visit they were covered with oil."

"When I visit Eddie and Ida they gather all religious articles and lay them on the floor for me to bless. Once there was a tiny little statue about one and a half inches high, and too wide for its height. It was in a little dish. At the end of the prayers I observed this statue. It was covered with oil and on the bottom of the dish there were about seven or eight drops of oil which accumulated during the time we prayed. A clear answer to those unbelievers who like to think that someone secretly put the oil on the religious articles. Besides, how to explain the fact that this oil dries up completely, nearly instantly, without leaving any sticky trace, when one takes home his religious articles."

"The oil was tested by two different biochemists and is documented as pure olive oil that can't be found anywhere on the market."

"Another miracle that the Lord is giving us at Eddie's place is seen on petals of roses. Since the summer of 1994 when the flowers dry and the petals fall, many of them show clearly or very clearly the picture of Jesus on the Cross; Jesus crowned with thorns; the Infant Jesus of Prague; the face of the Blessed Mother, etc. On one visit I began hearing Confessions and was a bit late for their prayers, so they sang songs as they waited for me. As soon as I entered the living room a little boy took a petal and put it in my hand. I looked at it and could see something was starting to form on it. I looked at it during the prayers and saw an image developing in my hand. At the end of the prayer it was developed further. Another time I was given two petals with something on them, but not definite. I keep those precious petals in a small cardboard box. After three months both are showing clearly the Infant Jesus of Prague."

Personal Testimony

Father Proulx concludes with his personal reflection. "These miraculous happenings are given us to strengthen our faith and support our convictions. These are so obviously miracles that nobody, with a minimum of good will, can deny."

"Someone asked me, 'Was there any investigation made by the Church about these surprising phenomena?' As if one **has** to wait for the result of such analysis to accept the Hand of God in his life. We have been exaggerating so much, for many centuries, on prudence. Jesus said, 'On this rock I will build **My** Church'. The building of the Church goes on from the death of Christ to the end of the world. Today, with the best of intention, authorities have undertaken the responsibility to build and protect the Church of Christ. It is done with so great devotion as to analyze the actions of God to make sure that they conform to what we recognize as the true teaching of Revelation."

"Yes, prudence is necessary. Satan always tries to deceive. One has to be careful, and Jesus gave us the norm: 'A good tree produces good fruit and a bad produces bad fruit'. The best attitude should not be to wait and see, but accept and see. Accept God's interventions and receive their graces. If the devil's intervention becomes clear, we reject it right away."

"God wants to prove that He does exist, though we know for sure that He does. He makes miracles like this that we can see, so that nobody can say that it's not true. If they say that the images on the petals are produced artificially, I disagree. There are no two images alike. I tried to place a petal on the overhead projector to see a large picture of it on the screen. It was only a black spot. When I looked at it, I noticed that the petal that I put on the glass was drying, because there was too much heat from the projector. The picture is still there. The petal changed colour but the picture is beautiful."

"I say this: In the autumn all the leaves of the trees fall and change colour. When a rose petal falls from the flower, God makes it dry the way He wants, printing a picture in it. The petal which is drying develops a picture. There is no other physical explanation. There is no paint involved in this process."

CHAPTER FOURTEEN

MARIAN LEADERSHIP

Bishop Roman Danylak of Toronto was baptized and raised in the church of Saint Josaphat, the first church of the Ukrainian pioneers to eastern Canada. He completed his high school studies with the Brothers of the Christian School, majored in philosophy at St. Michael's College University, and was the first Ukrainian student from this continent to complete his theological and seminary formation in Rome since the war.

He was ordained deacon on December 25, 1956, and priest on October 13, 1957, in Rome. With the defense of his thesis on a canonical collection of the Byzantine Churches, he obtained the laurea in Utroque Jure in Rome, in 1966. At that time he was assigned as assistant pastor to Saint Josaphat's Cathedral and chancellor of the eparchy shortly after. In 1978 he became pastor of the cathedral. He organized the Toronto eparchial matrimonial tribunal, and served as judge on this tribunal, the Toronto Regional Tribunal and the national appeal Tribunal of Canada until recently. For several years he was spiritual director to the Brotherhood of Ukrainian Catholics of the eparchy. He organized and directed the first Ukrainian Religious Radio Program with CHIN Radio International from 1969 to the present, and taught religion at the elementary and high school levels for many years.

In 1973 he was called by Pope Paul VI as a consultor to the Pontifical Commission for the Revision of Canon Law for the Oriental Churches until the publication of the Code in 1990. He was consecrated titular bishop of Nyssa on March 25, 1993 in St. Michael's Cathedral, Toronto. During the past few years he has spoken with Josyp Terelya, activist of the Ukrainian Catholic Church, at many Marian Conferences in Canada, the United States and the Philippines.

Bishop Danylak began visiting the Greensides farm in 1992 and continued to be a frequent visitor there. He notes, "In October 1994 I was in Marmora with a few friends and some people from Colorado. We made the Stations of the Cross and prayed before the Fourteenth Station. On our way back we looked for signs and in particular the miracle of the sun, since I had never seen it though other people described it to me. This time I saw it. The sun swelled and changed colour. Our faces were bathed in gold. At that particular Station Pat took two consecutive pictures. The first one shows the five of us. The second photograph shows bright flares around the group. When we sent the pictures for development, one of the women identified the flares as our angels. I think she is right. There were five of us and five angels."

Priestly Ordination

The bishop recalls his ordination to the priesthood on the fortieth anniversary of the apparitions at Fatima. He reflects, "It was my mother and I'm sure, the Blessed Mother in heaven who organized this. I was ordained at the beginning of my fourth year of theology rather than at the end. My mother knew that Archbishop Hermaniuk, Metropolitan from Winnipeg was going to Rome. He had been my pastor at Holy Eucharist Redemptorist parish in Toronto before I went to Rome. My mother contacted him and asked him if he would be so gracious as to ordain me when he went for the First World Congress of the Lay Apostolate, with Catherine Doherty and other luminaries present. The archbishop was happy with this role because he knew me personally. He contacted the rector of the seminary and the rector told me, 'You will be ordained by Archbishop Hermaniuk at the beginning of October. I rather resented this because I didn't want to be singled out for anything, although there were seven other Basilian scholastics and two other diocesan priests ordained at the same time."

"These two mothers had a lot to do with this event. Our Lady chose the anniversary of her appearance at Fatima for my ordination because it was also the conclusion of the Congress of the Lay Apostolate. I was ordained bishop on March 25, 1993 the feast of the Annunciation of the Blessed Virgin Mary. That feast was my choice. My name's day is October 1 or 14 depending on whether you use the Gregorian or Julian calendar. It is the feast of the Patronage of the Blessed Mother and also the feast of St Roman the Melodian, a great Marian poet and priest of Christian antiquity. All these Marian things are in my life."

"Because I arrived in the seminary on October 1, the feast of the Patronage of Our Lady, I wanted to dedicate my episcopacy to the protection of the Blessed Mother. I sought a Marian feast and decided to be ordained when most of the church celebrates the feast of the Annunciation. Mary's sign has always hovered over me."

Episcopal Election

The apostolic nuncio invited Bishop Danylak to meet with him in Ottawa on December 19 and 20, 1992, to ask if he would accept his episcopal nomination. He states, "The papal bull of my appointment was signed three days before by the Holy Father and I was asked only then if I would accept that appointment of my nomination. I did with some reservation and hesitation. It was made public on December 29 which was my birthday."

"As I drove back from Ottawa I decided to stop at Marmora to place myself under the protection of the Mother of God, to pray that she would look after our priests and bless this episcopal ministry. During the drive I thought concretely about the things that a bishop wears and does, the bishop's motto, my coat of arms. I prayed the Rosary and some ideas for the coat of arms became clear. I wanted to have a symbol of Ontario and Quebec because these are the extent of my jurisdiction for Ukrainian Catholics. I also wanted something to designate my spiritual heritage which is the eastern church of Ukraine, and something involving Mary and Jesus."

"I arrived at the farm around eight o'clock in the evening. No one was there so I parked the car and climbed up the hill to pray at the Eleventh Station. When I came down John met me. He was visiting his daughter, and returned to get Shelagh and Josie. We had tea together. Shelagh pulled out a bag of miraculous medals. I looked at the two hearts and knew that these were to be part of the coat of arms. For the slogan I wanted something that resonated with heart and charity. I asked Geraldine, a scholarly friend, to draft a design for me. She began working immediately, searched in her library, and developed an attack of asthma. The Lord said to her, 'Bishop Roman is my apostle. I'll look after him myself.' By that time the Lord had already put together what was to be in the coat of arms."

Pilgrimages to Medjugorje

Bishop Danylak made four pilgrimages to Medjugorje. He describes his visits. "I always had a singular and unique devotion to the Blessed Mother. I first visited Medjugorje in 1985 and went really for the celebration of the millennium of the passing of St. Methodius, who is one of the founders of the eastern rite and Ukrainian churches including Jugoslavia. I felt something special drawing me to Medjugorje."

"When my friend Father Joe asked me if I would like to go to Medjugorje I agreed. We spent the day there with the bishop of Zagreb. On the evening we arrived we attended the Croatian Mass and afterwards realized that the bishop made prior arrangements for us to have shelter in one of the homes. It was before all the billeting accommodations were built and I was really touched by the Christian hospitality of these people."

"My second visit was in 1987, the vigil of the Ukrainian millennium in 1988. My parishioners wanted to go and I agreed, provided they did the organizing. The Lord was very generous. Instead of our original plan to go in May, my sister Olga helped reschedule our pilgrimage in September. In anticipation of the celebrations of the millennium we planned to visit some of the areas from where Christianity came to Ukraine, Constantinople, Ochrid in Jugoslavia, and go to Medjugorje."

"We arrived in Medjugorje on Sunday morning October 11. It was a beautiful day. Throughout our visit we celebrated Mass in the chapel of the Apparitions, through the kindness of Sister Agnes. Another priest and I returned to St. James church for the evening Mass. It was stifling so we sat outside under the trees. He caught a cold. During the night a heavy electric storm poured down on the village. It seemed to relate to the messages we received during the next two or three days."

"On Monday the continued drizzling prevented us from local travel. I brought our people to Mostar on a bus and we returned around four o'clock. As we entered the compound at St. James Church a warm sun came out of the clouds and embraced everybody there. There was a statue of Jesus before the church at that time. Fascinated, I wanted to take a picture of it. A Mexican woman standing beside me exclaimed, 'Look! Look!' I knew she was witnessing the miracle of the sun and said to myself 'This is only October 12. I'll do my sun watching on October 13.'"

"The rain stopped after early morning Mass on Tuesday. My sister wanted to go to Podbrodo. Although I had been to Medjugorje before and had seen many pictures of the place, they related little to the reality. We saw people coming down Apparition Hill, but not by the regular route and we decided to climb the same way. I am not the lightest of men, yet I simply flew up the side of that hill."

"We saw a group standing by the Cross where Our Lady first spoke to the two girls. A group of Mexicans prayed there and we decided to join them. Afterwards a couple and their twenty year old daughter said to me 'There are more crosses up on top.' I zipped up the side of the hill and saw the crosses which I had previously seen in videos. I tried to shake the people who had come up with me and to do my own thing. The Lord said, 'Fine.'"

"Not knowing anything about sun watching I made a little horizontal crack through my fingers and peeked at the sun. The Lord, knowing my impatience, showed me immediately the most powerful experience of the sun. A disc spun around in front of the sun. The spinning sun continued for a long time. I asked myself, 'How long will this go on?' Not that it was boring. Suddenly it stopped. The sun plummeted straight down toward the earth. I prayed, 'Oh! my God!' Then it stopped and the small solar disc changed into a sharply defined white disc of the sun. Out of that disc was a sharply defined Latin cross. In between the arms of the cross delicate filigree rays emerged. It was like a huge monstrance in the sky. I stood there asking 'What does the Lord signify for His church? Later I understood that it was the glory of the victory of the Cross. It became more significant for me especially in the context of Medjugorje, after the previous day's storm when all hell seemed to break loose."

"In this triumph of the Cross, I believe Jesus was saying to me 'The Eucharist and the Cross and Mary are there." I took a slide picture of this apparition and it was one of the most beautiful slides I had ever seen. Many people saw different images in the slide. In my eagerness to show the slide to others I wanted to have prints made. The professional photographer said that there was indeed a cross in the print, and the figure of Our Lady at the foot of the cross. Behind the cross was Jesus with His outstretched hands. I had watched all this but only saw the initial part. The resulting picture showed the full image."

"Cathy whom I met in the Charismatic group in Toronto asked me what I was doing in Medjugorje. She called her friends who were with Bishop Lacey. That afternoon we returned again to the church for the evening Mass. It was not so crowded and we were able to be seated. I wanted to pray. During the Mass, sermon and intercession, I saw flashes of light all over the church. Then everybody stood up and looked backwards. My curiosity got the better of me and I too looked to the back of the church but saw nothing. I turned my gaze back to the altar. As I prayed, Our Lady came to me. I saw her from the back of my head and she said to me, '**My Son. Priest of my Son.**' I know Our Lady is in Medjugorje not only because of the millions of people going there but because of my own experience."

Visits To Marmora

During 1992 the Greensides opened their farm to friends of Our Lady with a Medjugorje Day. Bishop Danylak recalls, "On September 14, the feast of the Triumph of the Cross, Josyp Terelya was invited to speak. That is when Josyp saw the miracle of the sun for the first time."

"In the next three months Josyp visited Marmora several times. The big event was on the feast of the Nativity of Our Lady, September 8, 1993. That night when Josyp returned to Toronto he called me and said, 'Our Lady appeared to me at the Tenth and Eleventh Stations. She gave me a message.' Five days later she appeared to him in his own home. On October 13 I went again to Marmora as a pilgrim with my mother and sister. It was the first time I met the Greensides. They told me their story and how it related to Medjugorje. I could well appreciate it because of my own involvement at Medjugorje."

"At Marmora I saw the providence of Our Lord at work. I have not seen the Mother of God at Marmora nor has she spoken to me in an audible fashion, but I do know she is there. Usually when I drive to Ottawa I stop in at Marmora to pray, and Josyp accompanies me if the urge is strong for him to go there. I believe that Our Lady is truly very powerfully present. My first conviction is because of my discernment of Josyp and his messages. I came to know him well over the last eight years, especially when I heard and discerned the messages he received. I am convinced that they are truly from Our Lady because of Josyp's special mission as a witness, who gives testimony to the faith of the people of Ukraine throughout the years of persecution. Our Lady told him when he was in prison in 1972 that even though he was only through half his prison term he would be released and go beyond the ocean and Our Lady would always be with him, because his life was to be a witness. Because of my discernment of this, I evaluate positively the messages that Josyp received and the authenticity of his mission. I believe that he has truly seen Our Lady as he claims."

"I met the four or five young children who had apparitions there, visited their homes and know them to be simple and guileless. People like that don't concoct stories. I met Dory Tan. What overwhelms and touches me here, is the same thing that happened in Medjugorje. People by the thousands experienced the greatest gift of interior conversion, a change of heart. They discover the love and the compassion of Our Lord and His Blessed Mother, which for me is the most effective of these marvellous and convincing signs which I witnessed in both Marmora and Medjugorje."

"Stories of Medjugorje are very extensive. I watch people pray and listen to the experiences which changed their lives. People of Medjugorje have come to me for Confession as to so many other priests. Our Lady gave them the grace of seeing their own heart which resulted in the most beautiful and powerful Confessions."

"When the Holy Father responded to the events at Medjugorje he stated, 'Whether or not it is true that these are signs of the supernatural, whether or not Our Lady really comes there, that place has been made holy by the prayers of the millions of people who have gone there. We have confirmation of the presence of the supernatural from the testimonies of people relating their experience. The same thing is beginning to happen here at Marmora."

Josyp's Healing at Marmora

Marmora has become a place of blessing, conversion and healing. Bishop Danylak remembers his experience with Josyp. "On Saturday June 20, 1993 I was driving to Ottawa. At the last moment I invited Josyp to travel with me for the annual pilgrimage to our shrine in

Ottawa. He was happy to do so. On the way we paid a visit to Marmora, arriving around one in the afternoon. The Greensides invited us for tea."

"During tea Josyp asked to be excused. For the two previous months he had heavy nose bleeds because of his hypertension. Doctors had tried to cauterize his nose and stop the bleeding. His condition improved and so he came along on the trip. Suddenly his nose began to bleed. He went upstairs and wretched blood from his mouth for a half an hour. When he returned downstairs we prayed for him. He suggested, 'Let's go up the hill to pray.' By this time Dory Tan had informed the Greensides that Our Lady gave a special blessing to the spring at the top of the hill. Dory's husband and some friends were building a concrete foundation for the faucet of water. Josie told us how John was healed of the painful and bleeding growth on his hand by swishing his hand in the water."

"Praying and washing in the water didn't help Josyp. We went to a local clinic but they could do nothing, so we went to the hospital in Campbellford. They arrested the bleeding, packed his nose, then sealed it with a dressing, with the advice that he be checked in his home hospital on the following Monday. Josyp barely got back into the car when he began bleeding again. He stripped away the dressing and swabbed the blood as well as he could. We returned to the Greensides house and prayed as we administered ice packs to his forehead and the back of his neck."

"At this point Dory entered the kitchen and recognized Josyp. She lay one hand on his head and the other on his shoulder while the ice packs of frozen peas and corn continued to be held as previously. During the twenty minute prayer, Josyp stated, 'She took the whole weight off my head.' When Dory finally removed her hand from Josyp it was as if she removed the weight, pressure and pain. When he stood up he was weak because of loss of blood. Dory said ' You'll be O.K.' It was through her prayers that Josyp was healed."

"It was too late for us to drive to Ottawa so we returned to Toronto around 9:00 p.m. I suggested that we go immediately to the Emergency Department at the hospital but he declined, saying, 'I'm O.K.' That night he had another short spell of bleeding and his wife drove him to the emergency. He returned again on Monday. On the days that followed he used the water from Marmora and his high blood pressure came under control. Simple washing with the water had not helped. Continued use of the water enabled his healing. The Lord wanted to give us some discernment about Dory and her mission."

Hrushiv

The bishop comments on his visits to Hrushiv in the Ukraine. "I visited Hrushiv in the months of October and November 1993. It was my first time in the Ukraine and I wanted to go to Hrushiv chiefly because of the stories I had heard from Josyp. The subsequent February, June and July I visited Hrushiv again."

"I observed certain signs of the presence of Our Lady. In the cupola of the church of the Holy Trinity I saw well defined negative images of Our Lady. On the second visit I saw the negative image of the Annunciation on the larger dome. On my last visit in June or July I saw a small figure of Our Lady with white dress, blue mantle, hands outstretched, in three different positions as though she were moving in a certain direction."

"When most people see the Blessed Virgin they claim to see a little woman in black, bustling on the balcony of the church itself. They see it from only one spot, not from the church but from the area near the home of Maria Kisyn. That is how Maria first saw Our Lady on April 26, 1987. That date is significant because it is the first anniversary of the disaster in Chernobyl. Maria called her Mother. Her mother told her it was the Blessed Virgin and they both knelt in prayer."

"News of this apparition spread throughout all Ukraine. People mostly see the Virgin as this little woman in black bustling around. It wasn't until Josyp went a month later, May 9 to May 16, that he saw the Blessed Virgin, not as a little figure in black but as a towering image of light, in colour, standing over the cupola of the church at the height of two meters. Her own image was a twenty foot woman. That is where Josyp corroborated what he heard and saw with other people. Not only religious people observed what Josyp saw and heard what Our Lady said. This is one of the significant differences between the appearances of Our Lady. In Fatima and Medjugorje the Blessed Virgin appeared to three or six individuals. In Hrushiv Our Lady appeared for almost two months to hundreds of thousands of people and many heard her speak."

Reflection on Supernatural Phenomena

Bishop Danylak summarizes, "We hear reports of apparitions of the Blessed Mother all over the world. We hear stories of Eucharistic miracles being repeated. Everything has to be discerned, submitted to the sound judgment of the Church. I believe that many of these are authentic, and the Church whether in the initial stages or ultimately, has given some measure of approval to some of these apparitions, visions, such as Maria Esperanza in Betania, Sister Agnes in Akita in Japan. Others are under observation."

"One thing is certain. Our Lady is indicating to the world a haven of safety in the difficult times that are to come when we do not have access to our churches or the Eucharist. We will have these places of grace and these phenomena of oozing oil, springs of water for divine medicine to assist Christians, not only as places to visit. Jesus is giving us divine instruments of healing, holy water and holy oil, with the reminder of chastisement or more so purification, because the visitation of Our Lord is at hand."

"Our Blessed Mother comes firstly, as the one who prepares the Second Coming of Jesus, and secondly as the chief of the regions of angels. She is the great angel of whom we read in the Book of Revelation, who binds Lucifer with the chains of the Rosary, and casts him into the pit from which he will not emerge for a thousand years."

"She is not only a sign of the times to come. She is truly our Mother coming to us now to sustain us. We hear all these stories to encourage us to prepare; to return to her Son; to pray for peace. Had people responded in the numbers hoped for by heaven, she would have brought peace to the world as promised in 1981 in Medjugorje. Because people failed to respond and do not believe, chastisement and wars will surely come. It need not have been so. To all those who accept her she is truly there."

"Our focus should be on the Lord. We are not to fear the difficult times and the trials and persecution, but keep our hearts and our eyes focussed on Him."

Some Messages from Our Lady to Josyp Terelya Translated and Given to the Author by Bishop Danylak

The author appreciates the content and value of all the messages received, which will be incorporated into Josyp Terelya's upcoming book. Because of their considerable length, they have been abridged for inclusion into this publication.

August 21, 1992, in Marmora:

My children, why do you remain silent in sin? To you, my son, I say, you betray my Son through your silence. Hence do not remain silent in the face of sin. To those who do not want to repent I say, you shall not be condemned at the eternal judgement because you did not perform miracles, and did not theologize, oh unrepentant blind ones; but you shall be condemned because you did not lament your sins.

I am saying this to those who do not want to repent, who are priests and religious. And to you I say, pray. Pray as though you were conversing with Almighty God Himself. Through the Holy Spirit you will touch my Son. In prayer you will discover the spirit of prayer and the power of prayer, and through your sincere thoughts you will find deep and true faith.

Sunday, September 13, 1992

Josyp states, "I was making the Stations of the Cross around 4:00 p.m. in Marmora, Ontario, when the Mother of God, the Immaculate Virgin Mary, appeared – all in light, dressed in a white gown, a sky-blue mantle on her head, wearing a red coat. She stretched forth her hands; in her right hand, a Rosary. With tears in her eyes she pleaded:

Listen to what Heaven is saying to you. It is from this hill that I shall call the devout Christians to defend and not to lose the teachings of Christ the King. I am telling you that difficult times of trial are coming on this Godless world. I have chosen this place in Marmora, that I might pray together with believing Christians to entreat my Son, Christ the King, to have mercy upon sinners.

Let everything remain here as it is. Do not change anything, that devout Christians might have a place to pray in peace and in grace. Erect only a wooden chapel on the hill, between the Tenth and Eleventh Stations of The Way of the Cross, to the Immaculate

Heart of Mary, the sorrowful Mother of all who suffer in the world. You have seen how the chapel is to look. Obtain for this chapel an Eastern Icon. Pray constantly for Russia, for these people will suffer exceedingly again, and will perish in sins without grace and repentance.

Pray in this chapel for peace and love in this country, Canada. People are not aware that the prophesied times are already at hand. My heart grieves. I weep with material tears for all sinners, but what of this... people have torn themselves loose of all restraints. There is no authority; there is no peace; there is no truth nor justice. There is no true piety. My child, I tell you that the end times are at hand. My children, you are on the threshold of the day of judgment. God is now calling all to Himself as never before, to mutual understanding, to brotherly love among all.

The Son of God has come in defense of his Church and the faithful. Does everyone see the falsehoods and untruth behind the facade of fine words? All sorts of unchristian deeds are done in the name of my Son. Of what worth are fine words if there are no convincing deeds behind them? The Church today needs a radical purification from inactivity. This is why you should pray for the Pope. Pray for His good works. Pray that all may be one.

Everywhere we hear three words that Christians can't understand: collegiality, new rites and ecumenism. Remember, the Church of Christ is the Church of the Kingdom of God – theocratic, not collegial; for all ecclesiastical collegiality leads to chaos among the faithful and the Church leadership; and with this, the collapse of faith and the rise of inactivity. It is because of this that Bishops and Bishops' Conferences don't pay serious attention to the observations of the Pope. The authority of the Pope is being destroyed in disastrous fashion.

But God has given the Church strength even here. Through the pilgrimages of the Pope, the power of faith among Christians in the entire world is being renewed. Remember that Satan has infiltrated the very heart of the Church, and is spreading the idea of his ecumenical Christianity, of his new interpretation of the faith. This has led to today's indifference and neglect in the religious education of children and youth.

Friday, September 18, 1992

Josyp commented, "I fasted and prayed, that I might receive Confession and Holy Communion on Sunday. It was after midnight, around two o'clock, when a light appeared from the icon-painting I have from Denver. And then I saw the Mother of God, this time dressed in black, with a white mantle over her head; and in her hands, as always a rosary, this one of black and white beads. The Mother of God said,"

I have come because great events are pressing upon a Godless humanity, that no way wants to receive my Son. Josyp, my son, time is at hand. Until now there were so many lesser and greater events coming that affected many nations. But such an earthshaking event is approaching that will encompass the entire cosmos. A great war, the greatest that has ever been till now is upon you. And so many people will not survive it; only those who accept Christ the King and will obey God's Commandments.

I am telling you this in order that devout Christians might be able to receive information that will enable them to defend themselves. All this has been written in the Holy Book in the Gospel of Christ. Everywhere the servants of the Antichrist, the Sons of Satan, will proclaim peace and quiet, but Satan is preparing a great war, that has never been witnessed until now. His power is invisible, and this power will move people to arm themselves.

From my whole heart, and out of my great love for all of you, I say: may the Christians and all people of good will lay aside their religious hostilities, their political rivalry, economic profit, and calmly reflect upon the truth that the Lord God gave sinful man for his benefit. The Lord said: "Come, then, and we shall make our accounts". How my Mother's heart pleads for you . Obey the Divine Counsel. My child, do you know that Jesus informs me of that which is to take place, and I am telling you all: be obedient.

I beg you to pay special attention to the prophecy of the Holy Apostle John who says: "I saw three impure spirits like toads that came out of the mouth of the serpent, out of the mouth of the beast, out of the mouth of the false prophet. These are demonic spirits, who will work wonders, who go to the kings of the entire earth, to gather them for war in that great day of the omnipotent God." These words will soon be revealed. (Rev. 14-14)

Like little children who do not want to believe the truth, many people are in darkness and ignorance. I tell you this so that you might believe and repent, for obedience and repentance are the victory of God's forces over Satan.

How many priests and bishops today give glory to God in their lips but not with their hearts. How many are the priests who deny the Bible today, especially those sections which proclaim Jesus as the Saviour and King of the world. How little we hear in the churches today from the lips of priests that God's Kingdom in Christ remains the only hope for people in the entire world. How many are the Church leaders who unite themselves with the will of politicians and bank leaders, to place their hopes not in God but in the organization of the United Nations, calling it the only salvation for mankind.

Many of today's pastors have forgotten that God is the source of truth, for His word is truth. Did not Jesus say: "For this was I born, and for this have I come into the world, to give witness to the truth. Everyone who is in the truth hears My voice." (Jn. 18/37)

Pray, pray, pray without ceasing, and follow the path of God through penance and fasting, through your good works. Remember, all that is not the truth is a lie. The Lord says to all of you: "Satan is a devil and a liar. He is the father of lies. All the Holy Prophets of God from Abel to Saint Stephen suffered persecution because they spoke the truth. When Jesus, my Son, the great messenger of truth, came to earth, Satan set himself to destroy Jesus precisely because He spoke the truth. Today they persecute devout people because of truth.

In Russia preparations are under way for a worldwide revolution. The forces of hell which control the world will continue to say that everything they are doing is for the sake of peace and for the welfare of the people, but at the same time they will continue to deprive peoples of their freedom and free will.

December 4, 1992, in Marmora:

Defend the truth and search for the truth. Why do you remain silent at the unjust actions of those who fight God? They hate the Church of my Son because they are of hell and demons. They want to destroy the Crucified and Holy Church through their evil acts and lies. I tell you, especially you, my son, that the Church of Christ Himself is truth. And again I say to you, where we find the Holy Spirit, you will find the faith in Christ blossoming. The faith of Christ blooms in glory and in the purity of our thoughts.

Pray, pray with your whole heart with the prayer of the angels, and not just with your lips. Pray that the prophecies of the devil might be dissipated as smoke. Faith in God is living and salvific faith. Faith in the Antichrist is eternal hell and death, and that which is of death.

Seek prayers that speak clearly and which overcome the power of Satan. Pray with faith for the Lord is awaiting your prayers.

Wade Raley and Allan Young

Sandra Ruscio Presents Messages to the Holy Father

161

Marian Rodrigues

Virrey Home: Altar With Statues Oozing Oil.

Friends with Father Fernand Proulx, Eddie and Ida Virrey

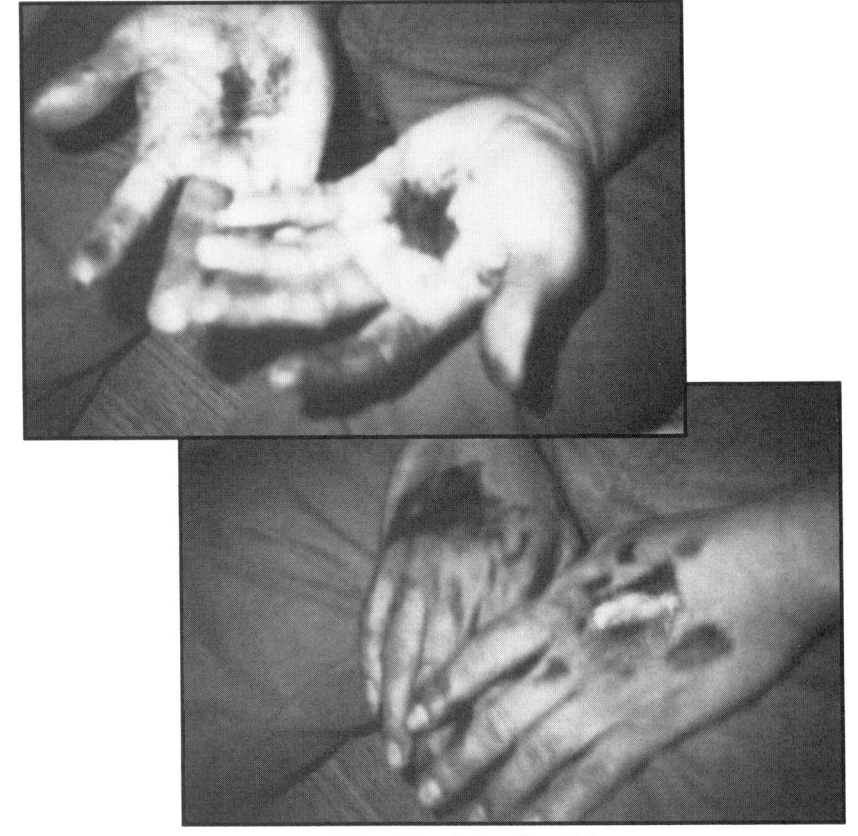

Eddie's Hands During Stigmata

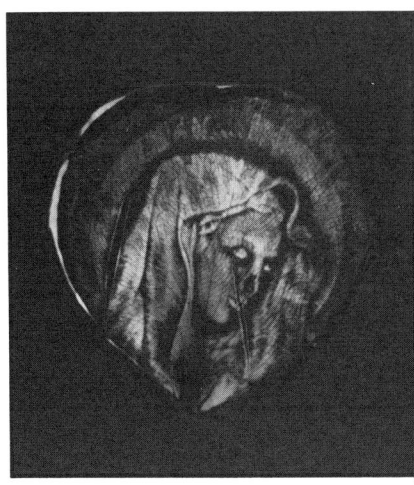

Phenomenon of Rose Petals.

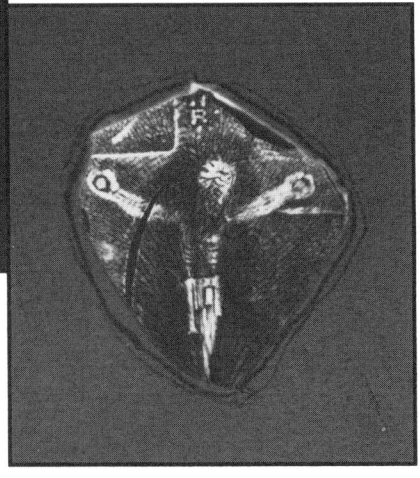

Bishop Roman Danylak with Four Friends....

....and the Light From
Their Guardian Angels.

Bishop Danylak With Our Holy Father.

CHAPTER FIFTEEN

OUR LADY CHANGED OUR LIVES

Ron and Janet Brown live with their son and daughter in Peterborough. Ron is self-employed and Janet works at Sears. Their statements complement one another, even while they demonstrate unique differences in the workings of grace in their lives and their family. Ron explains that his life style was like any other person in what he terms the evil empire of today where anything is acceptable. He states "I made up my own religion and took away from it whatever I liked. I rationalized my behaviour according to everyone else's actions."

The Beginning of Change

"In October 1993 my cousin's wife Val brought me a picture of Our Lady of Guadalupe to frame for her friend. I framed it for her and didn't think too much about it. I didn't even know it was Our Lady of Guadalupe until someone told me. A month later I saw a smaller version of the same picture at my mother's place. She is a practising Catholic and has visited Medjugorje. I asked, 'What are you doing with that picture?' She answered, 'That's a picture of Our Lady of Guadalupe and I'm praying a novena in her honour."

"I asked my mother, 'What's a novena?' She told me and I thought I'd be real smart and jokingly said, 'Maybe I will make one too.' She was so happy, that I decided I would really have to make one. I can't remember how long it was since I said the Rosary, probably not since I was eleven or twelve years of age. I went to church on Sunday, read the New Testament, and figured that I was doing great. During the nine days of the novena I said one Rosary every day for nine days. When it was over I felt self satisfied about what I had done and congratulated myself. I felt really happy."

"When Christmas was near I didn't have too much work coming in. Though I wasn't worried about it I thought that if I prayed the novena again, we might have a good Christmas. I had a picture of Our Lady of Seven Sorrows in my home and prayed a novena in her honour. Money came in and we had a good Christmas. Out of the blue around the end of January I thought, 'Maybe I'll make a novena.' On the last day I decided, 'I'm going to say the Rosary every day.'"

"Immaculate Conception church held a Marian week-end in May and I attended. In that church I gave my testimony for the first time. How I did that I will never know. The picture of Our Lady of Guadalupe was in the church that day, and I recognized it as the picture I had framed. I continued to pray two Rosaries a day."

"About a year later, the Legion of Christ Missionaries from New York gave a mini two hour retreat at Sacred Heart church with Mass, Confession and a short talk. A friend, Grace phoned me to let me know about it. The priests' message was that we try to go to Mass in the middle of the week and receive the Eucharist, in order to increase divine grace in our soul. That made sense to me and I decided to try it. I went to Mass on First Friday and the statue of the Mystical Rose was at the front of St. Peter's cathedral. Val told me that it was in honour of the feast of the Holy Rosary."

"The following Sunday I visited Marmora and met two Grey Nuns. They stopped overnight in Peterborough and stayed at my house. The next morning I drove them to Mass and began to attend Mass on a daily basis."

"My family talked about Medjugorje and Betania for the past couple of years. My son Jason went to Medjugorje and yet practises as a Baptist. I like to go to Marmora though I haven't seen any apparitions. I get a peaceful feeling there, and in the beginning, some small things happened to me. I didn't know what to read or what to pray for so I prayed for divine wisdom every day for about eight months, and still do. I learn something every day and read a lot. Books came to me through Marmora. A missionary in Marmora gave me a little book about the wonders of the Holy Name. I said the Holy Name of Jesus prayer and offered it up for the souls in purgatory."

"Another issue that changed for me was abortion. I thought the choice was up to the individual person. Whatever they wanted to do was fine with me. Now I am convinced that abortion is definitely murder. I go to every pro life demonstration walk that is held here."

Ron's Tattoos

Ron displayed the tattoos on both his arms. He explained, "Since I was fifteen years old I had tattoos of devils, snakes and things like that. One night in Sacred Heart church I looked over my shoulder for some reason and saw the Archangel Michael on the stained glass window. I decided to have my tattoos changed. Over the snake and the devil I chose a picture of Our Lord crowned with thorns."

"On my other arm over an old anchor, I selected a design of Our Lady of Guadalupe, the Rosary and some clouds to cover the old tattoo. We worked three separate times to design and tattoo the picture of Our Lady of Sorrows' heart on my forearm, but it was not until the third sitting that I realized what the design was going to be."

"In the Shepherd's Fold in downtown Peterborough I found a little picture of St. Michael the Archangel. This picture was in my head for a week and I was surprised when I finally found it. I do not remember ever seeing it before that time. It was exactly what I wanted and was the last tattoo to be done. Altogether there are six tattoos, including a ship which represents the bark of Peter."

Ron reflects, "I'm not perfect by any means but never thought I'd get as far as I have now. I have my religion and it all came to me through Our Lady of Guadalupe. Even the wall hangings and altar in the living room came through Our Lady from yard sales and antique shops.

Ongoing Transformation

Recently Ron and Janet invited Father Damien to bless their home. He did so, using holy water in every room and a traditional ritual for house blessing. Ron continues, "We live in a comfortable house with no evil in it. The devil was here for awhile when Jason played with the ouija board. Satan has been in and out of my life and tried to take hold of me many times. I figured that if I went to church and read daily a page of the New Testament, I was on the right road. I wasn't a true believer and recognized myself as a hypocrite."

"Although I do not drink now and have not taken a drink for eight years, I have sinned a lot over the years. In my mind I was an average person who got drunk at least once a week and thought that everything was fine. I missed that pattern for a while because that was the only way of life I knew. From Friday until Monday the family in which I grew up didn't inhale unless it was alcohol. We were no worse than anyone else, and went to church regularly. I don't have a job that's secure and I don't worry about to-morrow, whereas I used to worry all the time. I'm happier and more content than ever before in my life."

"I thought that I knew all there was to know about everything including religion, but found out I didn't know anything. I do know what the picture of Our Lady of Guadalupe did for me. It's like throwing a rock into the water and all the ripples flow out from it. The same thing happened to me since she came into my life. That image of Our Lady of Guadalupe had a powerful effect on me and a continuing impact on the people around me."

"I knew that Jesus was God and never put any stock in the Virgin Mary. Once Our Lady of Guadalupe and the Rosary took hold of me it seemed that Jesus went to the back burner and I prayed only to the Virgin Mary. I felt guilty about that for awhile until I realized that nothing makes Jesus happier than for us to love His mother."

"I learned a lot about Our Lady. On her feast days she releases from purgatory thousands of souls who were devoted to her on earth, just because she asks her Son to release them. I never thought I'd have another mother, but I figure she's my only true mother. It's the power of the Rosary. I thought it was weird to see someone wearing a Rosary around their neck, and carried mine in my pocket. One day it got in my way and I hung it around my neck. It's been there ever since."

Janet's Story

Janet describes herself as being a so-called lukewarm Christian all her life. She recalls, "The family attended church sporadically, and as children we were made to attend for two or three months at a time as a family. There was a lot of love as well as hurt in our family. When I was a child my mother always said that if anything bothered you to say your prayers and everything would be fine. For many years now, my parents have attended church regularly, and participated in the Charismatic renewal."

"I was spoiled and self-centered as a child and a little wild, but no matter what I did I knew enough to pray to God for forgiveness. I always had a sense of right and wrong and had strong faith and a close personal relationship with God. I was quite young when Ron and I were married and had children. I realized then that I should never be complacent because I felt that I didn't deserve our beautiful children. I prayed that God would use our first born son Jason for His work. Our own marriage was an up and down affair, since I was married at age seventeen, and had to leave my family in Prince Edward Island. I made a lot of mistakes but I loved being a mother. I would not want to change anything in my life."

"We moved to Peterborough and to this house when Jason was fourteen. Because he had never had the opportunity to attend a Catholic school, we wanted him to go to St. Peter's school. We were disappointed because they did not teach Catholic religion until Grade Twelve. Jason wanted to get closer to God. He walked to church in the morning in any weather and prayed the Rosary, but nothing happened to him. Then he met a group of people and went to their Bible study. Eventually he attended the Baptist church on Sundays."

"I recall Jason asking me to pray with him and I answered, 'Jason, that's something I prefer to do on my own.' He was reaching out to us but the time wasn't right. We weren't there for him and so he took another route. Now we pray that he will come back. He said, 'You know, Mom, I thought you and Dad were headed in the wrong direction, but now I know you're headed in the right direction. You're just taking a different route. Our daughter Shannon is a very good person, and although she keeps her beliefs to herself, I believe that they are strong, and that the example we set is a meaningful one for her."

"When anything happens to Ron it's like a bolt of lightning. I respond at a different speed. I'm more private. I don't want to tell people I wear a scapular because I think I'm bragging. I went to the Marian week-end with Ron and gained a lot from it. I realized that through the years when I said I didn't believe in Confession I knew better deep down in my heart. I went to Confession for the first time since my childhood and felt like a million pounds were lifted off my shoulders."

"Every day Ron and I pray the Rosary together. I wouldn't miss that for the world, but I don't make an effort to go to Mass every day. Some times I feel such strong emotion at Mass that I think I will fall apart. I find it overpowering. Everybody has their own speed of growth. A blessing for Ron and me is that we're one another's best friends. We don't have a lot of friends with whom to share in depth."

"I believe that there are many roads to God and you cannot tell another person what to do. For example, our mothers are quite different, yet one is not better than the other. I'm not afraid nor ashamed to share about my religion if a person gives me an opening, but I won't force my thinking on anyone, not even my own son, whom I love. I tell him that I pray that Our Lady will show him her importance as the activist and perhaps bring him back to our faith. He's a wonderful person with high morals. Any parent would be proud to have him as their son. It's more important to me that he is the good person he is, rather than simply call himself Catholic."

"What is important for me personally is to continue to learn, as Ron does, about Confession. My faith is a lot stronger and I'm wiser in spiritual matters."

Visits to Marmora

Janet explains, "I first went to Marmora with Ron in the spring of 1994. I sat on a bench while Ron knelt at the grotto in prayer. I prayed that any evil in me would leave. When I opened my eyes and looked at the ground I saw little streams of golden light. They moved in a pattern in front of me towards the grotto. The sun was not strong so I knew that these were not rays from the sun. I looked again and the rays were repeated twice and three times. At that point Ron asked me, 'Are you all right?' When I looked at him his face had that golden light. It scared me and I thought, 'Maybe that's the evil leaving me.'"

"When we got home Ron remarked, 'That was a nice trip. Too bad nothing special happened.' I told him what happened to me and he insisted, 'That was not evil.' Some time later we were told that the golden lights were a sign of the Holy Spirit. I was happy to have seen them."

Ron continues, "When we visited St. Augustine in Florida we stayed with Janet's aunt and uncle and their eldest daughter Bev, whom Janet had not seen for about twenty years. We went to the oldest church in

North America, and the next day Bev asked, 'If you're going to church would you pick up a holy card of St. Anthony for me?' I found the card and bought two, one for myself. I wasn't even near my conversion at the time, so used the card as a marker in my New Testament."

"We had no further contact with Bev. Two years after our trip to Florida we visited Marmora for the third or fourth time. I saw in the trees near the Tenth Station a little grotto with the statue of St. Anthony. It was approximately three o'clock. Janet and I finished the Stations of the Cross and went home. At five o'clock the phone rang. It was a cousin of Janet's with the news that Bev died at three o'clock."

"Val, Mike and I went to Marmora on the feast of Our Lady of Guadalupe. There were very few people there and that made it special for us. I believed we received a great deal of grace making the Way of the Cross and seeing the miracle of the sun. I have seen it many times and thought it was a normal occurrence seen by everyone, although Janet has not yet seen it."

Personal Reflection

Ron continues to let his thoughts unfold. "My message is to tell people, especially Protestants that the Catholic Church is the only one in which we have the Body and Blood of Christ. It's the only way to receive sanctifying grace in your soul after Confession. The Catholic Church has sacraments and missions to teach us what Jesus and His apostles taught even before the Bible came into print. This is the true faith and the true tradition of the Roman Catholic Church which has never changed. Statistics say that it's the largest religion in the world. I estimate that the largest religion in the world contains a small percentage of the true faith that will never die."

Ron's appreciation and love for Our Blessed Mother continue to grow as he experiences personal and sensitive communication from her. His gratitude is reflected in the following words, "A significant development for me is the teaching and messages which I receive from Our Blessed Mother. She taught me that the Church is her Son's garden. The flowers are those people who are consecrated to her, and she waters them every day with the radiant light which comes from the Sacred Heart."

CHAPTER SIXTEEN

ATTRACTION TO MARMORA

Jun and Diding Quiming live in Oakville. They agreed to be interviewed during one of their many fruitful visits to Marmora. Diding inherited a rich treasury of faith from her parents, while Jun knew virtually nothing about the Catholic tradition. Diding stated, "When I grew up I was very prayerful. My mother had great devotion to Our Lady of Lourdes because I was a sickly child. From then on I prayed every night, even a short prayer to Our Lord and to my favourite saints. I went to Our Blessed Mother with any problems I had. She helped me in all the crucial moments of my life."

"Meeting my husband was an answer to prayer. Jun believes in God and was baptized in the Roman Catholic faith, but did not have any proper religious instruction while growing up. He was like a Christian pagan, who goes to church regardless of its denomination. Jun said that before he met me, he asked the Lord, 'Please find a wife who is prayerful and who would lead me to a religious life.'"

Our Life Changed

Diding tells how their lives began to change in July, 1993. She was off work at the time and at school studying micro-computers. "I told my husband that my sister wanted to bring the statue of Our Lady of Fatima to our house. The first time this happened he agreed, but the second time he resisted, saying, 'No. You don't have the time.' I answered, 'I'll find the time, because the Blessed Virgin doesn't have a place to go. I would love to welcome her.' This transfer took place between my sister and me, and not through any prayer group. In spite of my husband's resistence, he finally agreed for us to have the statue in our home. During the stay of the Blessed Virgin, I was the only one who prayed, while Jun watched television in the next room. He wouldn't join me for the Rosary."

"On July 30, 1993, we had visitors for dinner. The day before they arrived I told Jun, 'I'm going to pray the Rosary so I won't forget it.'

When I woke up that morning I was so busy that I didn't concentrate any more on the Rosary until 3:00 p.m. when I knew that I had enough time to pray the Rosary. I looked for the new candles that I had lit two nights previously. I couldn't find them and asked Jun, thinking he may have hid them somewhere, but he said that he didn't touch them. However, Jun said that while he was cleaning the carpet he remembered that he noticed from the corner of his eyes that he saw the candles burning. It was a warning for him to start praying."

First Visit To Marmora

In response to being told about Marmora Jun and Diding made their first visit on Our Lady's birthday, September 8, 1993. Diding continues, "We arrived between 3:30 and 4:00 p.m., while the procession was coming down the hill. From that day onward, something kept nudging us to return. Maybe it was the Holy Spirit urging us, 'Go back to Marmora.' On December 26 we came in minus 46 degree F. weather, and many things happened to us that day."

"Jun picked up his sister who is married to a Punjab, who does not believe in our religion. His daughter Ursula is my godchild. During our visits to Marmora (almost every week) Jun's sister tried several times to convince her husband to take her daughter along. However when I called that day and Ursula answered the phone I invited her to come with us and she agreed. Thrilled, I exclaimed, 'Praise the Lord!' Because it was snowing Jun asked the Lord to give him a sign if we were to proceed to Marmora. Otherwise we would return home. The day was clear and the snow stopped until we arrived at Marmora which was knee deep in snow."

"One purpose of that day's visit was to purchase a Holy Bible from Josie's store. When we saw that the store was closed I said, 'We'll buy it another time.' At that moment, Josie came walking down the road, and opened the store for us, so we were able to buy our Bible. We met Bonita, an acquaintance who invited us to make the Way of the Cross with Dory Tan's group, and we accepted."

"At the First Station I smelled a strong odour of frankincense. It was very cold. Dory said, 'Whatever cold or freezing you feel in your feet and hands, offer it to the Lord. We did that. I could see my husband trembling because he didn't have a warm coat with him. At the Fifth, Seventh and Eighth Stations he felt so warm that he had to remove his gloves. At the Tenth Station someone told me that whenever the visionary prayed, you should also pray to the Blessed Virgin because she is there, so I prayed fervently."

"Suddenly I saw a silhouette near the tree, with the sun spinning and the rays of the sun coming down with tiny bubbles reaching to the silhouette. At first I thought, 'It's the condensation on my glasses, because I had been crying.' I cleaned them with lens cleaner. Then I remembered what a friend told me, and suddenly realized that the Blessed Virgin was present. That was my first experience of being in Our Lady's presence. From then on we returned to Marmora almost every week with Dory Tan, and I continued to have supernatural divine manifestations."

Grace At Work

Jun picked up the story from his wife, explaining that Our Blessed Mother and Our Lord Jesus Christ touched his heart in such a way that his life turned around. He comments, "For the first time in my life, I cried like a baby. Since then I started to grow spiritually through reading Christian books, listening to tapes and scripture reading. At this point in my life, the Lord has revealed to me that the more I seek the kingdom of God the more He shows the way of getting to know him personally."

"Jesus manifested Himself in so many ways that it has become a part of my daily Christian life. I'm so happy that Our Lord Jesus Christ sent Mama Mary to Marmora to touch lives like ours. Our Blessed Mother wants all of us to go back to her Son Jesus Christ, Our Lord and Saviour."

"On December 25, 1993, the Lord led us to meet the Fernandez family, who became an important instrument in forming the prayer group 'God-First'. We are happy to be with a community that is loving and compassionate. The bonding between members is so strong. I firmly believe that this is how every prayer group should be. The message of the Lord is for all prayer groups to unite with one another, because if they do like Our Lord Jesus said, 'Wherever two or three are gathered in

My Name I will be in your midst. Whenever two or three pray in one accord, whatever we ask shall be granted by Our Father in heaven.' Prayers will be answered by Our Father."

"We completely trust Our Lord to mend present divisions in the Church, and only He knows how to solve them. In our prayer group we constantly ask Our Father in heaven, in Jesus' Name, to grant all members of our community all the gifts of the Holy Spirit. The gifts of healing, discernment, anointed preaching and the gift of tongues were received by a few members after being baptized by the Holy Spirit."

"Our prayer group does not have a spiritual director, but we trust the Lord that He will lead us to obtain true spiritual direction. Since I turned around my life I try to resist temptation, which is the most difficult part of my conversion, and every time I succeed I praise the Lord for providing me the strength to overcome it. I would like to share with all my brothers and sisters in Christ that spiritual warfare begins in our mind by being aware of these things, and using the power of the Name "Jesus", we can defeat the evil one easily."

"I strongly believe that the main message of Our Blessed Mother is for us to 'Love one another', and she is directing all of us to her Son Jesus in order to follow His ways. In January, 1994, I received a prophecy from Our Lord Jesus Christ. He told me **Devote my time to all of you**. The message became clear to me when we started a prayer group in April 1994. He meant to be in our midst whenever we ask Him. Everything that we ask Our Father in heaven through Our Lord Jesus Christ He will grant, provided we follow His ways. It's as simple as that."

Power To Overcome Evil

Jun is firm in his conviction of the spiritual struggle which is taking place throughout the world. In dreams and messages Jun has been taught by the Lord. He shares fearlessly, "God wants all people to know that Jesus Christ is alive, that He dwells among us every moment of our lives. He talks to us at every moment. We have only to listen to Him."

"As we get closer to the Lord, we become aware that there is also a negative force which tries to draw us away from Him. Being aware of this evil thing allows us to defeat him with God's grace."

"In one of my dreams all the members of my community were on one side, and on the other side was the group of the negative force. I asked the Lord to give me the power and strength to defeat the negative force which was about to appear. Almost immediately I felt that strength and I know that Our Lord granted me the strength and the power to face and defeat this dark supernatural force. I waited for it to appear, expecting huge black monsters to emerge. What appeared were tiny creatures, smaller than I am, and I was thankful that the Lord gave me the courage and strength to face it. I believe that my prayer and God's grace totally vanquished the power of that dark force."

"Whenever we use the name of Jesus we overcome evil forces, as when we pray in the Name of Jesus, 'I command you, wicked spirit, Leave!' Any person who has strong belief knows that Our Lord Jesus Christ gives us the grace to expel this evil thing. We must be aware that there are two forces in constant warfare and call on the name of Jesus for the grace to overcome evil."

CHAPTER SEVENTEEN

NUCLEUS OF SPIRITUAL GROWTH

Emma De Guzman is a slight, radiant, vibrant widow who glows with good health. She has three children and two grandchildren and emigrated from the Philippines in 1986. She lives in Kingston with her younger son and his wife where they share a lodging with Sol, her landlady. Their home is an open centre where people from the United States and various parts of Ontario gather for prayer before the altar formed by several shelves of statues, some of which ooze oil.

Through Emma's cooperation with her spiritual gifts, clusters of La Pieta prayer groups developed in other cities, and indicate a possibility of continued growth. During the afternoon and evening of the interview approximately fifty visitors from different prayer groups gathered in Sol's home, in an atmosphere as exuberant as with any large family party. Prayer, healing, laughter, song and good food characterized this jovial group. To facilitate the interview Sol, a laboratory technologist, participated actively in the discussion, referring to extensive documentation of Emma's supernatural phenomena.

Visit to Our Lady Of Fatima Shrine

Emma described the events which unfolded in her life. "I received my initial spiritual gifts in Lewiston, New York when we attended Mass at the Shrine of Our Lady of Fatima on September 8, 1991. It was our first visit there. We went to the small gift shop and while I waited for my friends, I noticed a sign indicating a small chapel and decided to investigate. I saw the statue of Our Lady of Fatima in the centre, and on one side Jesus crucified. In front of the crucifix stood a tall man. I prayed there, then knelt before Our Lady's statue. The man beside me also knelt, and I knew that he also was praying, though I didn't see his face. I felt warm all over my body as though I were encapsulated, and an electric current flowed all through me. I was sweating and scared because I had never experienced anything like this before."

"From the right corner of my eyes I saw the man beside me. When I began to shake and perspire I meant to ask him for help but he was no longer there. I was distressed because I was alone and couldn't stand or move my body to walk. I crawled outside the chapel to the gift shop and Sol saw me crawling and crying. I told her what happened to me and together we went to Mass."

"During Mass I felt something strange in my body. Afterwards hundreds of people formed into a procession which went around the church to the shrine of Our Blessed Mother and then to the little chapel. We met a woman who was in a trance, and the Blessed Mother was in her. The woman prayed over people and we lined up for prayer." Sol continued, "When Emma was touched she fell to the floor into the position of a crucifix with her feet crossed and her hands stretched out on both sides. Two men tried to lift her but were not able to because of her weight. Two more men came forward to help. They commented 'She is so heavy.' The four men could hardly carry her, and placed her on a bench. As Emma came back to herself she cried and screamed because she had a vision of an accident with a bus load of children going over a cliff. She saw every person dropping out of the window and screaming. She described the children as having black skin. Two days later we learned on the news that the accident actually happened in Africa when a bus load of children were on their way to a sports event."

Initial Trance

Sol described the circumstances which preceded Emma's first trance. "Someone called our home in Kingston while Emma was out of the house and asked if they could bring a couple for prayer because the husband was very sick. I agreed and when Emma came home she was surprised, and asked, 'Why do they ask for me? I don't have the gift to pray for healing. What should I do?' I advised, 'Maybe you should place your hand on his head and ask God the Father to give you the right prayer for these people.' As soon as she laid her hand on his head and prayed, she went into a trance. This was our first experience. The Lord spoke through Emma with a very deep voice said, **I am thirsty. I am thirsty. I am thirsty.**"

"I asked my sister for water because I thought Emma was thirsty. Before I put the glass to Emma's lips another message came, **Father, forgive them for they don't know what they are doing**. When I heard those words I knew it was not Emma speaking, but Jesus crucified. His voice was soothing, compassionate, yet in agony. From then on almost every day, Emma suffered the Passion. When we prayed the Sorrowful Mysteries of the Rosary, she suffered terribly with each mystery. During the Crowning With Thorns we asked ourselves how we could stand seeing her this way, because we felt helpless."

Emma continued, "When I have pain it is so severe that I feel unable to endure any more. There is love in my heart and I accept the pain which is also love for people. I can't explain the depth of love I feel when I suffer. The pain is beyond what I can stand. Every part of my body and my flesh is like an open wound. I feel that I will die. My greatest pain was when I was crucified. It's hard to explain but the crucifixion is the most unbearable. During a trance, someone asked, 'Why Emma?' Jesus responded, 'Emma was chosen even before she was conceived.'"

The Crucifixion

Sol noted, "We spent Holy Week of 1992 in Scarborough. I received a message through Emma that she would suffer greatly during Holy Week. Our friends in Scarborough invited us to stay with them and they would support us since we had no experience with this phenomenon. Their house held more than a hundred people praying. That is the first time we experienced Emma's transformation into Jesus."

"When Emma was crucified her hands changed and became large like a man's. Her jaw, nose, face took on masculine features. Everyone pointed at her face because we no longer saw Emma, but JESUS. She looked so big lying on the bed. She felt the crucifixion, the nails. It started from eleven o'clock Thursday night until three o'clock Friday afternoon. She died with Jesus at that time. She was placed in a very deep sleep and didn't wake up until nearly midnight."

"During the time that Emma slept Jesus and Mary took her to hell, purgatory and heaven. Emma recalled, 'A door opened and I went inside to the first level. I saw many souls who tried to climb to the top and they slid back into boiling oil. When they fell, fire came out of their body. I cried, 'Oh! If people only knew what would happen to them because of their sins, they would stop sinning. But how can people know?'"

"Afterwards I went to the second level, which was purgatory. I saw many souls walking about who seemed to be praying. I saw a man there who is still alive. He was so sad. When I woke up I told Sol. I recognized his face but do not know his name. I know that he was still alive but died a short time later. I prayed and asked my prayer group to pray for him. Maybe he's already in heaven."

"I was taken to a gate of heaven, but did not see the whole of heaven. I heard a voice which made me happy, my body felt light, without burdens. I wanted to stay there rather than return to earth. When I heard angels singing I wanted to go farther into heaven and saw another door. I saw a priest wearing the brown Franciscan habit. He held a Bible in his hand. I asked him, 'Can I go through this door?' He answered, 'It is not time for you to go through that door because it leads to the heavenly Father, Jesus, the Blessed Mother, the saints and angels. When I heard these words I fell backwards, and when I opened my eyes I was lying on the bed."

Emma's Introduction To The Bible

Emma commented, "In December 1991 God the Father spoke to me and told me **Find a book where you will find the answers to all your questions.** I looked here in the house but couldn't find it. At the hospital I saw 'The Greatest Gift on Earth is Love' and thought it might be the right book. I took it home but my heart still felt closed and I knew it wasn't the right book. One day when Sol went to church she saw a brown covered book. Inside the front cover was an inscription, **Take me home and use me.** She brought the book to my place of work and showed it to me, wondering if it was the book for me to read. As I touched the book I looked up to the sky and saw a big cloud which opened to reveal about five or six angels moving in a circle in the middle of the open space. I wept. It was then that my heart opened and I knew that this was the right book. It is the Bible."

"I tried to live as a good person, but I didn't know the Rosary nor the Bible. That's why the heavenly Father told me to find this book. From then on I read the Bible and feel so close to God. I love Him. I offer myself to Him. Whatever He asks me to do I do it for Him. I am not the same person as I was previously. I love everybody even when I suffer. I have no more interest in going to parties or wearing fancy clothes, but only in prayer and the Rosary. Every morning around three o'clock I pray. I do not get tired praying. I am happy when I pray. That's when I feel God close to me and I feel so much love for Him."

Formation of La Pieta

Sol took up the narrative. "Our prayer group which originated in Kingston is called La Pieta Prayer Group. For a long time I wanted to form a prayer group but it never materialized. One time when Emma was in a trance I asked the Lord if He would let her form a prayer group. In October I went to a garage sale and in the rubble there lay the icon of La Pieta in an old frame of beautiful oak and stained glass. I bought it at a considerable discount, cleaned it and in December 1991 it went to Emma's first mission in Richmond Hill. From then on it went on missions every two weeks, and we are currently booked until 1997. Once I asked Jesus when He came to Emma 'What is Emma's mission, because she always asks me to ask You?' He answered, **Tell Emma her mission is for the people, for conversion and healing.**"

"We were invited to Washington, D.C. where they subsequently formed a La Pieta prayer group. The same thing happened in Hamilton, Toronto, and Syracuse. People in Baltimore want to form one when we visit them. A Toronto member returned to her home in Rumania where people were waiting for someone to lead a prayer group. We received a message from Santo Nino that she would go home to Rumania and carry a mission there. She formed a La Pieta group and from her town it reached out to another place, making two groups in Rumania."

"Not too long ago Jesus said, **I am the one who gave you the name La Pieta for your prayer group because you can see my suffering and my Mother's suffering in that statue. God the Father is so pleased with your prayers. You are special to my Father.** We are so thankful. Santo Nino said that there are more prayer groups to be formed. He told us, **Your prayer group will be known all over the world**. With the icon of La Pieta we also carry the statue of Santo Nino, St. Joseph, Our

Lady of Fatima, St. Michael the Archangel and San Lorens Ruiz, the first Filipino saint."

Healing Ministry

"Emma's healing ministry started in December 1991 when she went into ecstasy and talked to someone who was not visible to our eyes. She knelt with her eyes closed. She opened her mouth, put out her tongue and received something, then swallowed it. Afterwards she fell to the floor and lay on her back with her hands raised. She rubbed her hands from the tip of her fingers down each arm and seemed to be putting on a pair of gloves. Later Emma said that something very warm was placed on both her hands. We received a message that her hands are blessed. She can touch people to pray over them and bring them healing. Healing is not only physical but emotional, as with inner healing."

"One gentleman from Saudi Arabia heard of Emma and telephoned from there. He had a cancerous tumour on his spine and was to receive chemotherapy. Since he came from Iraq and worked in Saudi Arabia he was not able to have treatment. He pleaded with us to meet him in Los Angeles and he would provide all our requirements. Our time limitations did not allow us to travel that distance. After prayer and many calls we received the message **I will send Emma and you to this person at the right time and the right place.**"

"Later I suggested that we meet him in Syracuse New York. Emma said to me 'Don't tell me how he described himself to you on the phone.' As soon as he came down the escalator at the airport Emma went forward and gave him a hug. Prayers started the next morning and oil oozed from Emma's face, her hands, her chest, and her back. We raised the man's shirt and saw the large tumour on his spine. He said that when Emma touched his tumour he felt intense heat from her hands. He returned to Saudi Arabia and his recent Christmas card indicates that he walks without problem, his health has improved and he is working once more."

"A twenty eight year old gentleman from the Philippines worked in New York and Texas as a Physiotherapist. He developed a tumour of the spine and his doctor gave him two options. He could operate and leave him paralysed for the rest of his life, or leave the tumour alone and he could live possibly two years. He chose surgery and was sent home to the Philippines with braces, wheel chair and all the necessary equipment. When Emma and I went to the Philippines for a vacation a woman invited us to his house. That morning when Emma woke up she said, 'I think I'm going to a mission today because I can feel pain in my leg.'"

We went to the man's home where he was sitting on his make-up bed in the living room. As Emma opened the Bible and prayed for him, her face dropped on the Bible and leaked oil. Oil oozed also from her hands, and she immediately became crippled and couldn't walk. We carried her on a chair to the gentleman, took her hand and laid it on his knees and back. As soon as her hand touched his back he exclaimed, 'Oh!' and began to weep. Later he explained that there was intense heat from his back down his spine. Emma told him to stand up, but he resisted saying, 'I can't. I have to put on my braces.' Emma responded, 'No. You will walk. Just stand up.' Again he asked for his braces. Emma insisted, 'Just try. I will hold one arm and your brother will hold your other arm.' He did so. Then Emma instructed, 'Walk one step towards your altar. Now another step. You can see the Blessed Mother and Baby Jesus in front of you. Go towards them.'"

"He took one, then two steps and before he realized it Emma and his brother were no longer holding his arm. He reached the altar and started to shake. He wept and everyone in the room was crying. He returned to his bed and sat down. He stood alone and walked back and forth again. The next morning we went to the airport for our return flight. His brother ran to meet us with good news. 'We were wakened in the middle of the night because someone was in the kitchen making a lot of noise. When we investigated he was walking around there. Later Baby Jesus said, **He is getting better. He has only a little pain in his stomach.** My friend called and asked him how he felt. He answered, 'Just a little pain in my stomach but I'm getting better.'"

Emma commented about the transfer of pain to herself. When I pray for people's healing, their pain remains in me for two or three days. It might be back ache or cramps in my hands. If the person is very ill the pain may last up to five days, especially for cancer of the lungs or of the spine. When I prayed over the man from Saudi Arabia it took five days for my pain to leave."

Visit To Marmora

Sol noted, "August 23, 1992 was our first visit to the Greensides farm. We prayed the Rosary, the Stations of the Cross and the Chaplet of Divine Mercy. During the Rosary Emma almost fell at the podium where she had a vision of the Blessed Virgin Mary in a very bright light above the statue of Our Lady. Then she saw the form of Our Lady with her hands at her side pointing downward to us. After the Rosary Emma opened her eyes, looked at the sky and said, 'Do you see what I see?' None of us saw anything but the blue sky, while she saw a huge letter M written across the sky. A few minutes later at the same spot she wept because she saw Our Lady in a blue dress."

"We continued the Stations of the Cross. At the Fourth Station Emma had a vision of Our Lady in the trees, wearing a blue dress. The same vision occurred at the Ninth Station. Emma remained kneeling in prayer while the others moved on. After the Fourteenth Station we recited the Chaplet of Divine Mercy. During this time Emma witnessed the miracle of the sun. A few other people also saw it around 3:15 p.m. Emma saw a crucifix in the sun followed by different colours, red, yellow, violet and blue. All these colours reflected on Emma's face and shirt. Then she saw the Eucharist in the sun. I witnessed the sun dance and spin with different colours, and the dove, symbol of the Holy Spirit. Someone saw St. Michael the Archangel and another person saw the Sacred Heart of Jesus."

"Emma saw the Ecce Homo, with Jesus' mouth hanging open and His head bleeding, as He looked down on us. Emma cried hysterically and talked to Him, 'Dear Lord, is this why You sent me here, to see You like this? Forgive us, Lord, please forgive us our sins.' Then Emma saw three sacred words above the Lord's head. She uttered the words twice, even spelled the words to us, but these words are so sacred that she was told not to tell people of them, but to memorize them and keep them in her heart and her mind. Later on she will learn where to use those words."

"We returned to the hill and Emma knelt on the ground. She meditated and had a repeated vision of the Holy Face. She wept uncontrollably. I asked everyone to pray because the crowd stared at her and asked her questions. We sang 'Come Holy Spirit'. Emma's eyes remained focussed on the sky, and the Sacred Head never left her vision. The Lord's hand came out of the sky and tried to reach everyone. Emma reached upward for the Lord's hand. She cried 'Look! He is trying to reach for us! Can you not see Him?' Then her voice changed into a deep voice which said, **I am thirsty.** Jesus is thirsty for our love. Her voice returned to normal and she read the words written around the Sacred Head."

"Emma went into a convulsive state and we laid her down with people supporting her head and back, and the Holy Spirit entered her. Her hands were in a position of blessing then she went into convulsion and returned to normal. I called her full name and she nodded. She was pale and without strength. During this time a seminarian came to support Emma and prayed for her. With some of our friends he assisted Emma to the car and told her that he too is a visionary. We thank him from our heart and in Jesus' Name we bless him."

"On October 24, 1992 we returned to Marmora and made the Way of the Cross. At the Tenth Station Our Blessed Mother appeared to Emma and spoke with her. **Thank you for all your prayers. Continue what you are doing now. Come back to this place again this afternoon. I will wait for you.** We continued the Stations, then completed the Rosary Path and ate lunch. At 3:50 p.m. Emma became restless and said, 'I have to go. The Blessed Mother is waiting for me.' We went to the Tenth Station and Emma stated 'She is here now.'"

"One girl in our group took photographs from every angle. Emma saw a large ball of light come from the sky. It turned into a cloud and from it the Blessed Mother appeared clearly. She wore beautiful bright green with glittering stones. Emma asked her if she would show herself to the group or even to the children. The Blessed Mother responded, **I will give you something to prove that I was here and many people will see Me.** When the film was developed one of the photos showed the light of the Holy Trinity in three different colours. Above it were silhouettes of the Blessed Mother and St. Joseph."

Supernatural Manifestations

Emma continued her story. "On December 23, 1994 there were about fifty people in the living room. We prayed and many people placed their rosaries in my hands. I thanked Our Lord for bringing people here and asked Him to bless the rosaries which I held. I knew His presence was with us because the rosaries smelled of heavenly perfume. There is no scent like that on earth. When I returned the rosaries to their owners they had that beautiful scent."

"Our friend in Toronto asked us to take her statue of Our Lady of Fatima and place it on our altar. When I did so there was oil on her face. I told Sol, 'Look! The Blessed Mother is crying!' We called our friends to come and we placed the statue on the altar. We removed the oil which accumulated on her neck when she was in a horizontal position in the car. The next morning her face was wet, and she wept tears of oil. I asked Our Blessed Mother if I could video tape her and also that she would ensure a good reproduction. When I finished I was surprised that on the video Our Blessed Mother looked real and her neck moved in a sobbing way as though she were crying."

"One beautiful gift that Emma received is to be able to talk to souls in purgatory through the help of St. Mary Magdalene de Pazzi who introduced herself to Emma. Emma was chosen to witness the message written by St. Mary Magdalene de Pazzi through Emma's hand. She brings souls to Emma and they ask her for prayers. When we receive their names I make copies for our prayer groups and ask for their prayers. Within a couple of months they are lifted into heaven. Emma witnessed when the angels take them step by step up beautiful stairs to heaven. On the first, second and third step the souls did not yet have their halo. Once they pass the third step their beautiful bright halo comes on top of their head. The angels greet them and escort them with beautiful singing. St. Mary Magdalene de Pazzi is the last one who goes up the stairs behind them."

"Until now Emma has only witnessed one soul who died and became an angel. It was her three year old grandchild who died last year from a car accident. This year through Hilary, Baby Jesus spoke, **I have a surprise for you. I brought someone with Me.** He indicated a little boy in white named Adrian with bright face, wings, and a halo. Adrian is the name of Emma's grandson who died. Emma saw her grandson playing and singing with other angels."

"Sometimes when souls are being raised to heaven they try to take Emma with them, and Emma really wants to go to that beautiful place. During an ecstasy she levitated and witnessed souls going to heaven. They took her hand and asked her to go with them. We were afraid that Emma might die while going with them. About eight people leaned on her in an attempt to bring her body back to the floor. Her torso, legs, arms were so stiff that we couldn't bring her down. Then we formed a chain and connected our hands to her to keep her on the floor. Later Jesus gave us a message not to worry because He won't let Emma die during an ecstasy."

"On January 2, 1995, at 5:00 a.m., twelve souls from out list were lifted to heaven. St. Mary Magdalene de Pazzi gave this message: **My dearest friends, I want to say goodbye. My mission down here is finished. I will pray for all of you, especially Emma. Thank you very much.** We all felt so sad, as if we lost a very dear friend."

"Another of Emma's gifts is bilocation. My nephew saw Emma in the back seat of the car and said 'Auntie Emma, come inside the house. It's cold. Why are you staying in the car?' Emma waved to him to go ahead inside. When he entered the house he was shocked because Emma was in the kitchen talking and eating. He said, 'You were there in the car! How come you're here?'

"One day when Emma was baby sitting, the mother of the baby talked with her upstairs. When the mother came down to the kitchen, Emma was washing dishes. The mother said, 'I was just talking to you upstairs and left you there. How did you come down here?' Later we received the message that Emma's spirit sometimes leaves her body and goes to another place."

"Another day I asked Emma 'Why is your tooth brush always soaking wet?' Emma leaves the house early in the morning. I come home in the evening and her tooth brush is dripping wet. When Jesus came He explained, **Sol you wonder what is happening with the tooth brush. It is Emma's spirit. Sometimes it separates from her and comes here to use it.** (See Appendix One)

Miracle Of The Roses

Sol described the events which began on October 5, 1994. "During our prayer Emma went into ecstasy and had excruciating pain in her chest. She screamed with pain and tried to pull something out of her chest. When she did this Maria De Sousa from our prayer group saw something metal come from Emma. Then Jack exclaimed, 'Sol! Look at the roses on the floor!' I asked, 'What roses?' and thought they were artificial. Later on Maria asked 'Where is the nail? I saw the nail come out of her chest.' Another woman agreed that she saw something shiny like metal. Later on when Emma went into a trance Jesus came, and pointing at his hands He said, **You cannot receive my nails. So my Father gave you my flowers.**"

"One day when Emma went to the washroom I looked at her and warned, 'Don't get scared. Look slowly in the mirror.' There were three roses sticking out of her head, one on each side and one in front. Another time when we prayed Emma went into a trance and Baby Jesus came into her. He said, **I'm giving you a big surprise**, and pulled roses out of Emma's chest. He said there were ten flowers, but we saw only seven. He replied, **Yes, but three are for Emma. You cannot find any more.** That was at one o'clock in the morning during our meditation. In the afternoon of the same day Emma was folding her clothes in the living room and looked at Santo Nino. He held three beautiful roses in His hand for her."

"On November 19 we went on mission to Syracuse and drove into the parking lot of Sacred Heart of Jesus Church. Five roses fell on Emma's lap. We didn't know what these flowers meant, but one of the ladies from Syracuse suggested, 'Maybe they represent the five La Pieta Prayer Groups.'

"During the healing Mass in St. Stephen's Church, oil oozed from Emma's chest where she now bears the sign of the Cross. We had sixteen cars following one another and the people in each one claimed that the beautiful heavenly scent was in their car."

"Emma's first experience of the flowers was at three o'clock in the morning when she sang and giggled in her sleep. I thought she must be going into a trance so I went into her room and tried to wake her up. Her body was very cold and she was in a deep sleep. I was shocked to see that in her hand she held a fresh bouquet of flowers. I turned on the light and after twenty minutes I was able to wake her up. Afterwards Emma said that she was in heaven. She asked permission to pick flowers for her friends on earth and it was granted. These flowers smell of heavenly perfume. The members of the group asked if they could have even one rose petal. When Jesus came He said, **No. Maybe there is something special in store for the flowers. We will only give them away if we receive a message to do so.**"

Wounds on Emma's Chest

Sol continued, "The cross on Emma's chest was given her by the Holy Spirit at Marmora during the fall 1993 as we prayed the Rosary at the podium. Suddenly Emma screamed from chest pain and ran around restlessly. Then she ran to the hill saying, 'I have to go. The Blessed Mother is waiting for me.' Her feet were not touching the ground and we could not keep up with her. At the Tenth Station the Blessed Mother appeared to her and said to her, **My child, I place a sign on your chest, that my Son will always stay in you. Show it to your brothers and sisters.** She did and everyone there saw the cross in blood on her chest. It was painful and had a beautiful scent."

"Emma received another marking on September 25, 1994 in Hamilton. Our Blessed Mother came to Emma as she went into a trance and said, **I gave your sister Emma the Father, the Son and the Holy Spirit. When Emma wakes up she will see the markings on your forehead and on the palms of your hands.** When Emma's eyes opened she seemed to be in an altered state. The Holy Spirit looked through her as she gazed at every person's face, pointing at their forehead. She saw different markings, such as a cross, the head of Our Lady, Our Lady of Fatima, Our Lady of Grace, two hands with a little cross in the centre, the Divine Mercy. Around the cross on her chest are markings, 3, 3, 3, each one drawn three times. The meaning of these numbers is in Father Gobbi's book."(5)

"The Blessed Mother said that the followers of Jesus will be marked with a cross or the image of the Blessed Mother or of Jesus. The followers of Satan will be marked with the number 666."

Messages

"We received messages from a lady in the Philippines who also goes into a trance and the Blessed Mother enters her. She is a sister of one of our group members. Once the Blessed Mother gave a message for the people of Canada, **God the Father has a special mission for the people of Canada. Healing will happen, mostly of cancer that doctors cannot cure.** The woman said she believed that Emma would be the leader, and that possibly two of them will carry this mission all over North America."

"This year we received a message from Our Blessed Mother and Jesus. We were told to be ready especially when it comes close to 1998 and 1999 because evil will be at its full strength. That is why we have been given these markings so that the evil spirit cannot harm us. Jesus said, **I have put you aside,** and **I will go to many more places to ask people to come with me. Those sheep who will follow me I will join them with you. Those who refuse me I will leave behind.**"

Impact of Manifestations on Life Style

Sol commented on the dramatic change in their lives. "People tell us, 'With your mission you have no life. All you do on week ends is travel and go on mission.' We answered "The life we know now with Jesus and Mary is the only life. We know of no other.' We are happy after our mission and prayers. We sing, dance, eat and laugh. I would say that this is my third life. Once I almost died, then I nearly ended up in a wheel chair. I have advanced diabetes which affects my eyes, fingers, legs and toes. I have diabetic neuropathy and thought I would not be able to drive. Our mission was just beginning and I wondered how could I carry on with this full blown problem. Our Blessed Mother gave me a message, **In five days the pain in your legs will be gone**. It happened. Prior to that, no one could come near me or touch my legs."

Distinction: Trance and Ecstasy

"When Emma goes into a trance the Holy Spirit puts her into a deep sleep so that she does not know what is going on. Her spirit leaves her body. During that process her chest rises into a high arch. With a deep breath her spirit leaves and the Holy Spirit enters. When something like this is going to happen, Emma has no appetite all day because the Holy Spirit is cleansing her."

"When Emma goes into ecstasy she speaks to the Blessed Mother or to Jesus, with eyes open or closed, but mostly closed. Sometimes when the Holy Spirit touches her she falls to the floor and sees words coming out of a very bright light. She writes them automatically without knowing what they are until she returns to her normal state. If she is conversing with them or receiving messages I call that ecstasy. When she leaks oil she is in ecstasy. When she faints and receives the stigmata and bleeds, she is in ecstasy."

"Prior to this time Emma received deep red markings on her palms. Once her palms bled a little. Last Wednesday she screamed with excruciating pain and pressed her wrists together. When I smelled the beautiful scent I looked at her hands and saw them bleed, the left more than the right. Blood dripped from the middle of the mark to the wrist. The next day there was no visible mark."

"I received a message from Jesus, **I chose you to be Emma's helper. I give you full responsibility to take care of your sister Emma. When the Holy Spirit is coming in, make sure that no one touches her. Otherwise she will suffer.** The Holy Spirit taught me everything that I learned to do with Emma, through friends who had prior experience and taught me what to do, especially the group from Scarborough. They came here and taught me what they did and what I should do with messages from the Holy Spirit. I received some special prayers and the Holy Spirit guides me to give them to the right people."

"Not all people who receive gifts have them permanently. We know some people who have the gifts for only a few months and others for two years. Emma had her gifts for a full year and was given a break. We thought it was finished for her. Baby Jesus said, **I am leaving Emma now and I go to someone else.** It happened that Hilary received the gift. After a year the Blessed Mother had something for Emma that was heavier still. Emma said to ask the Blessed Mother, 'How long will I carry this mission?' She answered, **Tell your sister Emma, as long as she is obedient and lives according to God's will she will have this gift.**"

Emma continued, "Many people go into a trance. I don't know what happens to me when the Holy Spirit enters my body. Before I allow the Holy Spirit to come into me I accept it when I see a bright white light. When I see this I offer myself to God and surrender myself to the Holy Spirit. If that bright light is not there, if it is dark, I don't accept this spirit because I know it is an evil spirit. I go into a deep sleep and the Holy Spirit looks after me."

Sol added, "Before Emma experiences the bright light on the right side of her eyes she has a special prayer given her by the Blessed Mother.

She is the only one who can say that prayer. In English it is called the key to prayer. She says it seven times and the bright light comes. If it's a dull or grey colour she is not to accept it. With the bright light she opens her heart and mind and receives the Holy Spirit. The bright light comes closer and closer and forms into whoever it is to be, the Blessed Mother, St. Joseph or the Baby Jesus."

Emma recalled, "When I prayed the key to prayer to the Holy Spirit, I asked for the Spirit of angels to come upon me with the sign of a bright light. I feel as if floating in a deep sleep. When the trance is over I hear someone call my name and return to my normal state."

Spiritual Discernment

Sol remembered, "The first time I tried to explain to a priest what was happening to Emma, he advised that we observe her for a week, more likely in the hospital's psychiatric section. When I heard that I remained silent. Once when Jesus came to Emma I asked 'Dear Lord, shall we contact another priest for Emma?' He responded, **Are you not afraid of what will happen to your sister Emma? If the media learn about her she will suffer. Why don't you let the Holy Spirit handle this. I will send you the right priest at the right time and the right place.** We waited and after three years we met a priest who is the right one for Emma. The Holy Spirit gave us a message that he is the right priest. We thank God for that."

Sol refers to a message given by Jesus. **There are many people who will receive gifts like Emma. But there are some who will use my name and the name of the Blessed Mother for their own happiness. You must be careful of this whole process because you will meet these people. The Holy Spirit will give you the gift of discernment. It is from your hearts that we can feel whether or not it is true.** Many times we recognized false prophets. We do not judge them, but as Jesus instructed us, we pray for them."

"One day Emma had a vision of Pope John Paul II. His face was youthful, with a beautiful smile. He was being lifted by many angels into the sky. Later, Jesus gave this message, **My beloved Mother loves him very much, and when he leaves the earth, he will join me where I am.**"

Emma stated that the most important message she received from God is to be humble always; to love; be compassionate; and be one. "God told me that He loves me because I am nothing and I am little. I write messages during ecstasy in Latin, Portuguese, Italian, Greek and I don't know those languages. It is the Holy Spirit who writes these messages through my hands."

CHAPTER EIGHTEEN

A HEALING COMMUNITY

To visit with Mila Rose Bueno is to become part of a healing community in the home of Mrs. Maria Fe Barrientos, her landlady Fe, in Hamilton. The central focus of visitors who assemble nightly for prayer is the altar, which covers an entire wall in the living room. On the shelves of this altar are an array of different statues of Our Blessed Mother, including Our Lady from Marmora, Our Lady of Fatima, the Sacred Heart of Jesus, the Queen of Peace, Our Lady of Lourdes, Our Lady of Piat (from the Philippines), the Passion Face of Jesus, the Child and the Infant Jesus, special patrons such as St. Joseph, St. Roch, St. Claire, and St. Michael the Archangel, prince of the heavenly host.

The gentle camaraderie and good humour of these friends and neighbours are fostered by the experiences of several members of the prayer group. Mila Rose described its origin. "Our Lady chose thirteen persons from among them to form a network of healers, called the Mainstay. These thirteen persons receive apparitions, messages and manifestation of their gifts from Our Blessed Mother."

During the evening of the interview approximately fifteen people, including Mila Rose, the Mainstay and the author, gathered for the Holy Rosary and the Chaplet of Divine Mercy, with the blessing and permission of the Blessed Mother. Prior to the start of the interview a particularly moving event occurred. While Mila Rose and the author sat side by side on the sofa in quiet conversation, Our Blessed Mother came to grace and acknowledge the visit of the author. This was done through Mila Rose, when she went into a sudden state of ecstasy to receive a message from Our Blessed Mother addressed to the author.

Initial Visit to Marmora and Kingston

Maria Fe Barrientos, or Fe, as she is called, invited Mila Rose to Marmora for her first visit. Mila Rose explained, "I met several people who talked about the miracles which happened at Marmora, such as the dancing sun, the healing holy water from the spring below Our Lady's grotto, and the Way of the Cross that resembles the walk of Our Lord Jesus Christ to Mount Calvary. Fe invited me to go there a number of times, but something always prevented my visit. Eventually I accepted her invitation."

"The first visit was with Fe and her husband Frank, one week before August 15, 1994. At that time I did not feel anything particular or new. It was a simple, peaceful farm surrounded by a beautiful hill-top. I marvelled at the simplicity of the altar in the reception centre. I read the short story about the origin of the farm and the messages and prayers, but was particularly moved with the anti-suicide message composed by Nancy de Vivieros shortly before she died. I observed the faces of people who prayed at the kneelers. We walked to the Fourteen Stations, and ended our visit by offering the Holy Rosary at the top of the hill."

"At home in Hamilton, Fe persuaded me to visit Emma De Guzman, a gifted woman in Kingston. Emma is considered to be a mystic and a bilocator, and is known for her healing gifts. Fe desperately wanted to see her for prayers and for healing her painful shoulder. I had never heard of Emma, but was told of her oiling statues, and the thought of these statues enticed me to go there."

"On August 14, 1994 we organized a group composed of seven people with me as driver. We left Hamilton at 4:00 a.m. Sunday morning and arrived in Kingston at 8:00 a.m. We considered it too early to drive to Emma's house, and decided to attend Mass at St. Mary's Cathedral. Emma usually attended Mass at St. Joseph's Church, but on that particular day she also was present at St. Mary's Cathedral. By happy coincidence we were all gathered at St. Mary's."

"When we reached Emma's house, my passengers hurried eagerly inside, while Frank and I unloaded the van. While still in the parking lot I smelled a very nice scent coming from nowhere, but did not think seriously about it. As soon as I walked along the corridor in the house, I saw for a fleeting second the figure of Our Lord Jesus Christ crucified. When I walked into the living room and saw the crucifix hanging on the wall, I immediately recognized it as the crucifix I saw earlier. I shuddered with fear, but hid my feelings from the others."

"After introductions and a brief reception, our hostess signalled for prayer to begin, and we positioned ourselves comfortably in front of Emma's altar. During our prayer, the image of Jesus Christ crucified flashed before me. I closed my eyes and tried to ignore it, telling myself that my mind was playing tricks with me, and that I was tired from rising early and driving that distance. The image became more constant and pulsating. Then I felt something along my spine, as though the hairs on my back stood on end. I had goose bumps all over my body, and was becoming helpless, until Emma announced, 'Our Lord Jesus Christ is here.'"

"My heart beat very quickly, and I could not catch my breath. I became afraid, and flashes of my random sins went through my memory. I recounted them at full speed and confessed them to the Lord from within my mind and the depths of my heart. Then with a loud cry I begged for forgiveness. We were immersed in non-stop prayer for the whole day, and throughout that time I was in anguish for my sins. At the end I was consoled by Emma, when she handed me a rosary. The day ended with words of consolation from Emma, and we returned home. The group never knew what I experienced during prayer, and I decided to keep it from them."

The Statue of Our Lady of Fatima

The next morning, on August 15, at 8:00 a.m., while half awake, Mila Rose noticed a very strong light enter her bedroom window. She described its impact on her. "The light from the window was so brilliant that I could not see my bed nor my dresser. Everything in my room was totally bright. I thought I must be dreaming, but heard a commanding voice say, 'Come and meet me at Woolco Plaza.' I felt as though hypnotized, and without washing my face, I dressed to leave the house. When I went downstairs to the living room, Fe was busy putting finishing touches on a wedding gown. She asked where I was going, and I answered vaguely without telling her what I heard because she might not believe me."

"I drove to Woolco Plaza, and did not know what direction to take from there. My legs led me to the Bible book store, which I had not known to be there. The saleslady behaved as though she knew my purpose. She explained that she did not have a statue of the Virgin Mary, and referred me to two other stores in Hamilton. To save me any effort, she telephoned both stores, but unfortunately they did not have the statue of the Virgin Mary. I was told that it would take a month to receive one on order."

"I was very disappointed and drove home. On the way, a striking red light enveloped my car. I could not see my car, nor the steering wheel, nor my direction, but the car continued to move. A voice said, 'Go and pick up your landlady Fe and her cousin Zeny, and proceed to Marmora.' At home, I summoned up my courage to tell Fe what happened. She exclaimed, 'Mila we cannot go to Marmora. That's a four hour drive, and I am rushing this wedding gown. Besides, tomorrow is your flight to Japan, and you have not yet packed a thing.' As an alternative, Zeny suggested a store in Toronto where they had a large statue of the Virgin Mary."

Zeny explained, "We called Hilary, a visionary who knows Emma. She knew where the statue could be purchased in Toronto, and agreed to call the store and have them set the statue aside for us. Cancelling the thought of going to Marmora, we set out for Toronto, with Mila Rose driving. We were still within city limits, heading toward the Queen Elizabeth Way, when Mila Rose complained of a heavy head and a feeling of dizziness, so decided to stop the car. Immediately strange things happened."

Fe picked up the narrative. "Although in a parked position, the car rolled slowly across the road, blocking the oncoming traffic. Mila Rose was trembling with her head bent backwards. She spoke in tongues of different languages which we could not understand. I took my rosary from my purse and placed it around Mila Rose's neck. There was a great deal of confusion when the traffic light flashed green for the oncoming traffic. We rolled down the car windows and screamed for help. A doctor was the first person to pull up on the right of our car. With his medical bag, he rushed to our aid. A truck driver drove forward on our left and called out, 'Don't panic. You'll be all right.' Though Mila Rose's car remained in the park position, it continued to move, and blocked both sides of the road."

"With a great commotion, the paramedics, fire department, ambulance and police arrived. The doctor ordered Mila Rose to be brought to St. Joseph Hospital. I was left behind to look after the car, while the ambulance whisked Mila Rose and Zeny to the hospital. Zeny tried to explain to the hospital attendants that there was nothing wrong with Mila Rose, and that she did not need medical treatment. Since Mila

Rose kept repeating the name of the Blessed Mother and Marmora, they advised that a psychiatrist be called. Zeny insisted that she be left alone until she regained full consciousness. She pleaded for a spiritual advisor and the hospital chaplain arrived. She claimed that she had not personally experienced this phenomenon, but she understood what it was about. She consoled Mila Rose and Zeny, and suggested that if we proceeded to Marmora, Mila Rose ought not drive."

"After Frank and I arrived at the hospital, Mila Rose regained her normal condition. We decided not to go to Toronto, and with my brother-in-law Junior driving the car, we set out for Marmora regardless of the late hour. As soon as we passed Toronto, Mila Rose went into an intense trance. She spoke again in different languages, and we recognized words in Chinese, French, Italian, a mixture of Polish and Latin. She sang a beautiful song about Our Lady, which sounded like Aramaic."

"I asked, 'Is this really you, Mother Mary? We believe in you but please speak in English or our own dialect so we can understand your messages.' Mila Rose spoke immediately in our own dialect, **My children, you are all my children. Change, because the world is heavy with sin.** August 15 was the day on which photo radar was initiated, and all the cars on the 401 drove very slowly. I thought we would not make it to Marmora. A voice spoke through Mila Rose in French, **Speed up. No photo radar can pick up this car**. It took us only two and a half hours to drive to the Greensides Farm."

Mila Rose commented, "As we parked the car, we turned off the ignition and locked the car. We walked toward the washroom, and the car emergency lights went on and flashed quickly beyond the normal rhythm of lights. Spontaneously I looked at the sky and saw a ray of sun strike the large Cross at the top of the hill, move sideways to penetrate the statue of Our Lady on the hill, and simultaneously reflect on a statue of Our Lady in Josie's store. We entered the store and I identified the statue by means of the guiding light. I told Josie, 'I want to take that statue home.' Josie was amazed and asked, 'Do you know how much it costs?' I answered, 'I don't care. I want to bring her home. I'll pay you in cash.' I also bought ten brown scapulars without knowing to whom I would give them."

In Marmora, Mila had three trances, and described her experience. "After we bought the statue of Our Lady, a voice ordered me to bring it to the spring near the grotto, so Our Lady could bless it. We carried the statue up the hill and bathed it with blessed water from the spring. While pouring the water, I fell into a short trance. Later as I regained consciousness, I saw people around me, touching me all over, tugging at my shirt and holding my hands. We brought the statue back to the car."

"As we walked down the hill and into the parking lot, I looked at the sky and saw that the light became more intense. At first I saw the sun with brilliant rays which I could penetrate with my eyes. The rays came down and covered the whole of Marmora. Our Lady showed herself as tall as the CN Tower in Toronto. She was as though infinite. Her mantle and dress were crystalline white and sent forth sparkling rays all over Marmora. I saw pulsating rays of light emanating from her mantle, and closed my eyes when I could no longer tolerate the brightness. Even with closed eyes I still visualized her. Then the sky turned red and I saw the face of Jesus Christ fill the sky. He wore the crown of thorns. I felt myself fall backwards toward the ground."

Fe picked up the narrative. "A young couple ran to the Greensides' house for help. When Mila Rose fell into a trance again, the people on the hill converged toward us, because a beautiful scent spread over all the area. Mila Rose's sweater was already wet with oil. When she regained consciousness we prepared to leave the farm, and she was repeatedly in a trance on the way back to Hamilton."

"When we arrived home, we looked for a spot to place the statue of the Blessed Mother. Mila Rose immediately fell into a trance, and lay flat and heavy on the floor in the living room. Our Blessed Mother and the Lord Jesus came into her. She remained in that state from 11:00 p.m. until 5:00 a.m. The entire household and some relatives surrounded her in a kneeling position, as they listened intently to the words of the Blessed Mother."

"The Blessed Mother said, **I cannot bless this house unless everyone is purified. Wake the children and call them here.** Then she blessed all of us. Through Mila Rose, Our Lady placed her hands on each one's forehead, and did not remove them until each one repented of their sins, in mind or in heart. She knew when the confession was complete, and let Mila Rose proceed to the next person. We were all crying from fear of our sins, and with joy that the Blessed Mother was there with us. When the Lord Jesus came, the only questions He asked in a deep echoing voice were, **Do you know me? Do you hear me?** Then, **Behold thy Mother!**'" The Blessed Mother had private messages directed to the family circle, especially that of Frank and Maria Fe Barrientos, in whose home the group prayed.

Flight To Japan

Mila Rose continued her story. "My flight to Japan was booked for August 16, and I had not the time to prepare my luggage, so I threw articles into my bag, and rushed for the 7:25 a.m. flight. In the departure lounge of Pearson International Airport I saw the Blessed Mother and the Lord Jesus Christ standing among the passengers. I clasped Fe's hands and told her of their presence. Fe prayed, 'Mama Mary, Lord Jesus, please allow her time. She's leaving!'"

"The airport personnel told me I was late and might not be able to board the plane. I don't know how I was able to manage, but somehow everything went smoothly. On the flight from Toronto to Chicago and Chicago to Tokyo, the plane was wrapped in red light. Red rays penetrated every uncovered window throughout the flight. Angels multiplied everywhere like a three dimension movie in slow motion. I could not distinguish between the two levels of reality, and thought I would go crazy."

"When I felt the Blessed Mother's presence, I distracted myself so as not to fall into a trance. I was concerned that people might not know what to do if I fainted and fell down. I kept my mind busy by pushing the stewardess' light, but though the call light was on, no stewardess seemed to notice it. My eyes were heavy, but I fought sleep and reached for the head phone to listen to music, only to discover that there was no plug at the end of the cord. I gave up and asked, 'Mother Mary, is that you?' She answered with a strong **Yes!** I wanted to talk to the couple who sat beside me, but my lips got sucked between my teeth. During the remainder of the flight, they remained tightly that way, which resulted in a severe headache."

The Family Visit

Mila described the events which unfolded in Japan. "I usually go to Japan once a year to join members of my family at the anniversary celebration of our mother's death. Both our parents are dead. From the day I arrived in Japan, I constantly felt the presence of Our Lord Jesus Christ and Our Blessed Mother, and all I did was pray. I did not have the least idea how to pray. One day, alone in my bedroom, Our Blessed Mother came and taught my heart to pray. Afterwards I would spend my whole day praying. My family thought I was somewhat crazy because of it. I would not blame them for thinking that, as I was never a person of prayer. Nevertheless they tolerated the change in me, though they could not endure my hours of praying, especially the long kneeling."

"Japan is more into Buddhism than the Catholic faith. In our home we had a shrine with the statue of Buddha, and along with it the statue of Our Blessed Mother. My Japanese brothers-in-law were not concerned with this mixture, and we said our prayers together, theirs in Japanese, ours in English. Most of the time I was left alone to pray, because they finished long before me. It was usually in those hours that Our Blessed Mother placed me in the state of ecstasy, and would personally come to teach me the meaningful content of the Bible. In the beginning I did not know why she taught me about the Bible, aside from my spiritual growth, but I grew to understand its real purpose. She taught me many things which I am not to mention here, and she gave me the gift of wisdom when a situation calls for it. During my sleep, Our Blessed Mother filled me with dreams of the Rosary, and those dreams were fulfilled when I returned to Canada."

"The most fruitful part of my stay in Japan was when Our Blessed Mother led me to join the El Shaddai Movement of Japan and The Born Again Christian Movement, Japan Chapter. These groups of people form pious prayer groups for world peace and brotherhood."

Return To Canada

Mila Rose planned to stay in Japan until January 5, 1995. After she spent the minimum three months in that country, the immigration office allowed her two additional weeks until November 30, and refused any further extension. She claims, "My family were furious when the officer stamped my passport with the final extension date, and no number of guarantees could change their decision. With this short notice, I had only one day to prepare for my return flight to Canada. I went directly to the airline office to book a flight for the next day, thinking it would be impossible, because of the peak season. To my dismay the flights to Canada were available. I thought I would spend Christmas and New Year's with my family, and felt very sad at the disappointment. In the middle of the night an angel told me, **Behold your tears, as your brothers and sisters wait for you in Canada.** I slept peacefully that night, while friends and close relatives lamented my early departure."

Supernatural phenomena increased in intensity on Mila Rose's return. She recalled, "When I stepped into the car at the Toronto airport, I smelled the strong scent of roses, and my palms began to ooze oil. When we reached Hamilton, we stopped at a Chinese restaurant for supper. The scent of roses overcame the smell of fried chicken from the kitchen. Because the oozing oil from my palms made me very uncomfortable, we decided to take our food in a doggy bag and drive home. It was three o'clock, so we prayed the Chaplet of Divine Mercy. That first night was spent with all our friends in prayer of thanksgiving and the Rosary. From November 30 until the present time I have had no rest, and not even the opportunity to unpack my luggage. My winter clothes are still in storage."

"Intense miracles continued to happen. On the first Friday of December roses came out of my breast, my head and my back. I could not keep track of all the events, including abundant oil oozing from my forehead, my eyes and my back. Out of nowhere, I knew who would come to join us in prayer. I felt every doubting soul who came to the doorstep, heard whispers around corners, and detected concerns in peoples' minds. I prayed to the Blessed Mother asking her to take me slowly, as this was too much for me to handle at one time."

Phenomena Of Our Lady's Statue

Leticia Torio, one of Mila Rose's Mainstay, described further events. "The statue of Our Lady of Fatima from Marmora is miraculous. If we were holding an ordinary conversation in front of her, especially with regard to certain serious problems, she provided us with an immediate answer. I first saw the statue of the Blessed Mother shortly after Mila Rose left for Japan. My initial comment was, 'I have never seen a statue of the Blessed Virgin with such an old and sad face. Recently her features softened and became youthful and smiling happily. The statue's hands, which were fashioned tightly together in an upright position, are now beginning to open. We witnessed the hands move toward the right side of her breast and her crystal white mantle turn slowly into blue."

"Everyone in the house no longer wanted to sleep upstairs, and chose to remain in front of the altar, as the Blessed Mother usually comes between 4:00 a.m. and 7:00 a.m. The altar is bright with sparkling lights at this hour, and her statue radiates intense light for hours. Among the people who come here almost every night, Our Lady chose thirteen as the Mainstay. She gave us the gift of healing and other gifts which are unique to each one. This delighted us and no one slept that night, as the Blessed Mother allowed each of us to practise our gifts on one another. Other gifts were confidential within the Mainstay group."

Emergence Of Rose Buds

Leticia remarked, "On the first Friday of December at three o'clock, I placed a large hand towel on Mila Rose's back, which was oozing oil. That evening when I picked up Fe for Mass, she called me into the house. The glass bowl containing the oily towel held nine little rose buds. At ten o'clock that evening after saying the Holy Rosary, Mila Rose said that something was hurting her back. It was the staple of a flower. Three rose buds emerged from Mila Rose's back. Around eleven o'clock that night, Mila Rose told the women who stayed for the night, 'Mother Mary is going to give you flowers.' She took off her head band, and three roses came out of her hair, two in front and one at the back. Our Lady indicated to whom the roses were to be given."

"Before leaving for Marmora the next morning, six more buds came from Mila Rose's body, and later we saw another rose. Our Lady named the individuals who were to receive them. They were gifts from Our Blessed Mother through Mila Rose for members of the Mainstay."

Cely Bautista, one of the Mainstay, frequently visited the altar at Fe's house after morning Mass at the nearby church of Our Lady of Lourdes. Mila Rose and Cely were seated side by side on the sofa, when suddenly Cely fell into a trance. The Blessed Mother came into her and said, **My Son is suffering right now**. As she said this, Mila Rose, who was assisting Cely, fell down and began to suffer. The two women lay on the floor, while Fe and Frank tried their best to care for them. Fe and Frank witnessed the crowning of thorns and the Way of the Cross which Mila Rose suffered that afternoon. As soon as she finished the Way of the Cross, Cely, who was still in a trance, got up and cradled the lifeless form of Mila Rose, with both women in the pose of La Pieta. They cried in pain as they returned to their senses. In the evening, the Mainstay came for the usual hour of prayer, and that night Mila Rose ended the prayer with the experience of the scourging."

Teresita Abugan, a Mainstay member, shared another event. "Mother Mary promised that she would reveal herself to each one of the thirteen Mainstay, and she has begun to do so already. At three o'clock when I prayed the Chaplet of Divine Mercy, I asked Our Lady to reveal herself to me. As soon as I finished my prayer, I saw Our Lady's picture flashing brightly before me. I opened and closed my eyes, and the phenomenon repeated itself, as Our Blessed Mother revealed herself through different images. I was afraid, and called my husband so he could witness this as well. I did not want to go to sleep that night, nor leave for work the next morning."

Mila Rose commented, "The Blessed Mother already showed herself to eight of the thirteen Mainstay. Once I prayed to the Blessed Mother, because I was concerned about some visitors, and felt their doubts and wandering thoughts. I asked her, 'Mama, how come you don't reveal yourself to all those who pray to you? If you did, I would not encounter scepticism.' She readily answered, **I really would like to reveal myself as much as one wants. However, so few ask me in their time of prayer to reveal myself. People pray, but nobody asks to see me.**"

From the time the Virgin Mary manifested herself through Mila Rose on the feast of the Assumption, August 15, 1994, Frank and Maria Fe Barrientos opened their doors to everyone who wished to come, pray, offer intentions or petitions before the statue which they named Our Lady from Marmora. Daily prayers are offered, including the periodic recitation of the Rosary and the novena of the Chaplet of Divine Mercy, with visitors who come and go.

In all their prayers, the people gathered together focus on offerings, petitions, intentions for the souls in purgatory, conversion of sinners, reparation for sins, world peace, and the intentions of Pope John Paul II.

Messages

August 14, 1994, from the Blessed Virgin Mary, at Marmora:

Know that the end is at hand. Destruction on earth is fast approaching. All must ask for God's mercy. Pray, pray, pray.

The end of mercy is coming. The world is coming to its desolation. Oh, my children, you are all my children. Change now from your evil ways and be converted. I can no longer hold the hand of my Son. It's heavy, heavy, heavy.

Pray, pray, offer sacrifices, penance, atonement. Ask for God's mercy.

December 6, 1994, from the Blessed Mother.

The oil I give you Mila, is very special. It is blessed by me and my Son your Lord Jesus Christ.

The oil is salvation. It represents my Son's never ending love for mankind. It will draw crowds in millions all over the world. It will make the lost come home, the sleepy to waken, the unbelievers to believe, the blind to see. It will unite families and nations with heaven. It will strengthen the faith of the weak, heal the sick, and lift the burden of mankind.

While this oil brings peace and strengthens mankind's faith, it will evoke arguments, discussions and debates at home, in towns, cities, and nations all over the world. there will be commotion of all sorts.

Again, people bring disbelief and confusion to themselves, just as in the past.

The oil will be put to the test and scrutinized. The oil will be popularized all over the world. By the time mankind realizes what it brings, it will be the end of salvation and mercy. The Second Coming is near. So my dear children, while there is time for salvation, come to the Lord and repent. Let there be peace on earth. The oil is love.

Oil: Oil is love.

I showered the world with the flower rose. It is the flower's message that mankind should unite and love one another for peace, prosperity, and rest for the whole world.

Rose: Repent or salvation ends.

Final Note

Mila Rose commented, "The Blessed Mother's expression of these messages is deeply penetrating and soothing. Her voice is more than music to the ear. One would never wish to part from her. No one, I think, can ever in a lifetime explain the solemnity and peacefulness one experiences when with her. It is so difficult to part from her. I myself would never wish her to leave me, but whenever it happens, she always has a way of making her exit. It is something I cannot explain."

"Now, my daily living is dedicated to the service of her will. My movements and actions totally depend on her instruction. I am the soldier of Her Majesty's Immaculate Heart. I urge every one of you, my brothers and sisters, on behalf of the Immaculate Heart of the Blessed Mother, to come back to the house of our Eternal Father, which the Blessed Virgin Mary promises in this time of God's mercy. God blesses us all."

Ron and Janet Brown.

Fe, Mila, Emma (holding rosaries), and Bev.

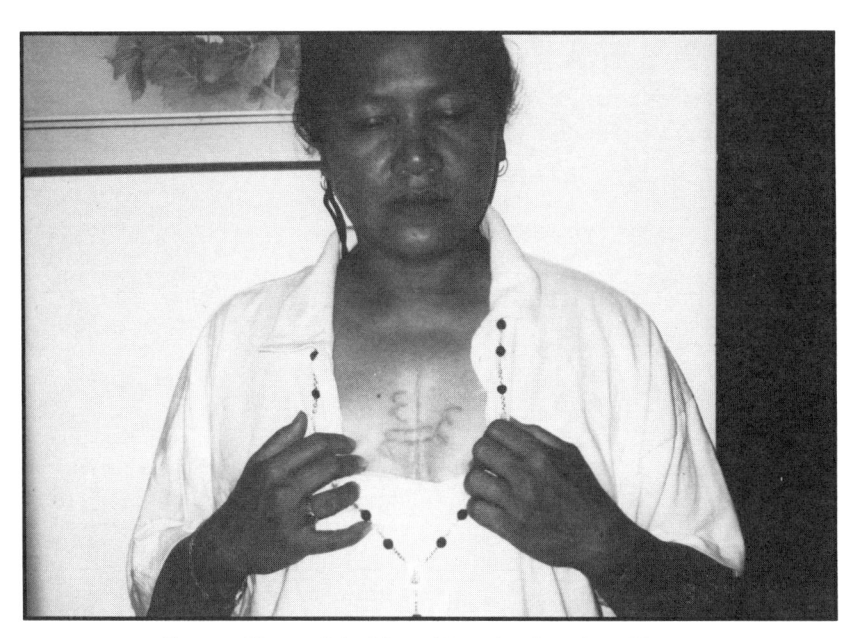

Emma Shows Markings Received on her Chest...

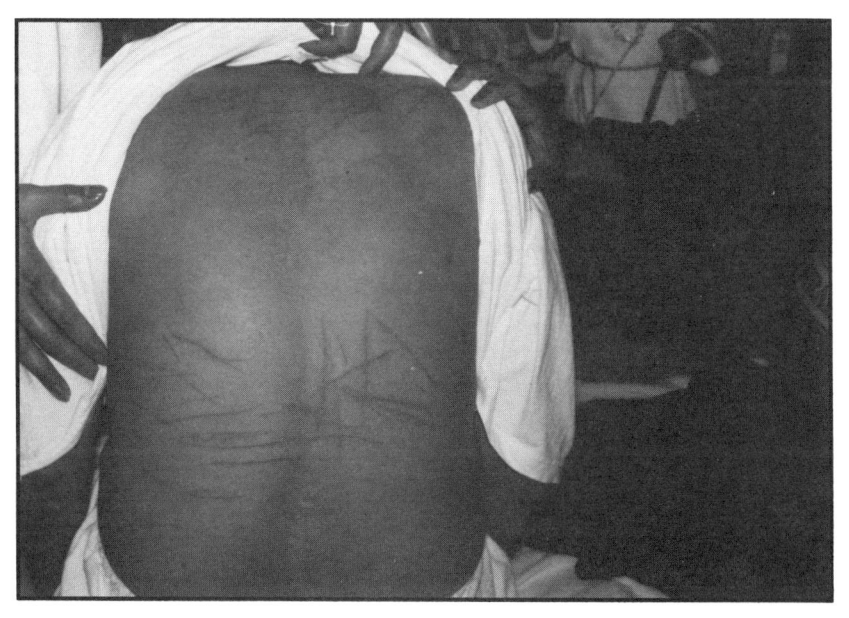

.... and on her Back, After She Experienced the Scourging of Jesus.

Emma's Helper, Sol Gaviola.

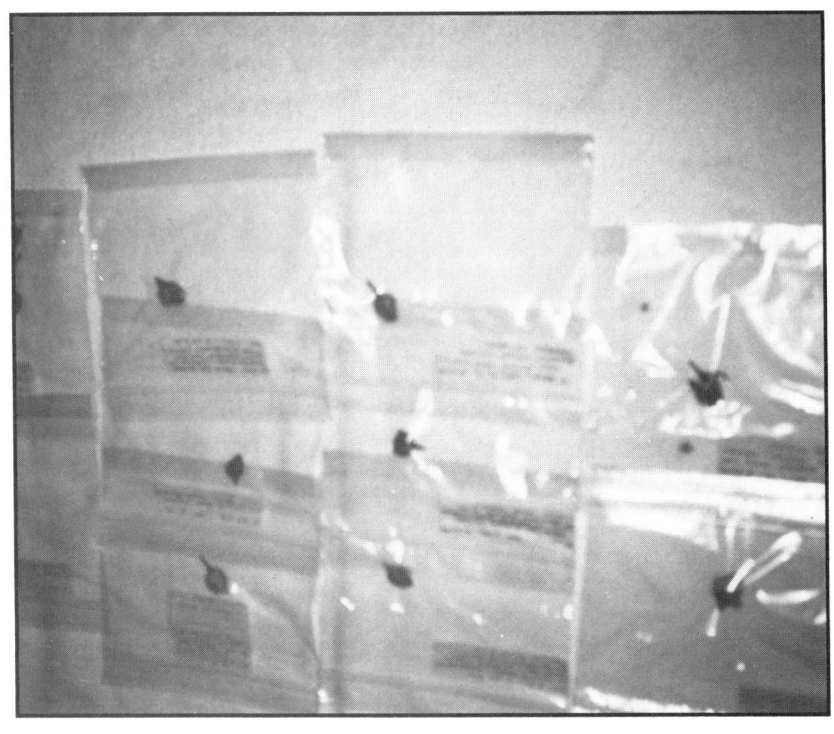

Roses from Heaven through Emma.

Members of Mainstay: Fe, Frank, Mila, Armando, Leticia, Virgie.

Miraculous Statue of Our Lady.

CHAPTER NINETEEN

Jesus, My Way and My Life

Hilary, the eldest of four children is an effervescent nineteen year old university student majoring in Science with an openness toward her future possibilities. She describes some experiences which transformed her life and led her into a new ministry even while her academic studies continue.

Hilary's First Retreat

"I attended my first retreat at St. Augustine's Monastery at Marylake in King City in February 1992. It was a spectacular, unforgettable weekend, probably beyond all my wonderful vacations put together. I was not feeling this excited when I first arrived. Actually I was overwhelmed with restlessness. In particular, the signs, '**Silence**' posted everywhere terrified me. I thought, 'How is anyone supposed to find Jesus in **Silence**?' Little did I know that at the end of three days I would find Him in **Silence**. One must understand that I was very accustomed to the cares of the material world. I was still on the dance floor of life, and harshly enough, Jesus was the last person on my mind."

"In fact one of the reasons I attended the retreat was because my best friend was attending as well. I envisioned a weekend of girl-talk, gossip, an exchange of make-up tips, etc. Not ever would I have imagined constant prayer and meditation in **Silence**."

"As soon as I entered the retreat house I wanted to leave immediately and return to the present century. Yet after the three days I didn't want to return home. I understand now, and give Him thanks with all my being for carrying me away from the dance-floor of life, melting every steel plate in my heart with His love, His unconditional love.

Initial Experiences

"My parents come from the Philippines. In December 1991 my Dad's cousin invited the family to go to Richmond Hill for a time of prayer with a group of people from Kingston. I hesitated about going, then thought there would be food there as well as time to visit with my cousins, so I decided to go along. They prayed and a woman by the name of Emma who was at the front of the room went into a trance. A man's voice came out of her mouth. It was astonishing because she was obviously a woman, and no woman on this earth could have such a voice as that. I was at the back of the room, crying because I could not make sense of it. It was very difficult for me and I left the room, only to return, leave again, and return. I felt an outpouring of tears and couldn't stop. I couldn't find words to describe what was happening."

"Soon after the Infant Jesus' Spirit entered Emma. He called all the children over and asked for ice cream which was given to the children present. At that time my sister and I were having a lot of fights because of petty little things. We were at each other constantly. The Infant Jesus spoke through Emma, **I want you not to fight any more.** I did not know any of these people and they did not know what was in our hearts or what our problems were. There had been no opportunity for them to get to know us. She could not be making this up. Those words released me and my sister."

"Because of that realization I believed in Emma, thinking it must be true. It made me aware of how the spiritual world can exist. As a family we weren't into the spiritual realm of things, nor did we incorporate the spiritual into our lives. That was one of the most difficult things at first, to understand the spiritual world and accept the Spirit entering the body of someone else. I sensed that Jesus wanted to let us know that He is truly spirit and truly human."

Local Headquarters for the La Pieta Prayer Group

In January 1992 the prayer group from Kingston went to Toronto. Hilary continues, "My Dad asked his cousin to bring the Santo Nino, the statue of the Infant Jesus, over for prayer. Afterwards it became an event every two weeks. Emma's group would come here to sleep and we loved it. Our house became the headquarters of La Pieta. As a family we went wherever the Kingston Group went, because the mission is to bring the statue to the host home, pray with their family, and leave the statue for two weeks. The group then return to pick it up and take it to another home."

"A typical day on the mission begins on a Saturday at 11:30 a.m. at the first house where the statue is located. We pray, sing, talk and eat with the host family. By 3:30 the same afternoon we go to another house and do the same thing for another host or hostess who ask for Santo Nino to come to their home. We are never insistent nor imposing on anyone."

"At the end of the mission day, everyone comes to our home and after supper we sing a lot. It's blissful. Everyone feels and sings from their heart. The meditation is at midnight. Half an hour earlier we settle down before the altar and surrender ourselves. We ask the Father to send forth His Spirit. If it is His will the Spirit comes through Emma or me or both, and manifests Himself in that way. This has gone on since 1992 when the Kingston group first came, and we continued to invite them to return to our house."

"Eventually our house and our family were transformed. A prime example of the lack of spirituality in the past was when we went to church on Sundays and always arrived late. We felt we had to dress up and that was a pain. We always sat in the back of the church and didn't understand what was going on. It was boring. My Dad didn't take Communion all through my childhood. I thought that if he didn't receive Communion why should I? The biggest conversion was that he went to Communion. It showed me that prayer works and is still working."

"1992 was a time of deepening my relationship with Jesus. I concentrated on Jesus and Mother Mary, meditated and considered how much we needed purification from our sins. As a family we were care takers because Emma was the chosen one. Our role as a family was to take care of her if she went into a trance."

"When Emma wakes up from an absolute trance she has no recollection of what happened. Sometimes you feel sorry for her in a way because all these special things happen to her, but she doesn't remember them. She doesn't know Jesus the way we know Him through her trance. She would say, 'You're lucky. You actually see. I know that I can see the same thing interiorly but it's not the same.' I knew at that time that my prayers are always answered because in the early stages when you first meet Jesus He answers practically all your prayers. I don't know why, but it's one of His ways of bringing you close to Him, like a honeymoon phase."

"I prayed that for one single moment Jesus would manifest Himself through me for Emma to see. I knew at that time, I was unworthy. I told Jesus, 'I know I'm the biggest sinner in the whole world, and will understand if You don't want to show Yourself through me.' Little did I know that Emma's experiences would happen to me. I can't say that I prayed for this to come, because honestly I didn't. I prayed for it to happen once and simply asked for Emma to be able to see Him through me. That was it. I thought it was an experiment and He wouldn't bother me again and I could go on living a 'normal life' with prayer. I didn't think it would continue for this duration. This gradual spiritual growth continued throughout 1992."

Ecstasy

Hilary distinguishes normal spiritual development from ecstasy. "I parallel the gradual process of spiritual development with the growth of the infant into childhood. In ecstasies I felt totally enraptured by Life and by Love. As a Science major I would explain it in logical terms if I could. Maybe I could ask Archangel Uriel the Archangel of Science to give me that knowledge and the right vocabulary to explain it. Maybe the best analogy for ecstasy is the dream. In a dream you feel that it's real and you know it's real. You wake up and you have no recollection of it. It's the same thing with ecstasy. I don't understand why I don't have the recollection of it. It bothers me, but I live it day by day. What happened yesterday helps me come to where I am today and that's fine."

"I remember in one ecstasy where Jesus came into me to the point where my physical body was transformed and crossed the line into the spiritual world. Those who were with me could see my body and my chest rising. It is awkward to see that type of position in a person. It was done to me and did not occur out of my own free will. My chest was pulled upward. Emma was beside me and when I awoke she was crying but I didn't know why."

"I don't fear the credibility of my experiences as compared with anyone else because I know His love for me and my love for Him. Gregory of Nyssa is the most wonderful mystical writer I have read. His analogy of the bride, the bridegroom, and the kiss, leaves me in awe every time I read it. It's surprising because how can He love me so much, wicked person that I am? At the same time He loves me so much and all I did was say 'I love You.' That's all. It's so simple. I feel the same way about Jesus as He feels about me. It really hurts me when people my age can't see the same thing, and I know of people whose lives are totally crippled, lacking love."

"I guess everyone coming out of high school and into university goes through that adjustment period, where you begin to understand and you really question your purpose in that program, and your purpose at that institution. I have experienced that too. But not so much as I have experienced the conversion of my heart and mind. When you experience the transformation of Jesus working in you, you know that you have a transformation of your mind."

"People commonly judge each other according to their exterior. This has a tendency to cause conflicts, misunderstandings and a lack of love for one another. Jesus and the Blessed Mother have taught me to revert back to childlike ways and look upon everyone innocently. Don't look at people's faults. Look at them for their innocence, their love, and the knowledge of who they are. In the first few months of school I felt really lonely because I didn't find a kindred spirit. Surprisingly, Jesus brought people into my life. The transformation, the ecstasy, the rapture in His warmth of love are truly inexplicable."

"I don't want to sound obnoxious but if I weren't preserved by His grace I would use my logic and my left side braininess to try to explain it. I know that it's happening. Some things are meant not to be explained. Though I try to explain how He feels for me I don't think it conveys that oomph!"

Spiritual Affirmation

At the beginning of her journey Hilary felt the need to talk to a priest about her experiences. She recalls, "As a child you have the idea that the priest is the ultimate being on this earth. Priests are special because they celebrate Mass and wear those vestments. I really wanted affirmation from a priest, but also remembered the saints and the difficulties they encountered when they brought their stories to the Church. I didn't want to be alienated from the Church because my whole perception of the Church changed into the Mass."

"For example, when someone says to me, 'Are you going to church?', in my mind it's not the building I am going to. Rather it is to visit Jesus through the Mass. I don't go to church to sit down in an uncomfortable seat. I learn through the Mass the special and important role of the priest. For now, I cannot bring myself to tell my whole story to a priest. I don't want to cause controversy but priests study a lot about theological aspects of Christianity. When Jesus wanted to teach through the saints and the mystic writers, the Church didn't want that teaching because I guess it was against their tradition."

"We need affirmation from the Church, even while Jesus is your ultimate Spiritual Director. God sends God-coincidence conversations with people through whom He works, who answer your heartfelt questions at such a time when you don't even expect it. God works in mysterious ways through the people you meet. A lot of people advised me to get a Spiritual Director and talk with someone who knows more about this subject. That's valid and human, but the time will come for that. I go to Confession through the Church and through Padre Pio, and directly to Jesus."

Supernatural Experiences

Hilary claims that she is never really alone. "One time when I was alone at home I phoned my best friend and asked her 'Are you alone at your house with no one there?' She said, 'Yes.' I said 'There's somebody there.' She insisted, 'No. Nobody's here.' Poking fun at me she added, 'Maybe my angel's out playing somewhere.' That's one of the gifts that Jesus gave me. He took away my fear and isolation and replaced it with rapture, the divinity, the communion of saints and all the angels. When I'm on the subway I look at people. They look so lonesome. I feel like laughing because these people don't know they're not alone."

"I do not have visions or apparitions. I am unworthy to bear the title of visionary. Ultimately and definitely I know in my heart the presence of the communion of saints, the angels. It's a force to be reckoned with and if I meet spiritual persons and they talk with me about their nature spirit or their guide, it's the same language of love. When they talk about their Mother Earth and I talk about my God, or they talk about their Mohammed and I talk about my Jesus, it's the same language. In February or March 1994 I went on a temple tour to the Buddhist and Hindu temples and the Jewish synagogue. It was the most wonderful feeling to feel that their God was in my God, and my God was in their God. It was a oneness that I cannot explain but I was in awe at the awareness."

Invisible Stigmata

On occasion Hilary has experienced the pain of Jesus. She comments, "I think that the extent of my physical phenomena is the invisible stigmata. In my heart I have not assimilated its meaning. I don't like to think about it because it brings me so much agony and grief. However, I am happy that He gave me the privilege to have even a little piece of His cross. It gives me joy to think that He gave me a little of the tiniest piece to help Him and to help His friends."

"The rapture of the love with which He envelops me is the same magnitude as the grief and the agony with which He enraptures me. He knows that I can handle it according to the seasons of the Church. During Lent it becomes more painful when Holy Week approaches. Holy Week is the most painful and agonizing period of the year because the Spirit lets me realize that Jesus suffers again for us. I picture the face of Mother Mary and what she went through. It's too painful to speak about. I'm in great pain which I know ultimately comes from Him. I'm in bliss because I know I'm helping Him."

"After reading about the spirituality of Padre Pio we became friends. I met other people who cherished Padre Pio not only because of his stigmata but because of his mannerisms toward God. He became as a grandfather to me and I love him a lot. I remember reading about his gift of sweet-smelling incense and after confessing my sins to him once, I prayed for affirmation of my experience and waited. Suddenly a smell of incense came swiftly but surely. I ran out of my room to my sister and asked her, 'Do you smell the incense?' She didn't. I knew for a fact that he heard me. Jesus used him as an avenue to change my life."

"In October 1992 on a week-end in Kingston, we were upstairs praying. Suddenly I felt like I was floating off the bed. Interiorly I felt light but my body was heavy. I knew that something was going to happen. It got to a point where I needed to be carried by four men because I couldn't pick myself up. I don't know why. It's common sense that the physical body weighs the spirit down. But when the spirit empties your body you're even heavier."

"On the living room floor of Emma's house I went into ecstasy and she did shortly after. During my ecstasy I felt painful wounds in my hands and didn't know what they were. They were so sharp. I did not connect with the fact that they might be nails. I needed to take them out. My body was very hot and my hands and feet were very cold. I couldn't lift my hands. They were being nailed to the floor with some sharp object. I asked Jesus to help me and to preserve me because I couldn't take the pain. I wished someone more capable of withstanding the pain had been chosen. I tried to bear it patiently. I put the sharp objects aside and those present placed my hands at my side. I felt the pulsating, throbbing pain at the centre of my palms. When I looked at my hands I saw a distinct indent on my left hand. I was ready to throw my hands away because I could not accept this. I felt 'How could He allow me to bear His pain when He knew that I couldn't bear it at first? Why would He do this?' I was confused and scared. These feelings made me want to throw my hands away."

Even then when I was not accepting the situation I remembered that Emma went into ecstasy at the same time. She wrote on the carpet, PIO. It was a sign for me that Padre Pio was there and he made himself known. I cried. That is one of my most vivid recollections of the beginning of my invisible stigmata. My consolations are the young people who are going through the same thing. Jesus chose us at such an early age and marks us now so that later on at His Second Coming the younger generation will already have implanted it in the hearts of the generation after them."

Visits to Marmora

Hilary and her group visited Marmora three or four times. She describes these occasions. "Our first visit was in the summer of 1992 when we saw the miracle of the sun. On our second visit it was raining. From the First to the Eighth Station Emma felt the same experiences as I did. A man helped her up the hill and through the trees. At one point she held the hand of an angel. The men who carried her felt her body suddenly become as light as an empty box. She felt pain and suffering through all the Stations. By the Eighth Station her pain became subdued. I didn't know the order of the Stations of the Cross and held on to someone for support. When we reached the Ninth Station I felt heavy and thought I was feeling sick. I fell to the ground because my weight which was the weight of Jesus was too heavy to continue. After that I was oblivious to everything except to the fact that people carried me because I couldn't stand."

"At the Ninth Station my eyes were closed, I heard what went on around me, and my body felt the weight and the pain of the agony. It was where Jesus fell for the third time. I prayed. We continued on through the remainder of the Stations until the Fourteenth Station when my body was at ease again. At that point I woke up. I believe that from the Eighth to the Fourteenth Station the Spirit used me to show the people around us what Jesus suffered. I'm accustomed to being in a private group and with a handful of people. When I awoke and saw a multitude of unfamiliar faces I felt scared. Then I saw the people I know with me and felt comfortable again."

Personal Reflection

"I still try to figure why it happened to me. I wondered why He chose me at this age and why He doesn't leave me alone now. I honestly know that without His help I would not be able to complete the Science course at university. I would not be able to have the courage to go on day by day the way I do. I would not have the patience to endure failing Chemistry all the time. I would not have the virtue of hoping that this will all get better. I would not have the joy of teaching my kids in Sunday school."

"I know I'm unworthy and sometimes feel that I'm not the right person, that someone else would be more effective than I. I thought that He would allow me to finish school and then use me. I like to do jobs one by one and accomplish each one to perfection before moving on. Now I have to learn to do many things at once. School and Jesus have to mix. They can't be separated."

"How can I summarize my life in a few words? They are Jesus, my Way and my Life. In my mind, Jesus is still growing, like Santo Nino. While He's growing I'm growing with Him. I think that Mary's role for me is in the picture of the Mother of Perpetual Help. You see Jesus running to His mother for help and his slippers fall. I'm probably a string on the slippers. I want to be there and I run to her when I need help. On Thursdays I go to the Perpetual Help devotions. Our Lady called me to be cantor and lector for these devotions."

"We know how important the Holy Family is, and that this year is dedicated to the family. I wish it would continue for many more years because a lot of my friends' families are torn up due to misunderstandings and materialistic attitudes and values. During our missions I try my best to convey the love of family. It doesn't matter what you have or how you look. If you have your family, that's all you need."

CHAPTER TWENTY

A CALL TO PLAN PILGRIMAGES

Mary Ann Dollard lives in Alden, a small village east of Buffalo, New York. She has organized pilgrimages to Marmora every second Sunday of each month and on special feasts of Our Blessed Mother, and witnessed a number of conversions and transformation of lives through Our Lady's intercession. She describes how she became involved with pilgrimages.

"Father Bob, a priest friend from Pittsburg, couldn't take a pilgrimage to Denver as he expected. The tour director asked me to replace him as a Spiritual Director. That's how I began my life of taking people to different areas in the United States, and now also to Canada."

An Early Call

Mary Ann described a calling in 1986. "It was to open my home and to start a Cenacle based on the teachings of Louisa Piccaretta, on the Gift of the Divine Will, given to Louisa by Our Lord in private revelation. I started the first Divine Will Cenacle on March 25, 1986 in my home. Soon I spread this gift everywhere I went. I started several hunded Cenacles of prayer throughout the United States and Canada, along with daily Holy Hours for priests and religious after the Holy Sacrifice of the Mass in parishes and homes. I worked with a missionary priest, Father Robert Rezac IMC, in starting Eucharistic Rosary crusades of reparation and atonement for all the sacrilegious acts committed against the Sacred Heart of Jesus and the Immaculate Heart of Mary, and also for an end to all abortions."

"For a period of four years, Father Bob and I held Enthronements of the Sacred Heart in the homes of families. When Father was recalled to Kenya, Africa for missionary work, I continued to renew the First Saturday devotions in many parishes, as requested by Our Lady of Fatima. I developed the Marian Movement of Priests Cenacle at my parish of St. Augustine in Depew, N.Y. on each Saturday. In addition, I conduct the Divine Will Cenacle on the second and fourth Wednesday of each month at my home in Alden."

Experience of Conversion

Mary Ann made a pilgrimage to Medjugorje in September 1987. While there she experienced a tremendous conversion of heart. She explains, "That's where all this began. God the Father showed me the sinful state of the world and my personal unworthiness. I asked, 'Why did you call me here? These pilgrims are holy people. I am not holy.' It was the feast of the Triumph of the Cross, September 14. When I looked down from Mount Krizevac, He showed me the crowd of people below. From that distance they looked like little jelly beans, then they turned into black and white spots. Some were very dark."

"As I watched this scene I saw the priests outside St. James church with massive lines of people going to Confession. They stood in line looking like spotted leopards and left like sparks of suns dancing in the air. The Lord said, 'See, they become reconciled to me in the Sacrament of Reconciliation, and they dance before me.'"

Mary Ann continued, "How I got that trip was even more phenomenal. A priest called me asking if I would give a retreat with him at Villa Maria College in Erie, Pa. I resisted claiming "I can't possibly do that. I'm not equipped to give a retreat. I don't know what I would talk about. I'm not a theologian.' He brushed away my comments, claiming, 'You'll be fine.'"

"I dismissed the retreat from my mind and went to New York to visit a friend. Before leaving I had a vision of Our Lady. She was holding a fifteen decade rosary made of mother-of-pearl. The beginning of each mystery was the most beautiful pink rose. She beckoned, 'Come. Come. Come. My Son is calling you.' I asked, 'Where do I go?' The next day I thought that I must have been dreaming."

"I went to Mass and prayed, 'Father, if this is from you, please show me. Before the Blessed Sacrament, He answered, 'I desire that you get a passport.' I exclaimed, 'A passport! I don't have two nickels to rub together, never mind a passport to go anywhere with. A passport means that I would go overseas. Where would I go and what is my purpose?'"

"The Lord answered, 'Don't worry about the money. Just go and get the passport.' I asked, 'How do I do that?' He said, 'There's a purse in your closet. Inside is an application blank for a passport.' It was as He indicated. I began to shake and asked, 'What do I do next?' He replied, 'Call the photographer and have a picture taken.' I obeyed. The photographer claimed it was his day off but he couldn't seem to leave his shop. He told me to come right away and I did."

"I asked the Lord, 'What do I do now?' The answer came, 'Go to the post office.' I objected, 'Don't I have to pay something? I only have three dollars.' He said, 'There are two cheques lodged behind the buffet. Now you'll have ample. Go to the post office in Buffalo. The postmaster there asked me, 'Where are you going?' I had not considered that question, and when I did ask the Lord, the answer was 'Medjugorje. Medjugorje. Medjugorje.'"

"I thought 'I can't possibly go to Medjugorje. But I have a friend who is working on the canonization of Blessed Nincio. I'll probably go with her to Italy.' The postmaster insisted, 'Lady, you've got to identify some place.' I answered, 'Put down Rome. That's probably where I'll go.' He asked 'When do you need this back?' I answered, 'By the twelfth of June.' This happened in May. I paid the money and forgot about it."

"Then I went to New York to visit my friend. On June 12 I called Father to cancel my attendance at the retreat which began the following day. He didn't give me the opportunity to cancel, but replied, 'I'm happy you called. See you tomorrow', and hung up. I cried and cried. The next day I went to Erie for the retreat. When I finished Father came to me looking as if he saw a ghost. He said, 'I have a gift for you. Our Lord spoke to me and told me to lend you the money to go to Medjugorje.' I asked 'When am I leaving?' He replied, 'September 11.' From there on my conversion continued and is still continuing. My call to bring pilgrims had begun."

Pilgrimages to Marmora

Mary Ann heard about Marmora when she took pilgrims to Denver Colorado at the alleged apparition site of Mother Cabrini Shrine. When she completed that pilgrimage she prayed, "Dear God, what do you want me to do next?" She recalled, "I spent a lot of time before the Blessed Sacrament. Interiorly I heard, 'I am going to redirect you in the way you are to go and what you are to do.' I waited."

"A lady from Pittsburg phoned and asked me to direct a pilgrimage to St Anne de Beaupre and St. Joseph's Oratory. I accepted. I received a letter in the mail from a man in Alaska saying, 'I think that Our Lord wants you to do something with this.' Enclosed was a newsletter from Father Heffernan, from the Queen of Peace Centre in Canada. I thought, 'What would Our Lord want me to do with that?'"

"I led the pilgrimage to St Anne de Beaupre and on the way back I stated, 'We must stop at this place called Marmora.' The lady in charge said that she had never heard of it, but I insisted, and gained the consent of the pilgrims."

"We arrived when it was already dusk and met Shelagh and John Greensides. When I walked into the house, I saw a terrific illumination of light. I asked Shelagh what was happening here. She told me the story of Marmora. Ironically, Veronica Garcia from Denver was one of the first visionaries to have an apparition here."

"After the pilgrimage I prayed before the Blessed Sacrament and asked, 'Is this what you want me to do?' I heard, 'I desire that you continue these pilgrimages on the second Sabbath of every month.' This is how I began bringing pilgrimages to Marmora."

"The experiences here do not consist so much of signs and wonders. I have seen people get on this bus with the hardest of hearts, broken and wounded, even destitute with very little hope for the future or hope for a relationship with Our Lord Jesus. Some people on the bus come with very hard hearts and return with hearts turned to flesh to be used for God's greater glory. Their hearts are filled with peace, love and joy, and filled with the Holy Spirit."

"I have seen individuals return by the droves to the sacrament of Reconciliation, and begin to partake daily in the Holy Sacrifice of the Mass. I have reports from different parishes saying that many of these people have become involved in missionary work with the poor, homeless, the abandoned. They seem to be healing the wounded people that they meet along life's path. Conversions which are taking place in Marmora are profound. There are manifestations such as the spinning of the sun, unusual photographs, rosaries turning gold, and the experience of God's love, which is personal for each individual."

"To me the greatest miracle is when a man of fifty years says to me, 'Could you find me a priest so I can go to Confession? I want to receive Jesus and I received Him sacrilegiously for fifty years, never realizing what a state of sin I was in. I come to beg forgiveness and mercy from

Almighty God, and give my unconditional 'Yes' as Our Lady did. Deeply shaken and with a repentant and contrite heart, he goes home a new man in Christ."

Mary Ann conducted pilgrimages to Marmora since August 1992. She claimed, "I was not going to come after October 1994 and told people that I was finished for the season. On the second Sunday in Marmora I felt so scattered, like an arm was cut off. I went before the Blessed Sacrament and asked 'What do you want me to do?' I could feel the presence of the Holy Spirit overpowering me. I heard, 'I desire that you bring two more buses, one on the second Sabbath and one on December 8.' I answered, 'Oh, Father, you know how cold it is and I can't stand the cold. He said, 'Does my love diminish for you with the seasons?' I answered, 'No, Father.' He replied, 'Then I desire that you go home and order the buses. Don't worry about the weather. I control the elements.'"

"I returned home and asked, 'How many buses do you want?' He said, 'Three, possibly four." I ordered three buses and one on standby. I said, 'Father I made an announcement on the last bus that I will not take any more pilgrimages for the whole year. What do you want me to do?' He answered, 'You will make three phone calls.' Immediately the names of three people flashed into my mind. I called them and explained that we had to go on pilgrimage in response to a special call."

"It was phenomenal. Within twenty four hours one and a half buses were filled. Within two weeks three buses were filled and in the third week the fourth bus was filled. There are people from different walks of life and varied religious denominations, Catholics, Protestants, Muslims, Jews. Their faith in Almighty God is strengthened and they grow in a deeper relationship with God the Father."

Impact of Pilgrimage

Mary Ann notes, "This is the year of the family. I have started prayer families, Cenacles in the home, with many of the pilgrims and children who have come to Marmora. Twice I brought a youth pilgrimage. These children are hungry, starved for God. They want to know the truth. They want to know about the sacraments. Many of these children have been to church only when they were baptized. Many children are broken because they come from broken homes and broken families.

They are now coming for religious instruction and returning to the faith."

"God the Father manifests His love to all people because He is a loving Father. Our only impediment is our human will. He wants us to surrender our human will so that His divine will can come and reign in us, because the kingdom of God is within each and every one of us. He wants us to enter into a deeper relationship with the Most Blessed Trinity. I encourage everyone to come to Marmora for the graces they receive, for the many blessings through the Mediatrix of all grace, the Co-Redemptrix, the Reparatrix. She is the most powerful intercessor for all our sinfulness."

"I ask those who have broken homes and broken families to turn to your Mother who was given to us at the foot of the Cross. When Jesus said to his mother, 'Woman, behold, your son,' and to St. John, 'Behold, your mother,' she became your mother and mine. She is the pure and immaculate spouse of the Holy Spirit who now comes to prepare her children for the Second Coming of her Divine Son Jesus Christ. This truly is a call to holiness through prayer, penance, reconciliation, reparation and atonement."

Reflection

To the question "How has this affected your life?" Mary Ann replied, "It has drawn me into a very deep relationship with the Most Blessed Trinity through the powerful intercession of the Blessed Virgin Mary. Even though I was always active in prayer, working in the mission field, starting prayer groups in church, homes and families, I had a special calling from early childhood to offer my prayers for the conversion of sinners, the salvation of souls, especially the poor souls in purgatory. I know it is through their intercession that I was able to grow in my spiritual life creating in my soul a great hunger and thirst to know, to love, and to serve God in the Divine Will."

"Through many pilgrimages to Marmora and around the world, Our Mother Mary brought forth the graces necessary to bring her childen back to God, their creator. She leads them to a deeper knowledge of the great love which God the Father has for them as they are led along the way of the Cross with His divine Son, Jesus. She guides them to personally experience this love, to be reconciled with God and one another through the sacrament of Reconciliation. Resulting grace allows them to be able to receive Jesus in His Body, Blood, Soul and Divinity in the Holy Eucharist."

"These conversions occur as the Mother of God touches our hearts with the flame of love from her Immaculate Heart. It brings forth a renewal in our hearts, homes, in our families and in the world. That conversion of heart invites people to return to prayer and into the knowledge and gift of the Divine Will."

"Many pilgrims who return home from Marmora are filled with the Holy Spirit. They call to tell me of physical healings, emotional healings, family healings. Most important of all are their spiritual healings. Today families are gradually returning to God in family prayer. Our Lord is pouring out extraordinary grace upon this world through the powerful intercession of His purest daughter Mary, Most Holy. Her words ring with profound truth, 'My soul proclaims the greatness of the Lord, and my spirit rejoices in God, my Saviour.'"

CHAPTER TWENTY-ONE

GRACE FLOWS ONWARD

Because of the sensitive nature of the sharings in this chapter, all names have been substituted to ensure a measure of privacy to the participants. Jeff is the supervisor of a group home for troubled boys. He was raised Roman Catholic but began drifting during the late sixties, and remained away from the Church for twenty-three years. His volunteer work at the Greensides farm was soon followed by a spiritual transformation which affects every aspect of his life and work. Jeff shares his experience.

From Drift to Avalanche

"As my life tumbled onward my sins started stacking up. I lost everything. Fire, a broken marriage and another lost relationship were the reward I reaped from my godless lifestyle. I became embittered. I believed that nothing I had would last for long, and lived from day to day, not wanting to give up momentary pleasures that satisfied me. Drugs, booze and physical pleasures were the order of the day. I tried various counsellors and therapists, all of whom left me empty inside."

"I prayed every now and then when I was in trouble, and promised the Lord that I'd mend my ways if He'd help me. My ultimate desire was not forgiveness nor the desire to be closer to Jesus. I simply wanted to get out of the mess I had created, in order to continue on the same path. Time after time I was given signs that the way to true happiness was to change my life and give it to Christ. I ignored them."

"During my most recent self-induced crisis, (another family break-up) I was affected by a number of people and circumstances that changed my life forever. Much of it was due to the example set by one of my workmates who saw my need for spiritual help and talked me into attending Christmas Mass and joining a group of people who were to become Catholic and for those who wanted to return to the faith."

Our Lady Intervenes

On March 25, 1994, Jeff went to the Greensides farm to celebrate the Feast of the Annunciation. He recalled that day. "That hillside with its Stations of the Cross, the hundreds of pilgrims and the complete peace that enveloped us brought me to tears. Two friends and I read the prayers at each Station. Numerous times one of us had to take over reading from the other, as our voices repeatedly broke."

"We witnessed people falling to the ground as the Spirit overwhelmed them. One lady dropped repeatedly. There was mud and slush on the trail, but her coat never got soiled. The farther up the trail we went, the more we felt a very powerful spiritual presence. The singing of hymns could be heard all over with none drowning out the others, but loud enough to distinguish the different languages of the singers. At the Tenth Station the multitude lingered as if anticipating the extraordinary."

Miracle of the Sun

Jeff had heard other people speak of the miracle of the sun at the farm. His experience was transforming. "I was afraid to look towards its brilliance, thinking I might be disappointed if I did not witness the event, or maybe I didn't feel worthy to see it. Finally I peeked at the sun and was amazed that I could look at it without blinking or having my eyes water. As I stared at it, the centre turned dark as if there were a total eclipse."

"According to my companions, I stared at it for about two minutes, turned away and looked back at it again. The centre was a dark disc, the rays around it were brilliant and danced outwardly. I was not aware of the lapse of time, apparently five or six more minutes, I was told. Near the end of the phenomenon the centre of the sun vibrated very quickly, still within the rays."

"As this was going on, a lady to my right dropped to her knees, held her hands outstretched and started speaking while staring directly at the sun. I believed she was in ecstasy as she was just beaming. When I looked towards her, I noticed that her face was golden. By this time I was not even aware of the sounds around me. I asked my friend if her face looked gold. He replied, 'No.' His face was its normal colour, so I looked around at the seemingly silent crowd. The majority looked normal, but every now and again I spotted another golden face. At first I thought it was because I had looked at the sun, but if this were so, everyone would look the same."

"During this time, a number of people took polaroid snapshots of the sun. Among those I witnessed a brilliant sun with a cross of light right through it, almost taking up the whole frame. Two other pictures showed the sun with a figure below and to the right. One was shaped like a statue of the Blessed Virgin, but had no detail. The other photograph was similar, but with what appeared to be a veil wrapped around the statue. One could distinguish the texture of the cloth."

"Other pictures showed a brilliant white door which covered the sun and portions of the trees. There appeared to be hinges on the door but no door knob. An Oriental lady, upon seeing the picture, remarked that she could never fit through this 'door to heaven'. She made it only as far as the next Station before she dropped to the ground. We completed the remaining Stations, fully aware of the evidence of the Holy Spirit working within the crowd."

Grace Reaches Out

The gift of faith is not only personal. By its very nature it reaches out to transform other lives. Jeff experienced the impact of this outreach. "Later that evening, my friend Frank's girl friend indicated that she wanted to go to Greensides farm. Although Frank was emotionally and physically drained from his earlier experience, he took her there. While they were at the Eighth Station, Moreen noticed a fire nearby. She asked Frank if that were normal. He was startled and both ran to the site. It was the Tenth Station."

"The flames were ten to fifteen feet high. While Frank and another person beat out the flames, Moreen ran to the farmhouse for help. By the time other people arrived, the fire was almost out. The Station and the statue of Jesus were not even scorched. Even the flowers below the Station were not harmed. Only a few beads of a large rosary hanging from the Station were melted. Another statue which was in the midst of the flames had totally disappeared. This fire should have done far more damage than it did. Moreen was so moved by the experience that she decided to pursue Christianity with the hopes of becoming Catholic."

Reconciliation

The grace of the Holy Spirit continued its action in Jeff's life. He continued his story. "That night I was so restless I hardly got any sleep. Even prayer did not settle me. We went to Sunday Mass the next day, where I participated in the sacrament of Reconciliation. I wanted to be one of the last in Confession so I wouldn't hold anyone back. Twenty-some years of sin takes a while to confess, and the priest was very kind and patient. After he gave me my penance, he suggested I pray the Chaplet of Mercy every day from Good Friday until the Sunday after Easter. He told me I would find it at the little book store, St. Joseph's Cabin."

"The next morning I went to the store but couldn't remember the name of the booklet. As I was about to give up, the priest who heard my Confession drove up to the store. This was only the second time I had seen him. He told me the title of the booklet and I purchased it. Since then I have had the most peaceful sleep I have ever experienced. For the first time in my life I have been able to forgive **myself**. Prior to these experiences I lived in the past, forever condemning myself and setting the stage to repeat my difficulties over and over again. I know that this is Satan's way to keep his claws in people, who become their own worst enemy and his staunch ally."

"There will always be problems in my life, but I deal with them through prayer and spiritual contemplation. I regularly attend Mass and receive the Eucharist to further strengthen my soul. I constantly examine my conscience and try to correct my sinfulness. I also try to turn my life over to Christ, but it's difficult to let go of old habits and thought processes. Daily prayer is proving that this is possible only through Jesus Himself."

Feast of the Immaculate Conception

Jeff's ongoing conversion developed during subsequent months. On December 8, 1994, he observed that the tremendous impact which Our Blessed Mother exercised on him also affected the boys in his care and other staff members. Once again she chose a special feast in her honour to pour out her blessings on Jeff and his friends. He described his experience of that day. "Shelagh and John asked me to help with the parking for the December 8 pilgrimage. It was my day off, and I was more than glad to help. I had been praying to Mary's mother, St. Anne, to help me keep my enthusiasm alive."

"Ed had voluntarily attended Mass a number of times with me. He had a problem with drugs, glue in particular. I suspect that a lot of his miscreant deeds were due to this behaviour. He had no school that afternoon, and asked the teacher to drop him off at the farm. Ed assisted with the parking for a few hours. I felt that his heart was elsewhere, so I told him to go make the Stations. He asked, 'What do I do?' I advised him to stay with a group of people and do what they do. I said a prayer to Mary, asking her to look after him. I learned afterwards that while Ed was making the Way of the Cross, someone asked him to carry the large Crucifix at one of the Stations. Ed is protestant, but afterwards told me that he was able to say the prayers with the group, without having known the prayers ever before."

"Later I attempted to make the Stations. I observed Ed at the Tenth Station, as I stood on a rock a few feet behind him, while he witnessed the miracle of the sun. I was also party to the conversation guided by the Holy Spirit through the little old lady, or possibly an angel, regarding drugs and glue sniffing. Ed's face changed. It took on a radiant, peaceful quality, and still remains that way. When the day ended, Ed returned to the group home and I went to my home. I apologized to Jesus for not concentrating properly on my prayers during the Stations. I felt happy for Ed, but disappointed with myself. That night I emptied my pockets, placed everything on the table, said my prayers and went to bed. The next morning at breakfast, I noticed that the silver chain on my rosary was now gold!"

Grace Flows Outward Gently To The Boys

Jeff describes the gentle movement of grace in the lives of the boys at the group home. He believes in the gentle nudges and whispers of the Holy Spirit as made manifest concretely in their subtle changes of behaviour.

"Jacob is thirteen years old with instability in his young life. He struggles with his decisions between right and wrong. When asked if he would like to attend Mass, he rarely refuses. Following one of Jacob's periods of life-threatening despair, Jeff spoke with him about Jesus, and how He would respond to Jacob. Then he suggested that Jacob say his prayers and go to sleep. That night, Jacob knelt privately in his room to say his prayers."

"On New Year's Eve we went to Mass. I had a little chat about sin and suggested to Jacob that he go to Confession. He asked me, 'What do I say?' I advised him to begin with 'Bless me, Father, for I have sinned.' He did this, and Father Timothy responded, 'Don't worry. I'm not going to hit you.' Jacob made his Confession, received Holy Communion, and confided that he felt like crying afterward. Now he claims that he won't miss Mass for anyone."

"Twelve year old Chris loves visiting Josie at St. Joseph's Cabin. He admired a statue of St. Jude, and she gave it to him. Later he asked me to tell him about St. Jude. I explained that we pray to him to ask God for difficult favours. One day he came home after school and said, 'You know that kid who wanted to beat me up? Well, I prayed to St. Jude last night to help me, and guess what! Today that boy came up to me, and we talked and shook hands!' After Mass one evening, Chris commented, 'I feel like such a man after Mass!' Chris wants very much to attend a healing Mass to obtain God's help in dealing with his anger."

"On New Year's Eve, all the boys wanted to attend Mass except Mike. The boys hid his Nintendo game and said they would return it only if he went along with the group. Mike did so. Now, if enough of his buddies go to Mass, he wants to go too."

"Every boy's story is rich with promise of what the Holy Spirit is doing in their lives. Whatever troubles they experienced in the past, they are open to receive God's help and respond positively to grace. The atmosphere in this group home reflects their positive outlook."

Impact on Staff

Jeff notes a gradual transformation among different staff members at the home. "With one fellow, the Holy Spirit brought about a release from guilt through the sacrament of Reconciliation. Another member is slowly allowing his skepticism and doubt to lift. The children's experiences are having a genuine effect on him."

Concluding Thought

Jeff truly feels the ongoing care and love which Our Blessed Mother showed him and his associates during the period between her two great feasts, which are nine months apart: the Annunciation and the Immaculate Conception. It is as though she has conceived new life again in the hearts and minds of these young boys, and brought them to a new hope, with the possibility of happy future. He remarks, "Jesus came to humankind through Mary. He came to sinners. One thousand, nine hundred and ninety four years later, again through Mary, in the power of the Holy Spirit, He came to this group home filled with sinners. Of all the places in our country, He came to our group home. It's a new Pentecost."

Ed's Miracle

Ed is an eager 16 year old who lives with five boys in the group home where Jeff is supervisor. Ed wanted to tell his own story. He is attracted to the Greensides farm which he visits as often as possible.

December 8, 1994 was an exciting day for Ed. As Jeff indicated, he got a ride to the farm and helped direct traffic for two hours, then joined a group of people to make the Way of the Cross. He describes his experience at the Tenth Station.

"People were looking at the sun and trying to see what other people had seen in the past. I looked up and saw a disc that looked like a Host spinning in the middle of the sun. I saw the sun's rays shooting out the sides of the disc and it was very pretty."

"One of the ladies standing beside me tapped me on the shoulder and asked me what I was looking at. I told her I was looking at the sun. She said that all she could see was blue. I told her to take off her sunglasses and look at the sun. She still couldn't see anything, then she drifted away in the crowd."

"When I met up with Jeff I told him what I had seen and what happened. Then I went to the washroom. On my way back I heard that Dory Tan the visionary was there. She talks to Our Lady. Dory said that Our Lady was going to appear to her at precisely 3:00 p.m. at the Tenth Station so everyone crowded around the Tenth Station."

"There were a lot of people there just before Dory arrived. The lady next to me started talking about our society and teenagers smoking drugs and sniffing glue so I wondered if it was a message for me. Even today I wonder why she said that to me."

"Just as I finished talking to her Dory arrived with her body guards. It took her at least ten minutes to make it through the crowd to the Station. When she finally made it, Our Lady told Dory to go into the woods by herself. When Dory went into the bush some people tried to follow her so it took Dory a while to get the message that she was supposed to get. Because of the crowd hardly anybody heard what she said, but I heard as clear as day."

"First she asked for a woman named June, but June wasn't there. Then she asked for everyone to move to the Eleventh Station. When everyone moved to the Eleventh Station everyone was supposed to be silent but not everyone was, so Dory left. When the crowd simmered down I found Jeff. He told me he heard something about Our Lady saying she wanted a chapel built at the Tenth Station."

"OOPS I forgot something! When Dory went into the forest the sun got brighter and brighter, but what I really noticed was the little beams glowing over the crowd of people."

"GOD BLESS THE WORLD"

CHAPTER TWENTY-TWO

SUMMARY AND CONCLUSION

The experiences related in this book demonstrated a significant change in the lives of those who received supernatural phenomena, and those to whom they ministered. They initiated a definite turning point in peoples' lives. The apparitions of Jesus and Mary made a significant difference to them. They became firmly convinced that God is real, that Jesus and Mary are real, and care personally for each individual.

In several instances this book moved beyond the initial book about Marmora. This book recorded experiences at the Greensides farm which transformed the recipients' lives. It also revealed supernatural phenomena which occurred to individuals in their own homes or in parish churches. These mystical experiences were not only external apparitions or internal visions, but also physical manifestations within their own bodies. As a consequence, these individuals felt impelled to minister to others in their homes or at the Greensides farm. Visiting the farm affirmed them and their ministry which resulted in additional conversion and healing.

It would seem that the role of the Greensides farm also underwent change during the past year. Individuals and groups who experienced supernatural phenomena in their own locale, and independently of any occurrence at Marmora, found affirmation during subsequent visits to the hilltop Way of the Cross. The phenomena recorded in this book occurred in different locations throughout central Ontario, yet during the same time period as those which began in Marmora in 1992. It was apparent that a cluster of visionaries encircled Lake Ontario and moved into Central and Eastern Ontario. From Stoney Creek, Hamilton, Burlington, Oakville, Mississauga, Toronto, Barrie, Scarborough, Kingston, Ottawa, visionaries' experience of transforming grace radiated to and from Marmora.

To several of the participants the Lord Jesus or Our Lady communicated messages for their personal conversion, edification of others, referral to the local priests, bishops, and also to the Holy Father. Their prayers and those of thousands of their supporters helped to sanctify the simple farm.

Some Historical References

History teaches that not all people respond the same way to the manifestation of supernatural phenomena. For example, resistance to unofficial use of spiritual gifts was documented in the time of Moses (6) and during the ministry of Jesus (7). During Paul's travels the early Christian Church received a severe warning against presumption in personally authorizing themselves as being gifted (8).

Mystics of the Catholic tradition experienced and described a range of spiritual activities and encounters. For example, St. Teresa of Avila documents occasions when God suspends the soul in rapture, ecstasy or trance. She notes, "One kind of rapture is this: though not actually engaged in prayer, the soul is struck by some word, which it either remembers or hears spoken by God."(9) She claims that if the soul has intellectual visions, they cannot be described, except perhaps after the soul has regained its senses.(10) She also insists that "if the soul does not understand the secrets God is revealing, they are not raptures at all."(11)

When St. Teresa refers to flights of the spirit she claims that the soul really seems to have left the body. It is clear that the person is not dead, but feels that he is in another world.(12) Distinct benefits of this experience are knowledge of the greatness of God, self-knowledge and humility, and a supreme contempt for earthly things (13).

St. John of the Cross comments on the desire and yearning through which faith leads the soul to seek God. He teaches that "the Beloved reveals to the soul some rays of His grandeur and divinity, which cause her to go out of herself in rapture and ecstasy (14). When asked how one becomes enraptured, St. John answered, "by denying one's own will and doing the will of God; for an ecstasy is nothing else than going out of self and being caught up in God." He adds that this is what he who obeys does. He leaves himself and his desire, and thus unburdened plunges himself in God.(15)

Tanquerey describes two elements which constitute the nature of ecstatic union, "the absorption of the soul in God and the suspension of the activity of the senses."(16) He comments further, "the suspension of the senses is the outcome of this absorption in God. It takes place gradually and does not reach the same degree in all."(17)

Referrring to some of the teaching of St. Teresa, Tanquerey claims that there are three phases of ecstatic union, namely simple ecstasy, rapture and the flight of the spirit.(18) He also notes that the principal virtues produced by the ecstatic union are a perfect detachment from creatures, an immense sorrow for sins committed, a frequent and tender vision of Our Lord's Sacred Humanity and of the Most Blessed Virgin, and a marvellous patience to withstand courageously the new passive trials which Almighty God sends, and which are called the purification of love.(19)

Common Characteristics of Visionaries Interviewed

The mystical phenomena of people interviewed in this book appear to be in line with traditional Catholic experience. They recognized that not all people readily endorsed their life style and special gifts. While they were aware that resistance to these phenomena had a long standing history in Church tradition they also showed wisdom and caution in using their gifts, and courage in confronting evil in their lives. They did not seem to take the undue risk of early imitators of St. Paul's disciples who left themselves vulnerable to demonic attack.

The visionaries had some traits in common. Their experiences of Our Lady always pointed to Jesus. They experienced physical sufferings. Sometimes their pain was excruciating. In the midst of pain they experienced the joy of God's love. They believed that Jesus allowed them to endure a portion of His suffering so that they could come to know the immensity of His unfathomable love. Through pain and love they were drawn into the mystery of God's glory, wisdom and knowledge. They were humbly confident in the truth of their supernatural manifestations and the grace of conversion which continued to unfold in their lives. They were extremely sensitive to the pain and suffering of others, whether physical, emotional or spiritual.

They recognized the gifts and the fruits of the Holy Spirit which were operative in their lives. They guarded against self-deception or deceit from evil sources. They received and valued appropriate spiritual direction. They recognized their call to minister to others and were generous in providing help. The spontaneity and stability of their personality was readily observed in their normal interaction with people.

Where they had been ignorant or dormant in matters of religion or negligent in church attendance or reception of the sacraments, their attitude and behaviour underwent total conversion. Their families and friends were enriched with deeper faith, devotion to the Church, and constant efforts at building Christian Community regardless of personal inconvenience.

Those visionaries who were interviewed appeared to be sustained by support groups which in some cases continued to grow beyond the original nucleus of prayer. These groups manifested radiant joy in knowing that they live in the presence of God and serve Him. They exhibited a decrease or total loss of interest in material goods. Individual differences existed between groups, such as their form of prayer, practice of Confession, and the nature of supernatural and physical phenomena among group members.

Impact of Manifestations on Clerical Authorities

The clergy who were interviewed in this book gave a tremendously positive testimony to the fruitfulness of their priestly vocation and their lives. They demonstrated that our Church has been blessed with bishops and priests who experienced supernatural phenomena in their own lives, and who are open to provide wise direction to lay people in their spiritual development. Many such clergy give faithful leadership to our people, and in turn feel supported by their loving communities.

While it is normal for people who have religious experiences to seek affirmation from their clergy, that caring support was not evidenced in the lives of all participants interviewed. In some cases visionaries met with suspicion, doubt, scepticism and dismissing fear from clergy. This may be understandable in the case of clergy who were possibly educated in classical philosophy and theology, parish administration and sacramental ministry, with little or no opportunity to discover traditional Catholic spirituality and the mysticism of the saints.

The persons interviewed recognized that their experiences were unique and were considered as private revelations. They knew that they had no official teaching authority to teach the truths of religion, but were subject to the teaching authority of the Church. Where their revelations indicated that they were to convey difficult messages for communication to the clergy, they endeavoured to obey, regardless of the veiled or open resistance with which they were received.

Apparently Our Blessed Mother took the initiative in guiding her people in the ways of prayer and traditional mysticism. These experiences appeared to be consistent with those of earlier Christians who experienced religious conversion.

Conclusion

While not claiming to be an authority in spiritual phenomena, the author believes in what she has seen and heard. In relation to unusual physical manifestations, she recognizes that in the light of Creation and the Incarnation, nothing will be impossible for God.(20)

The farm and hilltop Way of the Cross has expanded beyond the original prayer of John and Shelagh Greensides. Our Lord and Our Lady have demonstrated that they received the Greensides' dedication with gratitude, by pouring out spiritual gifts on all visitors. The lives of Shelagh and John have been abundantly blessed because of their simplicity and generosity. It will be interesting to observe the ongoing growth and development of the farm as gifted individuals and groups from Canada, the United States and distant countries return to give honour and glory to God in this place of blessing. The future of the farm is in Our Lady's hands, even as it was in the beginning.

With regard to the clergy, it seems to be vital to the life of the Church for priests to be open and prepared for a spirituality of the laity, which includes individual and collective supernatural phenomena, and profound prayer in groups who assemble regularly. These occurrences are transforming the lives of individuals who in turn help to transform the life of the Church. The ongoing process of conversion of the laity cannot help but enrich the clergy, since the recipients of these spiritual gifts demonstrate profound reverence for the Mass, priestly sacramental ministry, and wise spiritual direction.

For individuals who automatically disclaim supernatural manifestations, the words of Gamaliel may well apply: "Fellow Israelites, be careful what you are about to do to these men... For if this endeavour or this activity is of human origin, it will destroy itself. But if it comes from

God, you will not be able to destroy them; you may even find yourselves fighting against God". (21)

It would appear that the present manifestations are consistent with St. Peter's literal and symbolic Pentecostal speech in Jerusalem as he quotes from the prophet Joel:

> It will come to pass in the last days, God says,
> that I will pour out a portion of my spirit upon all flesh.
> your sons and your daughters shall prophesy,
> your young men shall see visions,
> your old men shall dream dreams.
>
> Indeed, upon my servants and my handmaids
> I will pour out a portion of my spirit in those days,
> and they shall prophesy.
>
> And I will work wonders in the heavens above
> and signs on the earth below:
> blood, fire, and a cloud of smoke.
>
> The sun shall be turned to darkness,
> and the moon to blood,
> before the coming of the great and splendid day of the Lord,
> and it shall be that everyone shall be saved who calls on
> the name of the Lord. (22)

The reader is reminded that apparitions and locutions are not recent phenomena in the Church. They antedate Christianity and are as old as Genesis. As people continue to gather at the Greensides farm they make it increasingly holy by their prayer, praise and sacrifice. Indeed where two or more are gathered in Jesus' Name, the Lord is in their midst.

To the believing Christian and non-Christian, the privilege is offered to be watchful and ready for the unfolding of God's mystery in our lives. This book is not an indicator of horrible tragedies to come. It is a challenge for people of expectant hope to wait for the coming of Jesus Christ according to His promise, as we observe God's continuing intervention in history through the signs of the times.

APPENDIX ONE

For readers who may be unfamiliar with some supernatural phenomena recorded in this book, the bibliography contains references with traditional Catholic teaching on these matters. In addition, the following excerpts may be helpful.

Tanquerey comments on Psycho-physiological phenomena as follows:

By this term we mean such phenomena as affect both soul and body, and which are more or less related to ecstasy. The principal phenomena of this kind are levitation; luminous rays; fragrant odours; prolonged fasting; stigmatization.

He describes levitation as a phenomenon whereby the body is raised above the ground and sustained in midair without any natural support. Sometimes the body rises to great heights; at other times it seems to glide rapidly over the ground. (23)

Both Tanquerey and St. Teresa of Avila devote serious consideration to Satan's attempt at tyrannizing people. Some excerpts from Tanquerey are as follows:

The devil, jealous of God's influence on the souls of the saints, strives to exercise his own dominion, or rather his tyranny, over men. At times he, so to speak, besieges the soul from without by assailing it with horrible temptations; at other times, he takes up his abode in the human body, which he moves at will as if he were its master, in order thus to afflict the soul itself. (24)

The devil can act upon all the external senses:
a) Upon the sense of sight, by appearing sometimes under repulsive forms to frighten persons and turn them away from the practice of virtue.
b) Upon the sense of hearing, by causing blasphemous or obscene words or songs to be heard.
c) Upon the sense of touch, by blows and wounds. (25)

Tanquerey emphasizes the need for extreme care in order to distinguish the differences between these manifestations of the devil and nervous diseases, since the devil can cause nervous disorders or other external phenomena similar to those of neuropathics.

St. Teresa of Avila's Struggles

In the book on her life, St. Teresa devotes two chapters to her struggles with the evil ones. She notes,

"I have had so much experience by now of the devil's work that he sees I know his tricks and so he troubles me much less with this kind of torture than he used to. His part in it is evident from the disquiet and unrest with which it begins, from the turmoil which he creates in the soul for so long as his influence lasts, and from the darkness and affliction into which he plunges it, causing in it an aridity and an ill-disposition for prayer and for everything that is good. He seems to stifle the soul and to constrain the body, and thus to render both powerless. Genuine humility does not produce inward turmoil, nor does it cause unrest in the soul, or bring it darkness or aridity; on the contrary, it cheers it and produces in it the opposite effects – quietness, sweetness and light." (26)

"Once, when I was in an oratory, he appeared on my left hand in an abominable form; as he spoke to me, I paid particular attention to his mouth, which was horrible. Out of his body there seemed to be coming a great flame, which was intensely bright and cast no shadow. He told me in a horrible way that I had indeed escaped out of his hands but he would get hold of me still. I was very much afraid and made the sign of the Cross as well as I could, whereupon he disappeared, but immediately returned again. This happened twice running and I did not know what to do. But there was some holy water there, so I flung some in the direction of the apparition, and it never came back. On another occasion the devil was with me for five hours, torturing me with such terrible pains and both inward and outward disquiet that I do not believe I could have endured them any longer."

"From long experience I have learned that there is nothing like holy water to put devils to flight and prevent them from coming back again. They also flee from the Cross, but return; so holy water must have great virtue. For my own part, whenever I take it, my soul feels a particular and most notable consolation. In fact, it is quite usual for me to be conscious of a refreshment which I cannot possibly describe, resembling an inward joy which comforts my whole soul. ... I often reflect on the great importance of everything ordained by the Church and it makes me very happy to find that those words of the Church are so powerful that they impart their power to the water and make it so very different from water which has not been blessed." (27)

Mystical Bilocation

The Catholic Encyclopedia defines mystical bilocation as follows: "An extraordinary mystical phenomenon in which the material body seems to be simultaneously present in two distinct places at the same time. Since it is physically impossible that a physical body completely surrounded by its place be present in another place at the same time, this could not occur even by a miracle. Therefore, bilocation is always an apparent or seeming bilocation. The most noteworthy cases among the saints are those of Clement, Francis of Assisi, Anthony of Padua, Francis Xavier, Joseph Cupertino, Martin de Porres, and Alphonsus Liguori. When bilocation occurs, the true and physical body is present in one place and is only apparently present in the other by means of a representation of some kind. This representation could be caused supernaturally, diabolically, or by means of a natural power or energy as yet unknown. If the apparent bilocation is caused supernaturally, the body is physically present in one place and represented in the other place in the form of a vision, i.e., through the instrumentality of angels or through an intellectual, imaginative, or sensible vision caused by God in the witnesses. Another possible explanation is that the body of the mystic was transported instantaneously, through the gift of agility, from one place to another and was returned in the same manner. In this case the apparent bilocation would be reduced to the phenomenon of agility."(28)

Nesta de Robeck devotes a chapter of the life of Padre Pio to the phenomenon of bilocation, as described by several witnesses. (29)

Blessed Sister Faustina describes a parallel personal experience. "This evening, a certain young man was dying; he was suffering terribly. For his intention, I began to say the chaplet which the Lord had taught me. I said it all, but the agony continued. I wanted to start the Litany of the Saints, but suddenly I heard the words, **Say the chaplet.** I understood that the soul needed the special help of prayers and great mercy. And so I locked myself in my room and fell prostrate before God and begged for mercy upon that soul. Then I felt the great majesty of God and His great justice. I trembled with fear, but did not stop begging the Lord's mercy for that soul. Then I took the cross off my breast, the crucifix I had received when making my vows, and I put it on the chest of the dying man and said to the Lord, "Jesus, look on this soul with the same love with which You looked on my holocaust on the day of my perpetual vows, and by the power of the promise which You made to me in respect to the dying and those who would invoke Your mercy on them, (grant this man the grace of a happy death)." His suffering then ceased, and he died peacefully. Oh, how much we should pray for the dying! Let us take advantage of mercy while there is still time for mercy."

"I realize more and more how much every soul needs God's mercy throughout life and particularly at the hour of death. The chaplet mitigates God's anger, as He himself told me." (30)

A Conclusion from Tanquerey

"These extraordinary phenomena, whether divine or diabolical, show on the one hand the mercy and the goodness of God towards His privileged friends, to whom He imparts, along with intense sufferings, such as in the case of stigmatization, the most signal favours as a foretaste of the glory He will one day bestow upon them in heaven; and on the other hand, the jealousy and the hatred of the devil, who seeks to exercise his tyranny over men by tempting them in a most extraordinary way, by persecuting them when they resist and spread the Kingdom of God, and by torturing some of his victims through taking possession of them."

"Thus, there are in the world the two Cities, so well described by St. Augustine, the two Camps and the two Standards mentioned by St. Ignatius. True Christians can not hesitate; the more completely they give themselves to God, the more surely do they escape the empire of Satan. If God permits them to be tried, it is only for their greater good. Even in the midst of their sufferings they can say in all confidence, "If God be for us, who is against us?... Who is like unto God?" (31)

APPENDIX TWO

This article is a reprint of a flyer made available to visitors in the home of Eddie and Ida Virrey.

RESTING IN THE SPIRIT
(formerly called Slain in the Spirit)

What is it?

It is the power of the Holy Spirit so filling a person with a heightened inner awareness that the body's energy fades away until it cannot stand. It is not fainting. The person keeps consciousness but is under the healing power of the Holy Spirit.

Is this Experience found in the Bible?

In the tenth chapter of The Acts of the Apostles, St. Luke speaks about St. Peter falling into a trance; in the description of Gethsemane, we read about the soldiers falling backward when Jesus spoke to them; and St. Paul fell to the ground during his conversion experience.

All of these experiences seem to have been similar to the experience that some have called "being slain in the Holy Spirit", and we are calling Resting in the Holy Spirit.

What is the Purpose of Resting in the Spirit?

Many people who experience Resting in the Holy Spirit experience not just rest and peace, but God himself in some way.

While under the power of the Holy Spirit, Jesus wants to release the person from the bondage of sin and heal some area of the inner person.

The Holy Spirit is free to do many spiritual actions in the person's mind, will, imagination, memory and emotions when one completely rests and relaxes in His love.

What should I do before the experience?

Do not make anything happen and do not prevent His power from coming upon you by being frightened about where you will fall and how you will look and what people will think about you. Release yourself from any of these fears. Relax in His love and gently praise Him for loving you. Release yourself from all guilt feelings about not being worthy. This is not an experience for the worthy, it is for those who need release, inner healing and infilling.

What should I do during the experience?

During the experience, relax in His love. Surrender to His love. Trust that something is happening in you even though you do not feel it emotionally. Stay in the position of relaxation as long as you feel you should.

What should I do after the experience?

When returning to the normal level of mind-consciousness, still inside of you any thoughts of self-condemnation, self-analysis, what will people think, disappointments that you didn't feel anything. Remaining in the resting experience for 5 minutes or for 5 hours is not a sign of greater sinfulness or greater holiness. Words of love and worship to the Father, to the Son and to the Holy Spirit from your sincere heart keep the healing flowing in the heart continuously. Be open to living in God's will every day. This experience of Resting in the Holy Spirit is only a beginning. The Lord will continue His work throughout the course to come in the remaining week, month, and maybe even years. That he would want to love us and let His Precious Blood cleanse us this way is indeed a great joy. No one praying with us or touching us has healing power. Jesus is the Healer and His Holy Spirit effects the healing because the Father wants it at this moment in your life.

BIBLIOGRAPHY

1. Pope John Paul II, <u>Angelus Meditations on the Litany of the Sacred Heart of Jesus</u>, Our Sunday Visitor Inc, Huntington, IN, 46750, 1985, p. 23.

2. Ibid, p. 77–78.

3. Anon, <u>The Miracle in Naju, Korea – Heaven Speaks to the World</u>, Mary's Touch by Mail, P.O. Box 1668, Gresham, OR, 97030, 1992, p.iv.

4. Johnson, Sister Alice, <u>Marmora, Canada: Is Our Blessed Mother Speaking Here To Her Beloved Children</u>? Amor Enterprises, Peterborough, ON, K9H 6R6, 1994, pp 61–70.

5. Gobbi, Father Stefano, <u>To The Priests, Our Lady's Beloved Sons</u>, The Marian Movement of Priests, Toronto, Ontario, M5P 3H4, 1992, pp 653–655.

6. Numbers 11/26–28

7. Mark 10/38–40

8. Acts 19/13–16

9. Saint Teresa of Avila, <u>The Interior Castle</u>, E.L. Dwyer, Philadelphia, PA 19131, 1985 p. 63.

10. Ibid, p. 63.

11. Ibid, p. 64.

12. Ibid, p. 66.

13. Ibid, p. 67.

14. Kavanagh, Kieran and Rodriguez, Otilio, <u>The Collected Works of St. John of the Cross</u>, Institute of Carmelite Studies, Washington, D.C., 1979, p. 406.

15. Ibid, p. 680.

16. Tanquerey, Very Reverend Adolphe, <u>The Spiritual Life</u>, Desclee & Co. New York, 1923, p. 684.

17. Ibid, p. 685.

18. Ibid, p. 686.

19. Ibid, p. 688.

20. Luke, 1/37

21. Acts 5/35, 38–39.

22. Acts 1/17–21.

23. Tanquerey, op. cit., p. 711 ff.

24. Ibid, p. 718.

25. Ibid, p. 719.

26. Peers, E. Allison, The Life Of Teresa Of Jesus, Doubleday, New York, 1960, p. 280.

27. Ibid, p. 288–9.

28. New Catholic Encyclopedia, Volume II, The Catholic University of America, Washington, D.C., 1967, p. 559.

29. De Robeck, Nesta, Padre Pio, The Bruce Publishing Company, Milwaukee, 1958, pp. 77–96.

30. Kowalska, Sister M. Faustina, Divine Mercy In My Soul, Marian Press, Stockbridge, MA, 1987, p. 393.

31. Tanquerey, op. cit., p. 726.